Praise for *The Disciplined Listening Method*

"One of the most talented presenters I have witnessed in person, Michael Reddington translates his gift into words with *The Disciplined Listening Method*, providing credible conversation techniques we can all implement. Leaders get paid by the conversation, and after reading this book, you won't see or hear conversations the same way again."

—**Jeff Dudan,** CEO of Dudan Group, Franchise Executive, UnderCover Boss

"A must read for leaders. Mike shows you the importance of listening to what is said and, equally important, what is not said. It shows you the need to observe and learn more about human communication. There's plenty of empirical evidence that allows the reader to move from theory into action. Invaluable for leaders who want to lead with vision and influence."

—**Anastasios Economou,** Founder of iGroup, YPO Global Chairman

"Michael's unique perception allows him to deftly apply investigative communication techniques to business and personal conversations in a manner that generates remarkable results. Since attending his seminars, I've applied Michael's techniques in my business, personal, and political conversations. I'm impressed with how he has outlined his approach in such depth in this book. *The Disciplined Listening Method* provides readers with a conversational approach that will open their eyes and ears to the opportunities they've been missing."

—**Pádraig Ó Céidigh,** Senator, EY World Entrepreneur of the Year Finalist

"In a world where social media encourages an abundance of noise, the ability to listen has shifted from a commodity to an asset. Michael's book gives its readers a framework to leverage the asset of Disciplined Listening and use it to close sales and build relationships."

—**Will Barron,** Managing Director at Salesman.org, host of the Salesman podcast

"I first met Michael Reddington when I attended a seminar he was facilitating. I was fascinated by his perspectives and techniques, and how they could be applied to my role as CEO. With this book, Michael elevates his material and expertly integrates his interrogation techniques with business research and best practices to provide a broader audience access to clear advantages in business and personal communications."

—**Neville Crawley,** CEO of OppFi

"If you ever wanted to read someone's mind, read this book! So much great advice and so many great stories, you won't regret it."

—**Simon Horton,** Founder of Negotiation Mastery

"Michael is a gem; a thoughtful person with no ego. He's an outstanding teacher on two extremely difficult subjects: speaking with the receiver front and center (focusing on what's being heard rather than what you say) and listening without your inner voice and ego in the way. His writing reflects his outlier talent remarkably well. And of course, getting him in person provides truly fantastic insights. In *The Disciplined Listening Method*, Michael teaches extremely eloquently. I strongly recommend this book to anyone who is looking to take their communications, and relationships, to a place where you will treasure your relationships and feel very accomplished."

—**Nooruddin (Rudy) Karsan,** Managing Partner at Karlani Capital

"I first met Mike Reddington as an investigator after a large diamond theft. I originally thought his main skill was uncovering lies, but it turns out that his deepest talent is in discovering truths. Learning how to listen is one of the most important skills that any of us can ever learn. This book will help you on that path. [This book helped me on that path.]"

—**Joseph Wein,** CEO at Hampden Watch Company

"Michael Reddington is a master of human interaction. He is one of the few guests who has an open invitation to join my show anytime because of his depth of knowledge, relatable style, enlightening stories and because I learn so much from him every time. With this book Michael generously shares the depth of his research and knowledge to provide readers with powerful tools for navigating a wide range of business and personal conversations."

—**Kwame Christian Esq., M.A.,** Director of the American Negotiation Institute and Host of the #1 ranked Negotiate Anything Podcast

THE DISCIPLINED LISTENING METHOD

HOW A CERTIFIED FORENSIC INTERVIEWER UNLOCKS
HIDDEN VALUE IN EVERY CONVERSATION

MICHAEL REDDINGTON, CFI

Published in association with Per Capita Publishing, a division of Content Capital®.

ISBN 13: 978-1-954020-19-1 (Paperback)
ISBN 13: 978-1-954020-30-6 (Ebook)

Library of Congress Cataloging-in-Publication Data
Names: Reddington, Michael, author.
Title: The Disciplined Listening Method / Michael Reddington
Description: First Edition | Texas: Per Capita Publishing (2021)
Identifiers: LCCN 2022901465 (print)

First Edition

CONTENTS

For Brooke and Gabriel.
Thank you for showing me the true meaning of love and happiness.

FOREWORD

I HAVE ALWAYS FOUND human communication intriguing. Many people think communication is simply two or more people talking and evaluating the words between them. In fact, most of the information we receive during a conversation is from the tone of voice, the pacing, word emphasis, and the physical behavior associated with what is being said.

As a Certified Forensic Interviewer (CFI) with years of interviewing experience, Michael is able to apply interrogation techniques and his communication skills to the business world using real-life examples to illustrate how to overcome communication difficulties in any setting. He stresses the differences between what we know as "active listening"—which most of us have been told is the best way to effectively communicate—and his Disciplined Listening Method.

The challenge with investigative interviewing is we are almost always trying to get information from individuals who are reluctant provide it. But the same principles that produce successful interviews can be applied for sales, negotiations, many business conversations, hiring new employees, and even conversations with family and friends.

From my perspective as the CEO of Wicklander-Zulawski & Associates (WZ), an international training firm focused on

Non-Confrontational Interview & Interrogation techniques, this book puts the most intriguing and effective parts of our job in an easy-to-understand, thought-provoking manner. WZ's Non-Confrontational Interview & Interrogation techniques are used by Federal Agencies, Law Enforcement, Military, Corporate Loss Prevention, and Human Resources as well as many others that are involved in investigative interviewing. As a result, we strive to hire the best available instructors to teach our techniques. In *The Disciplined Listening Method*, Michael provides masterful illustrations of how each minute movement or word plays a significant role within the context of our conversations.

I first met Michael Reddington in April of 2008. We needed another trainer who had a strong background in investigations in the corporate world, and three of our instructors knew of Michael's experiences and reputation and recommended that we hire him. During our evaluation process we require our candidates to provide us with a ten-minute video of themselves presenting on any topic they are passionate about; however, most applicants present a video of themselves trying to teach Interview & Interrogation, our area of expertise. As you can imagine, they come across nervous, dry, and often look unprepared.

Michael presented a video of a recent trip he took from New Hampshire to Massachusetts in a Black Hawk helicopter. He not only listened and thought deeply about our prompt, but the passion and excitement we observed in that video ensured Michael was the right person for us. It is easy to feel that same passion and excitement in this book as Michael guides the readers through the techniques and processes necessary to overcome the barriers to effective listening.

As part of a CEO peer group, we regularly process issues related to challenging conversations with business partners, some of which are family members, and often revolve around changes in ownership. In these scenarios, I've seen many CEOs stress over how to construct their conversations. The seven core behaviors outlined in this book are a perfect road map to easily plan and execute these difficult conversations—there is a reason Michael is a sought-after resource and speaker for CEOs looking to learn how to navigate tricky conversations and create better outcomes.

Negotiations, sales, difficult conversations, and interrogations all require a well-thought-out plan. These plans should include our goals and preferred outcomes while accounting for what might cause our counterparts to withhold truthful information or cooperate. With our plan in place, we allow the conversation to come to us, encouraging our counterparts to save face. This allows us to evaluate their verbal and nonverbal behavior to better understand what they are really saying and adapt our process and behaviors while keeping our goals in the forefront.

Many business leaders have been exposed to active listening, including myself. Active listening techniques work very well, making the speaker feel more comfortable as we give the impression we are listening—but are we? I can't tell you how many times I have been introduced to someone and by the time the handshake was over, I had already forgotten their name. I was too busy thinking of what I was going to say, what I was going to do, what I wanted to get done. We are all guilty of holding internal conversations with ourselves as we pretend to listen to our counterpart. These distracted conversations can be the difference between everyone leaving happy or leaving disappointed and unable to protect their self-images.

As both a CEO and a professional interrogator, I highly recommend this book to any businessperson interested in gaining a competitive advantage or those who simply wish to enhance their business and personal relationships with better communication skills. It's time to enrich our conversations by evolving from active listening to Disciplined Listening.

Shane Sturman, CFI, CPP
CEO/Senior Partner
Wicklander-Zulawski & Associates, Inc.

INTRODUCTION

"**CLICK, CLICK. I TURNED** my listening ears on, Daddy."

One of my son's daycare teachers taught him to turn on his listening ears when he was a toddler, and it has become his preferred phrase as soon as he realizes that he might be in trouble. He intends this statement to mean that he is attentive, obedient, and no longer needs to experience any consequences.

If only listening were that easy.

Given his age, there are several interesting dynamics that impact what he hears and how he reacts. He is in tune to changes in my wife's and my volume and tone of voice. He even appears to recognize (and emulate) our facial expressions. However, he most often reacts to the literal meaning of what we say. When we speak, he focuses on what we want him to do, how he might please us, or how he may get what he wants. As a toddler though, he often misses the nuance and intention behind our statements. All of this leads me to ask the question, is he listening?

Great listeners are rare. Precious few listeners possess:

- A strong sense of curiosity
- The ability to limit their internal monologue
- The capacity to control their emotions
- Enough discipline to limit distractions
- Ample awareness to uncover hidden value

- Sufficient confidence to empathize with people who harbor opposing perspectives

For great listeners, the value of learning and achieving some-thing new outweighs the risks associated with feeling vulnerable. Unfortunately, people are not typically born with these skills. Human beings are wired for the exact opposite. Stephen Covey, the author of the best-selling book *The 7 Habits of Highly Effective People,* writes, "Most people do not listen with the intent to understand; they listen with the intent to reply."[1] We are all pre-disposed to listen for opportunities to confirm or defend what we already believe, protect our self-images, and avoid individu-als and topics that make us uncomfortable.

> For great listeners, the value of learning and achieving some-thing new outweighs the risks associated with feeling vulnerable.

This fact is more pronounced now than ever before as we are increasingly incentivized not to listen. The collection and distribution of big data have awarded technology and media organizations with unprecedented influence over our thoughts, behaviors, and purchases. The abil-ity for these organizations to remain profitable is directly linked to their ability to reinforce and even alter our self-images, while also developing rivalries between perceptually opposed groups and individuals. We often have no idea how big data is weaponized to curate the information we see on TV and online, specifically for our personal consumption. This new reality rewards people for taking polarizing positions, reacting quickly as opposed to thoughtfully, valuing information that comes from sources with similar views, and highlighting differences as opposed to seeking commonalities. It reduces our ability to separate messages from messengers, and important details from larger messages with which we may disagree. Overcoming these popularized incentives requires uncommon levels of awareness, confidence, and empathy.

The Greek philosopher Plutarch is credited with saying, "Know how to listen and you will profit even from those who talk badly." His statement remains 100 percent true today. Listening is touted as one of, if not the, most critical business and personal communication skills to develop. However, knowing how to listen can mean many things, depending on a person's motivation. People can listen to, acknowledge, obey, respond, defend, attack, learn, understand, or achieve. Sometimes, all occur within the same conversation.

Carl Rogers and Richard Farson first defined the concept of active listening that many people are familiar with today. Essentially, they identified that listeners who strive to demonstrate that they grasp a speaker's entire message would affect change in others.[2] Mr. Rogers illustrated this idea when he stated, "We think we listen, but very rarely do we listen with real understanding, true empathy. Yet listening, of this very special kind, is one of the most potent forces for change that I know."[3]

Our personal brand as leaders is built upon how people perceive us as listeners.

Looking back, my journey as an observer and listener started decades before I was aware of it. For a variety of reasons as a young child, I was oftentimes hiding something from everyone around me. As a result, I honed my awareness skills as my fear of being discovered had me on high alert all the time. Fast-forwarding to a more responsible stage of life, my first attempt at a career was supporting children and adults with physical and developmental disabilities. Some of them were nonverbal, some had limited speaking abilities, and all of them bore the cognitive and emotional scars of their experiences. Learning to accurately determine what they were thinking, feeling, and requesting allowed my coworkers and I to preserve their happiness, safety, and dignity.

I went on to work in a customer service role and spent each day talking to hundreds of people who often did not know how to articulate their message or understand the complexities of their situation. These conversations were a crash course in sorting out confusing and emotional discussions to arrive at productive conclusions.

Eventually, I became a professional investigator and observed how people acted before, during the commission of, and after committing crimes. This period was also when I began studying non-confrontational interview and interrogation techniques. My earliest interrogations ignited a passion for understanding how and why people would choose to tell the truth in the face of real consequences, and why the most successful non-confrontational interview and interrogation techniques work so well. These pursuits motivated me to achieve my Certified Forensic Interviewer (CFI) Designation.

As a CFI, I was typically asked to engage with emotional victims, witnesses, and suspects who were motivated to withhold at least some, if not all, of the information I needed to resolve my investigations. These conversations often took place at inconvenient moments, in sub-optimal locations, and under tight time restrictions. Obtaining the truth under these circumstances was often predicated on my ability to evaluate the totality of the situation, observe my subjects, and identify unexpected approaches to encourage them to feel comfortable sharing sensitive information. The road to the truth was the same whether I was speaking with a victim who was previously too embarrassed to share her story, a witness too scared to bring forward evidence, or a suspect who had already lied about his actions to federal agents. Every victim, witness, and suspect brings their own story, fears, and motivations into the interview room. Inspiring each of them to commit to sharing the truth requires interviewers to empathize with people they may have very little in common with, and with whose actions they may strongly disagree.

Professional investigators are taught to look and listen differently. They know that everything they observe now could significantly impact the investigation in the future. What may look like a random action, sound like a throwaway statement, or appear innocuous, may be the key that unlocks the entire investigation. As a result, they are conditioned to collect all the potential puzzle pieces they find, because they can't be sure what the final picture will look like. Looking back on my career, the top ten lessons I learned in the interrogation room are:

1. I had more in common with everyone I interviewed than I initially thought.

2. There was always an opportunity to learn something from everyone I interviewed.

3. It was okay for people to lie to me! They had more motivation to withhold information than to share it. They were simply exercising what they believed was their last good option.

4. People *need* to save face and protect their self-images when they share sensitive information.

5. When I needed my subjects to share sensitive information, I was not in control of the conversation, they were.

6. The direct path is the path of most resistance.

7. Patience prevails—I obtained far more valuable intelligence when I allowed the conversation to come to me.

8. Keeping the "evidence" to myself helped me confirm what I was told.

9. Embrace excuses! They illuminate the easiest path to the truth.

10. I received more truthful information when I asked questions based on what my subjects needed to experience, not what I wanted to say.

I currently serve as an executive resource and have been fortunate to earn the opportunity to support leaders and businesses around the world. My experiences have taught me that we all have far more in common with each other than we think. Everyone has value they can add to a wide variety of scenarios. The depth, nuances, and contextual cues embedded in every message we receive offer a wealth of potential opportunities if we are aware enough to observe them. There are several common denominators that have led to my success in these roles. Creating the Disciplined Listening Method is the culmination of my unexpected journey. Specifically, this method is my application of *situational awareness, patience, strategic observation, emotional intelligence, and the ability to influence others.*

I developed the Disciplined Listening Method by integrating research and best practices from across the spectrum of business communications, with the world's leading non-confrontational interview and interrogation techniques. This marriage of material may seem counterintuitive until we consider two critical perspectives. First, the best leaders and the best interrogators capitalize on the same two core skills: vision and influence. A lack of big-picture understanding or the inability to motivate those around them stops leaders short of achieving their goals. Second, the cognitive road that leads customers to say, "I'll buy it," employees to say, "I'll do it," and suspects to truthfully say, "I did it," is essentially identical. This merging of business and investigative communication techniques positions Disciplined Listeners to prepare, observe, and engage their audiences at levels previously unattainable.

Many approaches to improving our listening skills focus on what we need to say or do to become better listeners. Unfortunately, this inward focus distracts us from the real problem. The most effective listening approaches are predicated on what our audiences need to experience before they commit to sharing the information we need from them.

The biggest keys to maximizing your listening and observation potential in all contexts may just be getting out of your own way, accepting the totality of what your counterparts share, and acknowledging where they are coming from. Unfortunately, these things are extremely hard to do when we are focused on our own perspectives, needs, and emotions. Modern leadership philosopher Simon Sinek says, "Listening is not understanding the words of the question asked, listening is understanding why the question was asked in the first place."[4]

Disciplined Listeners capture opportunities that others fail to see. Trained listeners in this method are able to intentionally combat predispositions and approach discomfort curiously and confidently, all while elevating their contextual awareness.

This book is designed to guide readers through a discovery process that culminates with a deeper understanding of themselves, an appreciation for others' rich experiences, and an approach to unlocking the unrealized potential of their conversations.

We will start by exploring the assumptions and shortfalls associated with active listening. With that backdrop in place, we will examine our individual listening styles, consider how to expand our situational awareness, and work on overcoming many of the common listening mistakes we are all prone to making.

Next, we will delve into the risks, myths, and misguided efforts associated with catching liars. At this point we will explore the seven phases of potentially contentious conversations, illustrate the seven core behaviors of the Disciplined Listening Method, lay out how to observe like an interrogator, and break down the potential meaning of specific verbal and nonverbal behaviors.

Finally, we will outline how to use the truth to your advantage with persuasive communication tools and enhanced questioning techniques. This entire text is also layered with opportunities for each reader to analyze their own business and personal experiences for opportunities to apply these lessons.

Before you go any further, consider the following questions:

1. What are the most valuable lessons you would like to take from this book?
2. What relationships can you impact with the lessons you learn?
3. What new opportunities can you create with the lessons you learn?
4. How can your previous success and missed opportunities reinforce the lessons you learn?

This book aims to provide readers with a game plan to overcome the obstacles that inhibit us from being great listeners. After completing this book, every reader should have a deep toolbox of new listening skills, perspectives, and techniques to apply in their business and personal conversations. They should have identified specific opportunities to apply what they learned, feel confident in their ability to do so, and be aware enough to reflect on their efforts. The lessons included in the following pages were taken from the interrogation room, the board room, the kitchen table, and research libraries. These ideas were packaged together to provide a holistic approach to improving how we engage with those around us. My desire is that the lessons and examples you will find in the following pages add significant value to your business and personal relationships.

CHAPTER ONE

PRETENDING TO
ACTIVELY LISTEN

I MUST ADMIT I was second-guessing my decision as I walked past the armed guards, stepped around the vehicle barriers, passed through the gate between the twelve-foot-high concrete walls, and strode onto the street to meet my driver. Choosing to get in a car with a stranger felt a little risky, but I believed it was truly a once-in-a-lifetime opportunity. I had completed my speaking engagement, and I had a three-hour window to explore the country before my flight departed Amman Jordan for Muscat Oman. My driver appeared to be a trustworthy man and had convinced me to let him take me to visit the Dead Sea. He told me he had lived in the United States for twenty-two years and seemed genuinely eager to show me his home country. I shook his hand, jumped in the back seat, and we set off. We fought our way through traffic that would've made Chicago proud and made our way out of the city.

We passed the forty-five-minute drive by talking about his previous homes in Dallas and Miami. I must confess, I wasn't totally listening to him. I was taken by the sights in a completely unfamiliar landscape, and I was working hard to memorize the roads and landmarks in case I needed to find my own way back. That being said, I definitely didn't want to upset the man who was in complete control of where I would end up next.

I kept the conversation going by occasionally meeting his eyes in the rear-view mirror, offering the intermittent "yeah," "cool," and "really?" A few times I even asked him if he had been to certain restaurants or venues to demonstrate that I was familiar with the cities where he had lived. I used these engagement techniques less out of actual interest in what he was saying and more to keep him happy with me.

When we arrived at the Dead Sea, we had to wait for a farmer to cross the road with at least one hundred goats. Once the herd passed us, we pulled into a parking lot at what appeared to be a public beach area. Both my driver and I exited the car and leaned on the hood. He gave me a few minutes to take it all in as I looked around in awe of the natural beauty that surrounded me, amazed that a kid from New Hampshire made it all the way to Jordan.

Our small talk continued for several minutes and he pointed out that the mountains across the sea were in Israel. I told him I had never been there, and he asked me what my religion was . . . suddenly I didn't want to participate in this conversation anymore. I know very little about world politics and religious conflicts, but I knew enough to be aware that I was on the precipice of a dangerous conversation.

I gave him an equivocated answer and did my best to illustrate that I understood religious conversations were personal and sensitive. He made several more attempts at getting a specific answer from me to no avail. Finally, he looked at me from across the hood of his car and said, "American, it's okay, you can tell me." I quickly responded, "Not if you call me American, my name is Mike." He smiled and said, "It's okay, Mike." I told him I was raised in a Christian family. He thanked me, and turned his gaze back to the mountains across the sea.

When his gaze returned to me, he sighed and told me that his family was from Palestine; he had wonderful memories of his family's olive grove. Within minutes we were both sitting on the hood of this car and exchanging childhood stories. Our business relationship was now intensely personal and all of our differences had evaporated. We talked about our families, our childhoods, and our favorite memories. At the end of the conversation, we both agreed that most people, and religions, have too much in common to allow division and wars to tear us apart.

After a few moments of silently staring out into the Dead Sea and the mountains beyond, he looked at his watch and said, "Quick, get in the car, we still have time." I jumped back in and he took us up a winding road into the Jordanian mountains to Mt. Nebo, where Moses is said to be buried. From there he took me to his cousin's office, where I sat in a back room and sipped lemon tea with five complete strangers. After our tea break, he took me to the town of Madaba where I could see a Greek Orthodox Church and a Mosque. I was stunned when I walked into St. George's Church and found myself staring down at a sixth-century mosaic map of the holy land that had been uncovered underneath the floor.

I was honestly sad as we hugged each other and said goodbye at the airport. I was fortunate to have had the opportunity to prove, in a spectacular way, that we all have much more in common with each other than we think. What started as a typical tourist excursion became an unexpectedly powerful experience when I stopped pretending to listen, accepted my vulnerability, and committed to our conversation.

Most conversations about listening inevitably include the phrase "active listening." Active listening has long since become the ubiquitous descriptive of good listening. Carl Rogers and Richard Farson are credited with establishing the concept of active listening in the late 1950s. The ensuing decades have seen a plethora of academics and practitioners add volumes of research and experiences to their work. Rogers and Farson's original approach to active listening was centered around the concept that listening is a powerful change agent. They believed that active, or sensitive listening, changes how people see themselves and others, and that these perspective shifts create breakthroughs in relationships.

Throughout the years, it has become widely accepted that active listening essentially means engaging with people in a manner that demonstrates attentiveness, understanding, and empathy to encourage them to share more information. To this end, active listeners are encouraged to maintain appropriate levels of eye contact, nod their heads, exhibit open body posture directed toward the speaker, mirror the speaker's body language, and even lean toward the speaker while displaying welcoming nonverbal behaviors.

Additionally, they're instructed to evaluate their counterparts' nonverbal communication. When active listeners respond, they are encouraged to use an engaging tone of voice and nonverbal behaviors, paraphrase what they've heard, reflect the speaker's feelings, and ask open questions.

Essentially, active listening equates to signaling attentiveness. As Carl Rogers and Richard Farson pointed out, people typically share more information when their audience appears to be fully engaged. There is also plenty of research that supports the idea that we like people who we believe share similar interests and ideas. Listeners who authentically remain engaged with their counterparts position themselves to obtain greater amounts of information and maintain stronger relationships.

The potential problems with active listening lie within the

execution of these behaviors, not the behaviors themselves. In fairness, any tool or technique will only be as effective as the person using it. It's not the hammer's fault if you miss the nail and hit your thumb. In the same way, signaling attentiveness doesn't equal listening or result in identifying unexpected strategic value.

APPEARANCE VS. ACTUALITY

The first potential issue with the traditional active listening model is that it creates the opportunity to appear as if we are attentively listening when we are not. There is a huge difference between appearing to listen and actually listening. I would confidently wager that many readers are quite skilled at maintaining eye contact, smiling, nodding, occasionally paraphrasing what they hear, or at least repeating the last word they heard with a questioning tone. This all while ignoring their counterparts, thinking about some other pressing issue in their world, or preparing their next response. We cannot fully focus on two conversations simultaneously. Our internal monologue wins anytime someone is talking to us while we are talking to ourselves.

> Our internal monologue wins anytime someone is talking to us while we are talking to ourselves.

Another common example of active listening backfiring is when we fail to deliver on a set of directions and expectations we have received. Maybe our spouse, boss, teacher, or friend has asked us to take care of something for them. From their perspective, we appear to be attentive and engaged so they believe we acknowledge and understand the request. Fast-forward to when we fail to follow through, and they feel personally disrespected because we have led them to believe that they had our commitment when we hadn't fully listened to what we had committed to.

Appearing to attentively listen should encourage someone to share more information. However, you may end up damaging the relationship if the roles reverse during the conversation and that person asks you questions you can't answer because your mind wandered. The same risk applies if people expect you to retain the information they shared, and you either never receive it, completely forget it, or must return to ask them again at a later time.

As dangerous as it can be to (unintentionally) deceive your counterparts into believing that you listened to them, it is far more dangerous to deceive *yourself* into believing you listened to them. Even when our minds wander, we still receive bits and pieces of the messages being shared with us. We may capture some of the words; we likely won't capture key contextual clues or important shifts in our counterparts' tone, volume, speed of delivery, word choice, or nonverbal behaviors. The few words or behaviors we do observe trick us into believing we have received different messages than our counterparts feel they have delivered. Our misguided confidence can create missed opportunities or strategic disadvantages, cause us to defend our erroneous beliefs, and ignite unnecessary conflicts.

The second potential issue with active listening is the perceived authenticity of the listener. Listeners who robotically respond, interject at awkward times, or consistently rely on the exact same verbal and nonverbal prompts can appear insincere and damage relationships as a result.

Many years ago, I went on a camping trip with another family. We were all sitting around the fire late one night when an unexpected argument erupted between another couple. The wife stormed off and I ended up sitting at the fire alone with the husband. He told me how he felt about the situation and asked me if I understood where he was coming from. I answered, "absolutely," because I felt like I truly did. He immediately looked at me and asked, "Do you? Because you always say 'absolutely.'" I was taken aback. I really did feel like I understood his position, and I definitely didn't want to appear humoring. Thankfully, I was able to recover and give him a specific example. That night, my unconscious response almost created a real problem, even though it came from an authentic place.

This risk runs especially high when listeners attempt to mirror a speaker's behavior. Yes, it is true that people naturally mirror each other when they experience rapport. In fact, there is a fun way to determine if a stranger is paying especially close attention to you in a public establishment: When you believe they are watching you, casually bring your hand to your face and make an adjustment (scratch your eyebrow, adjust your glasses, fix your hair, glide your fingers across your goatee). If the observer in question touches their face, he or she is likely quite in tune to you at that moment.

When people teach mirroring as a listening technique, they are encouraging you to artificially leverage behavioral connections that occur naturally when people experience rapport. Attempting to force or jump-start rapport by mirroring someone's behavior becomes dangerous. The biggest potential problem with using mirroring as an engagement tool is that unnatural behavior almost always appears forced and awkward. Mirroring our counterpart's behavior often requires us to demonstrate behaviors that may not align with our emotions or statements, or that we may not even be comfortable displaying. Both your relationships and your credibility can be irreparably harmed if your audience picks up on your discomfort or incongruencies.

I spent several years teaching investigators how to identify and apprehend shoplifters. New investigators were often surprised when I would start the lesson by asking them to describe how most honest customers behave when they are shopping.

18

Most people have never thought to break down what honest people look like while completing normal activities. Once they outlined how honest shoppers typically behave, I would ask them to look for people in their stores who are trying to *act* normal. This resulted in observational breakthroughs for many new investigators.

For most people, trying to act normal is an awkward proposition. Their behaviors typically appear mechanical, choppy, inconsistent, and conflicting. Typically, the harder one tries to act normal, the less normal they appear, which exposes their ulterior motives. I feel awkward in many social situations—especially standing in line at passport control in airports. I know there are both uniformed and undercover agents who are attempting to identify criminals and threats by watching for people in line who appear to be acting out of the ordinary. I'm also keenly aware that the harder I try to act normal, the more I'm likely calling extra attention to myself. People would find it hysterical if they could hear my competing internal monologues as I try to act normal, and catch myself not acting normal, while I'm anxiously waiting to have my passport stamped.

The same is true for listeners. A listener can quickly destroy trust if a speaker, especially an emotionally vulnerable one, senses that a listener is intentionally mirroring their behavior in an attempt to manipulate the conversation. Think how you would feel if you were nervously opening up to someone and realized that he or she was faking their nonverbal behavior in an attempt to make you more comfortable.

A similar and safer approach is matching your counterpart's behavior as opposed to mirroring it. Mirroring essentially means displaying the exact same behaviors they are, whereas matching their behavior means simply displaying similar behaviors, which is (and comes across as) more authentic and comfortable. This technique will still create the benefits of mirroring while reducing the likelihood of being perceived as insincere.

A third issue with active listening involves the potential for our verbal reflections of the speaker's perceived feelings harming the relationship. The overwhelming majority of adults do not enjoy being treated like children, especially when they are feeling vulnerable. Telling someone what you believe they are thinking or feeling, or what you believe they should be thinking or feeling, can be received as an assumptive and parental approach, which might shut your counterparts down.

In fact, the word "you" is among the most dangerous words in the English language. The more a listener responds with the word "you," the more the speaker may feel his or her self-image is being attacked, which risks putting them on the defensive. We will discuss this idea in greater detail in chapter 13. This trap can be avoided by framing your response around the issue, not the person. For example, don't say: "I can see that you're angry." Say: "Being treated that way can easily make people angry." Don't say: "You're clearly upset." Say: "People can only take being ignored for so long before they become upset." Or "Feeling upset is a valid response."

The same risk is present when we tell someone, "I understand." If a speaker shares emotions or unique experiences and the listener responds by saying, "I understand," it can feel assumptive, disingenuous, and breed suspicion and distrust. Listeners will be well served to illustrate their developing sense of understanding without making blanket statements.

Examples include:

- "I believe I'm starting to understand."

- "My current understanding is . . ."

- "From my experience, I believe the piece I understand best is . . ."

- "As I start to try and understand . . ."
- "From the outside, I could never completely understand."

When someone challenges us by saying "You don't understand," our natural reaction is to defend ourselves and try to
convince our counterparts that we do indeed understand them—
especially if we believe it to be true. Unfortunately, this reaction
often creates a new argument that we cannot win. There is usually nothing we can say to convince a person that we understand
their situation if they do not want to believe it. This conflict can
be avoided when we respond in acknowledgment of their unique
experiences. This is an important step toward finding common
ground with one another.

The responses in the above graphic acknowledge your audience's perceived unique experiences, sidestep the unnecessary
argument, and create opportunities to find common ground
together. Similarly, paraphrasing can be a double-edged sword.
Paraphrasing is an amazing listening verification tool when we
have pre-existing bonds with our counterparts. It can also be
extremely beneficial if your counterparts do not believe that you
are listening.

Effectively paraphrasing becomes challenging when we are engaged in contentious conversations. Paraphrasing typically involves providing our audience with a summarized version of what we heard them say. This summarization often requires us to drop specific words they used and share the meaning we inferred. Presenting our summaries in our own words may provide the fuel someone needs to escalate an argument, no matter how accurate our summarization was. In these scenarios, they may shoot back with, "That's not what I said," "That's not how I said it," "I knew you weren't listening!" or the tried and true, "You clearly don't understand!"

How we introduce our paraphrasing can significantly impact the potential resistance we encounter. If we start our paraphrasing efforts by saying, "What you're saying is . . ." we open the door for them to fire back at us. We can avoid stepping into these metaphorical bear traps by introducing our paraphrasing with room for feedback. One alternative is to lead with, "What I believe I heard was . . ." We can layer on additional empathy and capture more of our counterpart's attention by preceding that statement with, "Please correct me where I'm wrong."

"Please correct me where I'm wrong," is much different than saying, "Please correct me if I'm wrong." The *if* implies that we expect to be right, and can be perceived as arrogant. The *where* implies that we may not be correct, and reframes our audience's listening perspective. This typically helps us capture a greater level of their attention and encourages them to either approve or educate us at the end of our statement, which returns the perceived power in the conversation back to them.

Carl Rogers and Richard Farson believed that listeners must apply unconditional acceptance and unbiased reflection to truly perform active listening.[1] Demonstrating unconditional acceptance can range from difficult to impossible when listeners engage with people or topics that generate strong emotions. It is hard for people to listen to and find potential value in messages that offend their personal, moral, ethical, religious, political, and cultural beliefs.

The next time your emotions flare, you feel offended, or start to get defensive, remember that acceptance doesn't mean agreement. Accepting what a speaker says means recognizing that they believe their perspective is valid, attempting to understand where they are coming from, and withholding immediate judgment. You don't have to agree with what they said, you just have to avoid immediately challenging them or writing them off because of what they say.

> **Accepting what a speaker says means recognizing that they believe their perspective is valid, attempting to understand where they are coming from, and withholding immediate judgment.**

As an example, most of the time leaders, parents, investigators, and sales professionals become furious when someone gives them an excuse or explanation that deflects accountability. They feel personally insulted and angry that their counterpart is abdicating responsibility.

On the contrary, you should be *happy* when people give you an excuse or explanation for why something did or didn't happen. In giving you the excuse, they are acknowledging the situation in a manner that helps them to save face. They are signaling a willingness to talk about the issue at hand on their terms. Leaders must instead put their ego in their back pocket, accept (not agree with) the excuse, and work backward from the excuse to accountability. The process may take longer, but it is far more effective. It is typically much easier for people to accept responsibility at the end of conversations rather than at the beginning.

Achieving unbiased reflection is also a very difficult task. We all have 175 cognitive biases that have been hard-wired into our brains in order to increase the efficiency of our decision-making processes and reduce discomfort.[2] The only way to overcome our biases is to remain alert to when they are impacting our judgments, and intentionally consider additional alternatives and perspectives, which we will delve deeper into in chapter 4.

This process is further complicated by the demands on our time and increased distractions since Rogers and Farson penned their first thoughts on active listening. We are increasingly connected to more people in more ways, twenty-four hours a day. Any direction we look finds us bombarded with information we may or may not want. This bombardment can instantly challenge our priorities, focus, and emotional balance. It can become nearly impossible to be truly present and completely focused on what someone is communicating when our brains are running at ten thousand miles per hour.

Finally, there are two opportunities that active listening doesn't expressly address: What should we be specifically looking for during our critical conversations, and what do we do with our observations? Active listening illustrates how to convince our audiences that we are intently listening. Active listening focuses on evaluating the words spoken, observing body language, and emphasizing the importance of responding empathetically. However, the process doesn't go into great detail on how to increase the power and accuracy of our observations, or how to activate the valuable intelligence we focus on picking up.

USING OUR INTEL

Creating the perception that we are engaged with our counterparts can breed trust, establish connections, and lead to real breakthroughs. In their original work, Rogers and Farson made several statements that are especially useful today and relate to the Disciplined Listening Method. They noted that direct attempts to change someone's self-image are perceived as threatening and force people to either defend themselves or deny the experience. They also noted that active listening is contagious, a growth experience, and carries an element of personal risk. When a leader demonstrates the patience and vulnerability necessary to truly embrace the totality of another person's communication experience, they are setting both the example and the standard for everyone around them.

Active listening is often believed to represent the entire process of listening when it only really addresses one component—signaling attentiveness. Active listening focuses on convincing our counterparts that we are listening; it does not address the techniques and behaviors necessary to increase our situational awareness, pinpoint strategically valuable components of our counterparts' communications, and apply our observations to achieve our goals.

The Disciplined Listening Method goes well beyond signaling attentiveness, focusing on maximizing the value we obtain from our conversations. It starts by understanding how any conversation you participate in can help you achieve your long- and short-term goals. Disciplined Listeners embrace their perceived weaknesses to prepare for important conversations and maximize their observation opportunities by patiently allowing conversations come to them. Disciplined Listeners then observe the totality of their counterparts' communications within the context of the situation and adapt their approaches by quickly applying their observations. As a result, they elicit more information and create stronger relationships by always encouraging their counterparts to protect their self-images, while also building trust equity by following up after important conversations. We will explore the seven core behaviors of the Disciplined Listening Method in chapter 8.

The issues and opportunities we explored in this chapter open the conversation into what it means to be truly engaged, how to engage with others, and how listeners can increase the strategic power of their observations. We will begin our journey toward arriving at these answers and becoming Disciplined Listeners by both examining how we listen as individuals and how other people perceive our listening skills.

CHAPTER TWO

INDIVIDUAL LISTENING APPROACHES

THE POTENTIAL POWER OF great listening skills is undisputed. Most people understand that listening intently is key to developing strong relationships and identifying elusive solutions in any business or personal context. Tuned-in listeners perform three critical tasks simultaneously:

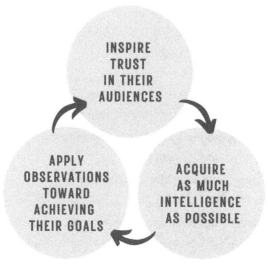

INSPIRE TRUST IN THEIR AUDIENCES

ACQUIRE AS MUCH INTELLIGENCE AS POSSIBLE

APPLY OBSERVATIONS TOWARD ACHIEVING THEIR GOALS

People and organizations often have different operational definitions of what exactly it means to excel at listening, and academia has no shortage of available definitions. Many of these definitions are similar with unique components specific to the researcher's focus area. The process of listening is generally accepted to involve receiving, retaining, and interpreting information prior to responding.

One study breaks listening down into three processes: effective, behavioral, and cognitive.[1] The effective process includes our thoughts and motivations related to listening. Not surprisingly, listeners tend to capture much more information when they are properly motivated to pay attention. The behavioral process involves the actions listeners can take to signal that they are paying attention, which would include the questions they ask and their corresponding nonverbal behaviors. Exhibiting the proper behaviors often results in speakers sharing more valuable information. The cognitive process includes receiving, understanding, and interpreting the information we observe. Accurately interpreting our observations usually results in clearer mutual understandings, shorter paths to solutions, and stronger relationships.

Judi Brownell went even further and systematized the listening process with her HURIER Model.[2] According to Brownell, listening involves six distinct steps:

1. **Hearing:** listeners must fight through internal and external distractions and focus on receiving the right information.

2. **Understanding:** involves comprehending the literal meaning of words they hear.

3. **Remembering:** a critical component of how attentive listeners are perceived to be.

4. **Interpreting:** listeners must consider all the available cues to accurately determine the speaker's intentions and full meaning of the message.

5. **Evaluating:** when listeners judge the messages they receive and arrive at conclusions based on what they've observed.

6. **Responding:** when listeners create an opportunity for speakers to assess their listening efforts.

These steps can be employed independently or sequentially. Systematically dissecting any process increases our opportunity to improve our execution. Anytime we realize that our listening efforts may have fallen short or have misled us, we can reflect on the HURIER model and attempt to identify where our deficiencies may have been. We can ask ourselves:

- Did I hear them correctly and focus on the right information?
- Was I truly clear on what they meant?
- Did I accurately recall their message throughout our interaction?
- What contextual factors did I fail to consider as I interpreted and evaluated their message?
- How did my response affect them?
- What was my motivation?
- How can I learn from these opportunities to improve my next interaction?

Systematically dissecting any process increases our opportunity to improve our execution.

Answering these questions is a good start toward developing heightened awareness and stronger connections. Our reflection and development will be even more accurate and effective when we understand how we listen as individuals.

THE FOUR LISTENING STYLES

In 1995, Kittie Watson and her team reported that people have four primary listening styles: a focus on *people, content, action,* or *time.*[3]

People-focused listeners tend to be more successful identifying emotional cues and common areas of interest. Action-focused listeners often pinpoint inconsistencies or mistakes in messages and prefer concise, organized, and logical explanations. Content-focused listeners tend to be a little more patient and pay attention to the entire message and supporting evidence. Time-focused listeners often prefer to get the information they need as quickly as possible and typically aren't shy to remind speakers of that fact. Watson suggests we all may use each of these in different situations, but we typically default to one style. Understanding our own listening style preference(s) can help us understand how we receive, retain, and interpret information, as well as how we respond during conversations.

> Life is a series of solvable problems. We can choose to focus on the problems, or we can choose to focus on the solutions.

Life is a series of solvable problems. We can choose to focus on the problems, or we can choose to focus on the solutions. The people- and content-focused listening styles focus outward on the speaker and offer more solution-oriented approaches. Choosing to tune in to your counterparts' emotions and patiently evaluating the entirety of their message positions you to maximize your understanding and generate successful solutions. These approaches may be uncomfortable and add additional time. Think of it as an investment in your relationship. More often than not, your commitment will be rewarded with the additional intelligence you receive.

The action- and time-focused listening styles focus inward on the listener and present more problem-oriented approaches.

Few things will erode trust and damage relationships faster than calling out someone's mistakes and forcing them to comply with your preferred listening style. You may very well be correct in your assessments of your counterparts' errors, and it may be much easier for you if your counterparts could present their stories more logically, but it doesn't matter.

Our emotions play a significant role in stressful conversations, and often there is a direct correlation between the amount of stress we are feeling and the perceived importance of a conversation. When emotions run high, peoples' stories are likely to be presented inconsistently and out of order. Due to heightened emotions, as well as the telling and retelling of their experiences, it is common for both victims of crimes and innocent suspects to share inconsistent stories that investigators must patiently sort through. In fact, experienced interrogators often view perfectly seamless and logical stories as red flags that require further investigation.

Time is the enemy of empathy.

The time-focused listening style is likely the most dangerous of Watson's four listening styles. Anyone with a background in production or design knows that when time is prioritized, quality suffers. This is true in relationships as well. Let me be clear—*time is the enemy of empathy.* It is impossible to truly focus on what someone needs, feels, and communicates when we are focusing on the ticking clock in the back of our mind. When we find ourselves in these time-pressed scenarios, it is critical that we ignore what we cannot control (passing time), take a deep breath, and focus on what we can control (our attention and interaction).

Everyone feels defensive and de-valued when they believe they are being rushed through a conversation. This is true with interrogation suspects and their interrogators, parents and children, coaches and athletes, sellers and buyers, and leaders and their employees. The most common professional example occurs when we are on our way to a meeting and an employee stops us in the hall to ask for assistance. Typically, the conversation transpires as follows:

> **Employee**: "Excuse me, do you have a minute? I have an issue I'd like to get your input on."
>
> **Leader**: "I'd love to help, but I have a meeting with Bob in five minutes. Can we catch up later?"
>
> **Employee**: "This will only take a second."
>
> **Leader**: "I'm sure. I'm sorry, I really can't be late for this meeting. I'll catch up with you after."
>
> **Employee**: "Okay."

At the end of this exchange, both parties often walk away with opposing perspectives of the conversation. Leaders often walk away feeling like they listened to the employee. Additionally, the employee understands their priorities and knows they will try to follow up with them—and now the employee has the opportunity to either figure it out on their own, or ask someone else for help.

Conversely, the employee walks away feeling ignored and that they are not worth five minutes of their leader's time. Everyone is busy, and employees know that; they would only approach their leader if they considered it necessary. Over time, these interactions breed resentment, impact productivity and morale, and drive employees from the organization.

Now let's replay this same situation. This time, the leader understands the potential value of every interaction with her team, allows the conversation to come to her, and values quality over time.

Employee: "Excuse me, do you have a minute? I have an issue I'd like to get your input on."

Leader: "Sure, what's going on?"

Employee: "I'm worried we are going to miss our deadline. We are having a really difficult time staying focused, the customer keeps changing their demands, and my teammates keep getting pulled away to help with other projects. I'm getting really stressed out and am running out of ideas to keep us on track. I don't want to upset this customer, lose the contract, or have my bonus impacted. What other options do I have?"

Leader: "Thank you for coming to me. That sounds like a lot, and we should probably sit down and talk through it. I do have a meeting in about two minutes with Bob. Can I come see you at 3:00 when it's over? It would be super helpful if you could outline the specific challenges, where we are on the project, and what ideas you have and haven't tried. That would allow us to create a pretty solid plan together."

Employee: "Okay. Thank you. I'll have it ready for you."

Now both parties walk away from this exchange with much improved perspectives. Sure, leaders may now be concerned about additional infringements on their calendar and other tasks they would rather be doing. However, if the employee and project are important enough, dedicating the time to resolve this issue could easily be in their best interests. The employee walks away feeling much better about the situation. They felt valued, listened to, and supported. Assuming the leader follows up as promised, this interaction can set the tone for how all future issues are handled.

When we recognize the potential value of our relationships and invest in the minutes we share with our employees, customers,

partners, and family members, we may be saving hours of unnecessary stress and problem solving down the road. Just as business
owners have to invest money to make money, we all have to invest
time to save time.

The people who rely on you for leadership, advice, and guidance may feel like they face hundreds of unique problems. There
is a strong chance that if you sat down with them and had them
categorize all their problems, they may only
end up with four to six categories. This
means very few of the problems they deal
with are truly unique. When we invest the
time to teach them how to solve one problem, we're actually teaching them to solve
multiple problems, which saves us much
more time over the long run.

> **Just as business
> owners have to invest
> money to make money,
> we all have to invest
> time to save time.**

A research team led by Graham Bodie updated the initial
writing on Watson's four listening styles in 2013. Their Revised
Listening Styles Profile reframed Watson's styles as goals that
listeners can focus on during their interactions.[4] The four goal-oriented listening approaches that Bodie's team presents are relational
listening, analytical listening, task-oriented listening, and critical
listening. Each of these styles have optimal and suboptimal conversation applications. Our preference for any of these styles may
be influenced by our personality, job title, relationship history,
and relevant pressures we are facing.

According to Bodie and his team, relational listeners generally
have more concern for their counterparts' emotions and feelings.
The relational listening approach could be perfect if you're talking
with someone who you know has more emotional needs, has been
through an emotional experience, or is discussing an emotionally
charged topic. Analytical listeners tend to think systematically
and attempt to listen to the entire message prior to making any

judgments. This approach can be very beneficial when you're participating in negotiations, project development or investigative conversations, and learning unfamiliar topics. Task-oriented listeners prefer for people to remain on topic and are concerned with how much time an interaction may take—they often don't enjoy listening, display verbal aggressiveness, and struggle to respond empathetically. Critical listeners tend to focus on the consistency and accuracy of the messages they receive and prefer to have time to critically examine people and information; it may be wholly appropriate for any investigative or fact gathering/checking conversation.

SELF VS. OTHERS LISTENING

Bodie's listening approaches can also be categorized into self- and other-focused categories. Listeners who apply relational and analytical listening approaches are focusing their attention on their counterparts' feelings, messages, and needs. Listeners who apply task-oriented and critical listening approaches are focused on satisfying their own perceived needs, potentially at the expense of their counterparts.

It is likely that listeners who default to each of these four approaches will defend their preferred style as the best style, and why it works best for them. While this is understandable, it is also short-sighted. Leaders, parents, sales professionals, and investigators will all be more successful if they allow their audience, goals, and the situation to dictate what listening approach they use. This can be accomplished by asking yourself, "What listening style will help me achieve my goal as I interact with this person, in this situation?"

ASSESSING PREFERENCES

Discovering and exploring our own listening preferences is an important exercise. It allows us to understand how we prioritize information and outcomes, as well as recognize how other people experience us during our conversations.

It also mirrors one of the biggest issues with personality quizzes and other similar assessments. The process of completing, evaluating, and reviewing these assessment results can either motivate a person to increase their awareness or negatively reinforce a person's self-image. To share one example, let's say an executive takes a personality assessment and the results show that he prefers a dominant communication style. He has two options for how he applies this knowledge. The first option is to understand how his dominant approach can shut people down and make an intentional effort to be less dominant in his communications. His second option is to view the assessment results as confirmation of who he is, a justification for his dominant communication style, and tell his employees they need to adapt to him. If we polled a large population of executives, we may be surprised by the number of respondents who believe their employees should accept and conform to their default communication styles. These same executives likely also lament the amount of critical and timely information they don't receive from their employees.

You may be thinking, *I would love to change my communication style and be more cognizant of the impact I'm having on others, but I can't. This is who I am.* Anytime we say, "I can't," we are leaving one word out of that sentence—"easily." Essentially, we are experiencing a disconnect between either the perceived cognitive, emotional, and/or physical effort we need to commit, and the perceived reward we will receive for our

> Anytime we say, "I can't," we are leaving one word out of that sentence—"easily."

efforts. If the efforts outweigh the reward, we feel like we can't do it. If the perceived rewards outweigh the perceived efforts, we feel like we can. Moving ourselves, or anyone else, from "I can't" to "I did" starts with recalibrating the perceived efforts and rewards involved with the change in action or beliefs you're requesting.

Let's consider that many professional and personal conversations feature at least one person who is looking to obtain information and at least one person who may be asked to share information. People seeking information have two choices. They can either adapt their approach to fit the needs of their audience, or they can attempt to force their audience to comply with their default communication approach. This choice highlights an unfortunate reality that many leaders, sales professionals, investigators, and parents have difficulty accepting. *If you are talking to another person who has information that you need to obtain, you are not in control of the conversation, regardless of your title or position.* The more you try to demand con-

> **The more you try to demand control of the conversation, the less control you have.**

trol of the conversation, the less control you have. The person with the information is in total control because they will eventually choose what information to share or withhold, and why. Most of the time, they will almost certainly choose the option that makes them feel better, regardless of the perceived consequences. Listeners who are captive to their default approaches and refuse to adapt to their audiences are leaving information on the table—and definitely blaming other people for not sharing this information with them.

This next statement will almost certainly feel counterintuitive. The best way to maintain control of most conversations is to allow your counterpart to feel as if they are in control. Metaphorically speaking, if you push someone, their first reaction is to push you back—harder. Then you respond in kind, and the situation quickly escalates. If you don't push someone, they don't have to push back. If they aren't pushing back, you are in control of the conversation and can patiently follow their lead to guide the conversation where you want it to go.

For much of my career, I conducted non-custodial interrogations. This meant that my subjects were not under arrest, I could not hold them against their will, and they were free to leave anytime they wanted. As a result, I started every conversation by telling my subjects they were free to leave at any point.

When people would threaten to get up and leave my interrogations, I would respond by saying, "Go ahead, you're free to leave anytime you want." That answer defeated the argument they were hoping to start and they continued participating in the interview. Of course, I've had a few people just sit in front of me for an hour and refuse to say a word, but it took eleven years for someone to actually get up and walk out.

I was interrogating a human resources executive who was accused of taking a drug test for her younger brother, an employee at the company, because she knew he couldn't pass the test. She and her brother were under investigation because her brother had made a series of mistakes. His biggest mistake wasn't doing drugs while working for a company that prohibited and tested for drug use. It wasn't even asking his sister to take his test for him, or telling his girlfriend (a coworker) the whole story. No, his biggest mistake was breaking up with his girlfriend after he told her. Hell hath no fury, as they say. His ex-girlfriend responded to the breakup by telling the company everything she knew, and they started an investigation.

During the interrogation, the HR director threatened to get up and leave three times but chose to remain in the room. The fourth time she told me she wanted to leave I started to respond with, "Like I said, you can—" and she cut me off by saying, "I don't want to listen to your stories anymore, I quit," and walked straight out of the building, got in her car, and left.

I honestly have to give her credit. If the accusations were true, she fell on the sword for her brother, and quitting saved her from being terminated. She also took the opportunity to warn her brother before I could speak with him. He was very polite and professional when he walked into the office I was using, and had the self-control to not say one single word for over an hour. He was later relieved of his job for operational reasons.

A few interactions have reaffirmed this lesson in control for me. My former boss, Dave Zulawski, and I were once reviewing one of my interrogation videos together; he became particularly attentive as I was attempting to expand the suspect's initial admission. She had confessed to a small amount of theft and I was attempting to encourage her to share additional theft activity along with possible accomplices. After suffering through my attempt for a few minutes, Dave paused the video, looked at me, and calmly said, "You sound too needy. The more you sound like you need this information, the more power it gives her and the less likely she is to share it with you." It was sage advice that I've been applying in all my important interactions ever since.

This lesson is constantly reinforced by none other than my dog. My wife and I chose to buy a house out in the country because we enjoy the tranquility. We didn't realize that we had purchased a home in an area where people commonly release dogs they no longer want into the woods. We've found, and helped rescue, a dozen dogs since we've lived here. We chose to keep one for ourselves and she is a loving (and crazy) little girl. She also has a strong will, loves to play, and usually only listens when she wants to. It's pretty common for her to run out into the yard when I let her out at night. If I chase after her, she runs away. If I call her a few times and open the door as if I'm going inside without her, she runs back to the house. She is only going to come back inside when she wants to, and my approach has a significant impact on her decision.

THE SIX LEVELS OF LISTENING

Our perception of our own listening skills isn't nearly as important as how our audience perceives our listening skills. To this end, Jack Zenger and Joseph Folkman outlined six levels of listening that simultaneously improve both our listening ability and how we are perceived as listeners.[5]

They describe level 1 listening as creating a safe environment where difficult and emotional issues can be discussed. Level 2 listeners remove all distractions (yes, including and especially your cell phone) and maintain appropriate eye contact. Level 3 listeners seek to understand the substance of the message they are receiving and confirm the accuracy of their understanding. Level 4 listeners observe nonverbal cues. Level 5 listeners empathize with their counterparts by identifying, acknowledging, and validating their emotions without conveying judgment. Finally, level 6 listeners ask questions to clarify their assumptions and help reframe the issues being discussed—without hijacking the conversation.

Zenger and Folkman's levels range from common displays of respect (a private setting and no open phones or computers), to high levels of attention (observing nonverbal cues), to strong emotional intelligence (seeking understanding, demonstrating empathy) and high levels of curiosity (asking questions). The levels and behaviors each listener commits to is directly related

People view how you communicate with them as proof of how much you respect them.

1 CREATE A SAFE ENVIRONMENT

2 REMOVE ALL DISTRACTIONS

3 SEEK TO UNDERSTAND THE SUBSTANCE AND ACCURACY

4 OBSERVE NONVERBAL CUES

5 EMPATHIZE WITH COUNTERPARTS WITHOUT JUDGMENT

6 ASK CLARIFYING QUESTIONS AND HELP REFRAME THE ISSUES WITHOUT TAKING OVER THE CONVERSATION to the value they associate with each conversation in which they participate. All these levels tie into one very important concept to understand: *people view how you communicate with them as proof of how much you respect them.* This perception includes all aspects of how we listen and how we communicate.

Leaders have two risks to consider when determining how much effort and attention to dedicate to each interaction. The first risk is dedicating more effort and attention than necessary—which negatively impacts the leader. The second risk is not dedicating enough effort and attention because they underestimated the potential value of the conversation—which negatively impacts both participants. All things being equal, leaders are far better served committing too much time and attention than too little.

AM I READING YOU CORRECTLY?

To this end, it is important to stop and consider a few of Margarete Imhof's research findings into the perception of listening behaviors.[6] She found that assessments of good and poor listening behavior are directly related to the perceived status of the listener. Her research found that listeners in subordinate (i.e., employee, child) positions are expected to behaviorally orient themselves toward speakers with superior status, send clear attention signals, and ask questions. This means that superiors believe their subordinates are good listeners when they remain quiet, don't interrupt, aren't distracted, appear focused and patient, and ask clarifying questions.

Conversely, subordinates are considered to be poor listeners if they appear preoccupied, distracted, unprepared, look around, interrupt, change the subject, don't ask any questions, or ask a superior to repeat what they've said.

Leaders will benefit from a little contextual awareness before jumping to these conclusions. It is a good discipline for leaders to consciously offer their counterpart the benefit of the doubt. For example, even if their counterpart appears to be looking around, perhaps they are either processing what they are hearing or experiencing elevated stress levels. Subordinates may also appear preoccupied or distracted when they are trying to create an acceptable answer or recall important information. Finally, any interruptions, lack of questions, or requests to repeat statements may be a result of communication failure on the leader's part. Here is a list of reflection questions that a leader might first ask themselves before they jump to conclusions:

- Am I engaged and connected?
- Am I bullying the conversation?
- Am I speaking too quickly?
- Am I speaking abstractly or concretely?

When the relationship is flipped, Imhof found that listeners with a superior status (i.e., leaders, parents) are viewed more favorably by their subordinates when they display an open-minded and caring attitude. This means that subordinates feel their superiors are good listeners when they are calm, refrain from judging, demonstrate empathy, are honest and helpful, and show interest both verbally and nonverbally. Conversely, subordinates feel that their superiors are poor listeners when they jump to conclusions, appear self-absorbed, or are judgmental.

It is worth saying again—*time is the enemy of empathy.* These behaviors present further rebukes of the inward-focused listening styles and approaches: action, time, task-oriented, and critical. Maybe the hardest part of listening as a leader is suppressing the belief (verbally and nonverbally) that you know how the movie ends before it starts. The two most divisive things leaders in any context can do is pass judgment on their audiences and make the situation about themselves. Statements such as "I think," "I believe," "I feel," "What I need," "What I need you to do," "What you need to do for me," and "I give you permission" could offend subordinate audiences because they indicate this conversation is all about the leader. Every one of these statements creates the perception that the leader is treating their employee like a child; the negative effects of these kinds of statements multiply the more they are used.

Leaders can benefit from several small changes in their delivery to remove these unhealthy parental connotations. One option is to drop "I think" from the sentence and start with whatever your recommendation is and replacing the statements above with questions such as:

- "Considering where we are in the process, what needs to be done next?"
- "What should we do next to avoid falling behind?"
- "Keeping our end goal in mind, what is our best next step?"

Other helpful replacement phrases include:

- "It may be worth considering . . ."
- "Another option could be . . ."
- "The next step in the process . . ."
- "In order to ensure that we stay on track, the next step is . . ."
- "Based on what we currently know, it appears best if we . . ."

It is important to note that these questions and statements should all be delivered with a curious tone, and not a judgmental one.

THE DISCIPLINED LISTENING LEADERSHIP TEST

All our team's leadership advising engagements start with the same first step. We begin every one-on-one executive engagement by presenting our clients, as well as their peers and direct reports, with the Disciplined Listening Leadership Test. It only consists of three questions, yet the results provide us with tremendous insight. The three questions are simple: Are you calm? Are you consistent? Are you making people better?

We are in great shape if the executives, their peers, and their direct reports believe the answers to all three questions are "yes." We have a lot of work to do if everyone agrees the answers are "no." We have the most amount of work to do when leaders believe the answers are "yes" and their peers and direct reports believe the answers are "no." Perception is reality. *We do not get to decide if we are good listeners or communicators; only our audiences do.*

Calm leaders are perceived to be better listeners and communicators, exercise more control during stressful situations, and are intelligent/aware enough to thoughtfully consider alternatives. Additionally, calm is contagious. Calm leaders inspire calm teams. Simply put, if you're okay, they're okay. Consistent leaders are perceived as trustworthy and predictable. Their teams experience less stress because they can be relatively sure how the leader will respond or react. Finally,

> **We do not get to decide if we are good listeners or communicators; only our audiences do.**

leaders who are perceived to prioritize others over themselves generate much higher levels of trust, commitment, and engagement. If you feel like you always, often, or frequently experience difficulty communicating with people, please stop and ask yourself, "Am I the common denominator?" If your communication difficulties extend across multiple people and/or groups, and you are the only common link, you are almost certainly doing (or not doing) something that is contributing to the issue. To steal a quote from one of my favorite TV shows, "If you run into an asshole in the morning, you probably ran into an asshole. If you run into assholes all day, you're the asshole."[7]

A FINAL REFLECTION

Let's take a few seconds to acknowledge several facts as we wrap up this chapter. Listening is a key leadership skill in all contexts. Listening is hard. It requires a dedicated effort. The more power someone has in any situation, the easier it is to falsely believe that they don't need to listen to anyone else. All of this leaves us with a final question to consider. What is more important—forcing people to comply with your preferred communication techniques, or obtaining information and developing the relationships you need to achieve your goals? If you need someone to commit to something they may not want to do or say, forcing them to conform to your preferred communication style will almost certainly be counterproductive.

This sentiment is often greeted with the same response from our executive clients: "I shouldn't have to change my style." Whenever you consider adapting your communication approach and you think, "I shouldn't have to do that"—STOP—and recognize two realities. The first one is, you are most likely right; you shouldn't have to do it. The second is, this is exactly what you need to do. In this context, anytime we think, "I shouldn't have to do that," we've almost certainly identified the right thing to do. More often than not, the thing we need to do the most is the thing we want to do the least.

The Disciplined Listening Method is based on the belief that we have the ability to increase the value of our interactions. It is impossible to execute successfully if we apply

> **More often than not, the thing we need to do the most is the thing we want to do the least.**

self-centered styles in our conversations. It is easier to commit to this approach when we think of vulnerability and discomfort not ~~as~~ are weaknesses to avoid, but ~~as~~ investments in our professional and personal relationships.

Even our most well-intentioned efforts can be short-circuited by common conversational errors. In the next chapter we will discuss how to identify, avoid, and overcome some of the most common mistakes leaders make in their business and personal conversations.

CHAPTER THREE

COMMON LISTENING MISTAKES

CONSIDERING HOW IMPORTANT LISTENING is in every aspect of our lives, it is incredibly difficult to do well. There are a myriad of internal and external forces working against our best efforts. Distractions, emotions, perceptions, competing priorities, and the complexities of communication make the processes of accurate evaluation and value identification exceedingly difficult.

The process of listening includes three opportunities to mislead ourselves. The first is what we actually observe (and what we believe we observed). The second is how we interpret and internally react to what we observe. The third opportunity is how we respond to what we observe. Mistakes or misjudgments in any of these three areas can create inaccuracies within our assessments, missed opportunities, and damaged relationships.

Unfortunately, we've all been exposed to myths and misinformation about listening and observing. We've been taught that many behaviors have specific meanings that are either completely untrue, or only occasionally accurate. These widely accepted myths are wonderful for misinforming observers.

MYTH BUSTING

One of the most common myths is that when people cross their arms, they are closed off and defensive—and this is simply not true. I've had numerous suspects cross their arms immediately prior to confessing their crimes. People generally cross their arms for two reasons: physical comfort and emotional vulnerability. It is very common for people to cross their arms when they are cold, if they find it is a comfortable position to rest in, or it helps relieve physical pain or discomfort.

Emotional vulnerability is more complex than simple defensiveness. When people are feeling vulnerable, they will commonly use their arms and hands to cover the areas of their body that their skeletal system leaves open—their abdomen and their neck. People may feel vulnerable if they are considering a new idea, or an idea that contradicts their beliefs. They may also feel vulnerable when they decide to share sensitive information. People often feel uncomfortable in novel situations and yes, people can feel uncomfortable when they become defensive. Next time you're having a conversation with someone and they cross their arms immediately, ask yourself two questions: What event appeared to cause them to cross their arms? And what does the rest of their body language say? If they crossed their arms at a random time, it may mean they were physically uncomfortable. If it happened when the air conditioner turned on, it may mean they are cold. If it happened when the waiter returned to the table, he may make your counterpart uncomfortable. If they crossed their arms when you accused them of making a mistake, they may feel defensive.

Single-factor decisions are dangerous and should be avoided whenever possible.

Single-factor decisions are dangerous and should be avoided whenever possible. This is true both in life and when evaluating communication. Just seeing someone cross their arms does not provide you with enough information to accurately determine what your counterpart is feeling. Quickly look at their face and the rest of their body language. If they exhale, droop their shoulders, and drop their heads, they are likely about to tell you something very sensitive. If they are nodding their head from side to side, pursing their lips, and tapping their feet, they may be considering various alternatives. If they turn their shoulders perpendicular to you and snarl, they are likely angry. Like placing pieces in a puzzle, the accuracy of our evaluations increases when we observe multiple components of behavior shifts.

Another extremely popular myth is that people avoid eye contact when they lie. In fact, Charles Bond conducted two extensive research studies covering seventy-five countries and over 4,800 participants and found the number one behavior people associate with dishonesty, globally, is gaze aversion.[1] This myth is 100 percent untrue. The scientific community has repeatedly proven that there is zero correlation between breaking eye contact, maintaining eye contact, or looking either to the left or to the right, and dishonesty.[2] Yet across the globe, it is the number one behavior people associate with liars.

People break eye contact within their own cultural and personality norms when they feel stress, and they generally maintain eye contact within their norms when they are comfortable. Honest people are just as likely to break eye contact when they feel stress telling the truth, as dishonest people are if they feel stress when they are lying. On the flip side of the coin, dishonest people who feel no stress lying will have no problem maintaining eye contact throughout their deceptive communications.

Once again, single-factor decisions are dangerous. Broken eye contact needs to be evaluated along with any additional corresponding verbal and nonverbal behavior shifts within the context of the situation.

When I was young, I struggled to fit in, and my struggle often manifested itself in behaviors that my teachers and principals weren't pleased with. As a result, it wasn't uncommon for my parents to receive a call to inform them of my unfortunate behavior choices. I usually wasn't in a hurry to tell my parents exactly what happened and often tried to avoid the conversation or minimize the details.

My father would counter my diversionary tactics by saying, "Michael Garrett, look me in the eye and tell me the truth." I'm sure part of his statement was to make sure he had my full attention. He was also likely fueled by the false belief that people break eye contact when they lie. As a young child, looking him in the eye resulted in me telling him the truth because of the stress his eye contact induced.

This tactic produced positive results for my father when I was in the first grade. However, this was only a temporary win for him. These conversations occurred so many times in my early school years that it didn't take too long before looking him in the eye no longer generated a stressful response. By the time I was out of elementary school, I had no problem making eye contact and telling him whatever story I thought might work that night. Practice makes perfect, as they say.

Crossed arms and broken eye contact are not the only two widespread myths with regard to evaluating communication. Tim Levine reviewed all the relevant studies into deception detection from 1981 to 2011 and found an extensive list of behaviors people erroneously believe indicate dishonesty.[3] Some of the highlights include acting nervous, shifting posture, contradictions, sounding uncertain, feeling less friendly or cooperative, talking faster, and taking long pauses before responding. None of these behaviors have ever been scientifically linked to deception.

As Levine's work continued, he found that we often judge

others as honest or dishonest based on their overall demeanor. He clarified that people who exhibit behavior clues such as confidence and composure, appear friendly and engaged, and give plausible explanations are very likely to be perceived as honest. On the other hand, he noted that people who exhibit behavior clues such as gaze aversion, hesitance, excessive fidgeting, appear tense or nervous, sound uncertain in their tone or words, and portray inconsistent behavior are often perceived as dishonest.

Again, none of the behaviors on either list directly correlate to truth and deception. Liars who are practiced or comfortable lying will likely demonstrate all the honest demeanor traits. Regretfully, honest people who are uncomfortable sharing a message will likely exhibit many of the dishonest demeanor traits. Paul Ekman refers to failures to recognize these dangers as the *Othello error* and the *Brokaw hazard*.[4] The Othello error occurs when people fail to realize that honest people experiencing stress sometimes exhibit behaviors typically thought to indicate deception. The Brokaw hazard occurs when observers fail to consider individual differences that may lead liars to show zero deception clues and honest people to exhibit deception clues. Education, contextual awareness, and both pre- and post-conversation fact-checking are the most powerful tools observers have to protect themselves from these erroneous evaluations.

Many of the behaviors typically associated with dishonesty are actually reflections of discomfort. There are dozens of reasons why someone may exhibit behavior that makes them appear nervous or uncomfortable. Lying is only one of them. The people you engage with may appear uncomfortable because they are embarrassed, confused, surprised, or unprepared. They may lack knowledge of, or confidence in, the topic you are discussing. They may also feel like they are under mounting pressure. Additional factors such as cultural differences, language barriers, or previous life experiences may impact their communication, or they may be in a hurry to go somewhere or do something else. They may be worried about perceived consequences you're not even considering. The physical environment may be impacting their behavior. It may even be the result of a misunderstanding and maybe, just maybe, it's because they find you attractive. Assuming discomfort equals dishonesty is a potentially disastrous decision.

DANGEROUS EXTERNAL DISTRACTIONS

In addition to observing the wrong behaviors, assigning value to the wrong behaviors, and falling prey to these communication myths, we often mislead our observational efforts without realizing it by distracting ourselves.

One way that we distract ourselves from picking up on the nuances of our counterparts' communications is when we multitask. Our brains aren't capable of fully focusing on two separate things at once. This is why texting and driving is so dangerous. Think about the last time you tried to talk on the phone and send an email simultaneously. How many times did you speak what you wanted to type, type a word said on the phone, and mixed up both messages? It's very likely that neither conversation was completely coherent.

Multitasking is the archenemy of listening.

Multitasking is the archenemy of listening. We cannot fully focus on the messages we receive when we are doing something else. Rule number one for participating in critical conversations is to remove any distractions. Shut your cell phone off. Take your smart watch off. Close your laptop or shut off your desktop computer. Simply leaving your phone in your pocket or turning away from your computer isn't enough. Our brains produce dopamine every time our devices buzz or beep, to alert us to new messages. This dopamine hit immediately distracts us as we start guessing who the message may be from, what it may be about, and fighting (or succumbing to) the urge to check the message. Shut off your television. Turn off the music. Position yourself so you're not facing potential distractions. Stop engaging with other people. Focus on listening.

Distractions cause more damage than we may initially anticipate. While they reduce the intelligence we observe, distractions also destroy relationships. Remember, people interpret how you communicate with them as proof of how much you respect them. When your counterparts perceive that you are prioritizing your devices, other people, or other activities over them, they determine that you don't value them. In turn, their determination negatively impacts how they communicate with you. We often blame poor communication on our counterparts without realizing we may have caused it. This classic lose-lose situation is far too prevalent; we may be distracted as much as 75 percent of the time during our conversations.[5]

INTERNAL DISTRACTIONS

The external distractions are obvious. The internal distractions are more sinister. The single biggest distraction that creates the greatest negative impact on our ability to listen is the voice inside our own heads—our internal monologues. No one can have anything more important to say to us than we have to say to ourselves. Our internal monologue wins every time.

The first danger is that it tricks us into believing we have observed our counterparts' messages accurately when we have missed the point altogether. We pick up enough pieces of what they communicate that we believe we understand the totality of their message. In reality, our brains connect the dots and insert the missing pieces based on our perspectives, expectations, and assumptions—not what our counterparts told us. This dangerous mistake is often compounded by overconfidence.

Another danger is the mathematical imbalances our internal monologues create. According to Rodney Korba's research, our inner speech (as he refers to it) is capable of producing up to 4,000 words per minute,which is 10 times the rate of our outer speech.[6] This disparity often leads us away from the intelligence we need to be observing, reaching into the past or jumping into the future instead of focusing on the present conversation.

How fast our internal conversation races away from us is a problem. Where it usually races to is even more problematic. Often our internal monologue focuses on how we feel, confirming our expectations, and what to say next. All three of these alternatives can produce disastrous results.

Human beings are emotional creatures. All of our observations and decisions are filtered through our emotions. As the team at Vital Smarts illustrated in their book *Crucial Conversations*, there is a four-step process that leads us from observation to action.[7]

The first step is our *observations*, what we choose to see and hear. In the second step, we give our observations meaning by *telling ourselves a story*. We can't see our counterparts' intentions, so we fill in the gaps. The stories we generate are based on our expectations, perspective, biases, and assumptions. Sometimes, they are accurate. These stories have the potential to lead us off course, cloud our judgment, and unconsciously judge our counterparts based on our own thoughts and feelings.

Once we tell ourselves a story, we *generate an emotion*. We typically believe the emotion is directly based on our observation, but it is not. The emotions we feel are a direct result of the stories we tell ourselves. Their words or actions don't make us happy, mad, or sad. Our *interpretation* of their words and actions make us happy, mad, or sad. Blaming our emotions on our counterparts' actions is another misstep that limits opportunities to generate new value in our conversations.

The fourth step, *taking action*, is based on the emotion we feel. Our actions are two steps removed from our actual observations, and we typically do not realize this. We believe that how we respond to our counterparts is a direct response to what they say or do, and we justify our behavior accordingly. Oftentimes, this is not the reality of the situation.

CHALLENGING OUR PRECONCEIVED NOTIONS

We carry expectations of value into every conversation we participate in. These expectations may be positive, negative, or neutral, and they absolutely impact the amount of observational effort we exert. They also determine what information we retain and interpret. People react the strongest to what they first observe. We literally look and listen for the very first verbal or nonverbal indication that either confirms or violates our preconceived expectations.

People react the strongest to what they first observe.

Several very interesting research studies have addressed the question of just how quickly humans make their initial judgments during their conversations. The answer is lightning fast. A research team led by Dr. Phil McAleer at the University of Glasgow found that we are capable of judging someone's trustworthiness and dominance (among other factors) in as fast as *300–500 milliseconds* just by listening to them say the word "hello."[8]

Another research team from Princeton University led by Janine Willis and Alexander Todorov found that we are capable of judging someone's trustworthiness, aggressiveness, and competence in as fast as *100 milliseconds* just by looking at their face.[9] A third study conducted by Tiffany Ito and Geoffrey Urland from the University of Colorado demonstrated that we are capable of categorizing people, specifically by their gender and race, in *100– 150 milliseconds.*[10]

Think about this for a moment. There is a high likelihood that in the first fraction of a second you meet someone you've already judged their trustworthiness, competence, and attitude, and categorized them within one of your pre-existing mental categories. Right or wrong, these immediate judgments cast a shadow over our conversations and direct what we observe, how we interpret our observations, and how we respond for the duration of our interactions.

Admittedly these instantaneous determinations aren't always bad. They can be game-changing and life-saving realizations when we are in highly competitive or life-threatening situations. Thankfully, most of our conversations don't fit into either category, although our body can trick us into feeling like they do.

Anytime we feel threatened or vulnerable to a high enough degree, our fight-or-flight response kicks in. When this happens, our rational brain shuts off and our emotional brain takes over with the singular focus of getting us through perceived danger; we lose the ability to see the big picture and think strategically, and we make short-term, tactical decisions to relieve the discomfort we are facing. Fight or flight is not called "stop and think" for a reason. The blood and oxygen that our brains need in order to think clearly rushes away from our brains and down to our extremities. When we are under stress, we go to what we know. We default to communication approaches and action sets we are comfortable with. These approaches can often be defensive, resulting in us communicating in a parental style and treating counterparts like children, and frequently drive us to achieve short-term success at the expense of others. The best way to center ourselves, think strategically, and elevate our observations is to intentionally slow the situation down and take a deep breath.

ARE YOU IN OR OUT?

Our snap judgments are based on our life history, perceptions, and stereotypes. In their book *Blind Spot*, Mahzarin Banaji and Anthony Greenwald discuss the fact that stereotypes connect groups with shared attributes.[11] They illustrate that any stereotype is partially true and partially false, and that group stereotypes are typically negative.

These stereotypes assist in instantaneous categorization. According to Banaji and Greenwald, our category-forming capacity is so great that we can envision a complete person when they are described by a set of six unfamiliar dimensions. Once our brains possess that tiny amount of information, we are capable of connecting the rest of the dots, and feeling good about it.

The categories we place people in are often filed within our perceived in-groups and out-groups. In-groups are groups of people with whom we believe we share important traits. We often perceive our in-groups to be people who look like us, share the same beliefs and interests we do, and come from the same places we do. These may include your family, friends, fans of the same sports team or music groups, graduates from the same universities, people from the same city, members of the same church or political group, and teammates. Out-groups are for people who we don't perceive to share important traits with us and who we perceive to have opposing views or experiences.

The power of our in-group and out-group perceptions cannot be overstated. Dan Ariely is one of many researchers whose work has demonstrated our increased willingness to listen to, support, defend, and even commit crimes for members of our in-groups.[12] The same research illustrates how we often behave in unexpected ways when we interact with people from out-groups. We are far less likely to listen or support them. When we communicate with members of our in-groups, we often listen to confirm our similarities, whereas when we communicate with members of our out-groups, we often listen for opportunities to validate our disagreements and de-value their ideas, as it would violate our self-image to be in agreement with someone "on the other side." This self-image violation is why it can be extremely hard to separate messages from messengers.

DRESSING THE PART

One of the earliest lessons I was taught as an interrogator was to dress slightly more professional than the people I interviewed. Dressing too casually or too formally has the potential to hurt an interrogator's perceived credibility.

With this lesson in mind, I arrived on site wearing khakis and a button-down shirt for an investigation at a manufacturing and distribution facility in rural Oklahoma. It was a typical theft case involving multiple suspects and no evidence. About halfway through my interviews, I believed that I had identified the culprit and decided to interrogate him. There were several times I thought he was going to confess, but he didn't. I had no evidence, so about sixty minutes into the conversation, I had to excuse him to go back to work. Later that afternoon, another employee provided me with some unexpected evidence that confirmed my suspicion, and my client agreed to let me re-interrogate the main suspect the next morning.

That night I sat in my hotel room, reviewing my game plan and lamenting the fact that the next day's interrogation would be exponentially harder than the first conversation. Aside from adapting my approach to essentially pick up where we left off, I made one other change. I decided to show up the next day wearing jeans and a short-sleeve golf shirt.

The next morning, when the suspect and I sat across from each other, his demeanor quickly relaxed. Not only did he confess to a substantial amount of theft, he also confessed to working for his company's biggest competitor on the side and providing them with proprietary information. I'm sure several factors converged to motivate him to tell me the truth. I'm also confident that the fact that I was wearing jeans made it much easier for him to identify with me and rationalize telling me the truth.

COMMUNICATE FROM COMMON GROUND

Human experiences are far more universal than we may expect. People across the world share common journeys, feelings, and wishes. Focusing on these commonalities opens our minds to potentially hidden opportunities to create value in our conversations. Conversely, focusing on our differences virtually ensures division.

Human beings are hardwired with bias. These biases typically serve as shortcuts to save us time and energy, while increasing the comfort we experience with the decisions we make. There are several biases whose impacts on listening are particularly significant and are worth highlighting.

Confirmation bias is likely the biggest. Our brains are wired to look and listen for information that confirms what we already think and believe—and ignore, or explain away, information that doesn't. When confirmation bias sets in, we find exactly what we are looking for every time. If we believe someone is trying to take advantage of us, we will latch onto the first potential verbal or nonverbal indication that verifies our assumptions and use it to validate our preconceived expectations.

Confirmation bias also ties into another inherent danger of observational interpretations. One of Robert Cialdini's countless contributions to the world of influence and persuasion is the idea that we often mistake what is causal for what is focal.[13] Meaning that if we are focusing on our counterpart's job title, years of experience, clothing, age, gender, race, or other factors, we can easily believe that the single factor we are focusing on is the root cause of their statements or behavior. This trap may provide a quick and comfortable judgment for us, but it drastically restricts our situational awareness, reaffirms our biases, and reduces our ability to connect with others and resolve conflict.

Another related mistake observers often make is assuming that correlation equals causality.[14] The example Steven Levitt and Stephen Dubner use in their book, *Think Like a Freak,* is that just because married people are often happier than single people, doesn't mean that marriage makes people happy. People who were happy prior to getting married are likely still happy, and people who were grumpy prior to getting married are probably still grumpy.

Determining the actual cause of the communication we observe is a key skill Disciplined Listeners intentionally work to develop. Separating our momentary focus and correlated traits from actual causation requires observers to recognize when their biases are impacting their evaluations and increase their situational awareness. They must observe to learn as opposed to observing to validate. Two questions we can ask ourselves to help with this process are, "What am I missing?" and, "How are my assumptions driving my decisions?"

A similar bias with real negative potential is diagnosis bias. Diagnosis bias often occurs when we fall in love with snap conclusions, based on incomplete data sets and our preconceived assumptions, and fail to investigate other potential explanations or alternatives. The negative impacts of diagnosis bias are often reinforced by our confirmation bias as we look to validate our choices.

Our brains love nothing more than to experience consistency and comfort. When we are presented with information, or act in a way that deviates from our beliefs, we experience cognitive dissonance. Perhaps the most common example of cognitive dissonance is buyer's remorse. When this dissonance creates discomfort, we rationalize or justify our new beliefs or actions so they fall in line with our previous ones. The best way to avoid falling prey to diagnosis bias is to maintain a curious, learning mentality. If we continue to test our ideas and educate ourselves, we are less likely to fall victim to diagnosis and confirmation bias.

INVESTIGATE FOR INNOCENCE

Earlier in my career I taught investigators how to complete investigations. Many were taken aback when I told them that our job as investigators was to conduct our investigations with the mindset of proving people innocent. This thought is often counterintuitive to people who have dedicated their professional lives to catching criminals.

If investigators conduct investigations with the intention of proving their suspects guilty, they will reliably find a piece of evidence that confirms their suspicions. Once they find this piece of evidence, they will more likely fall prey to confirmation and diagnosis bias, cut their investigations short, and claim they have solved the case. While they may have found the guilty party, ending their investigations early may stop them from identifying other crimes the suspect has committed, accomplices, and additional incriminating evidence, while also creating potential liabilities for the prosecution team. Or worse, they may try and prosecute an innocent person based on circumstantial evidence that confirmed their initial suspicions, while the guilty suspect goes free.

When investigators proceed with the intent of proving their suspects innocent, it forces them to leave no stone unturned and no lead untraced. If at the end of their investigation, they cannot prove that their suspect is innocent, they are more likely to have identified the guilty party and developed a thorough case with stronger evidence.

Two more biases that impact the observation process are legacy bias and recency bias. How often have you heard someone answer a question with "because we've always done it that way." This is a common vocalization of legacy bias. Often, it's because we value comfort over learning; it is reinforced by our preconceived assumptions and devalues new communication opportunities.

Recency bias is the opposite. This occurs when we overvalue new information and discount previous experiences that may add value to our current situation. We fall victim to recency bias when we make decisions based on what people have done for us lately as opposed to what they've done throughout the relationship.

There is one more bias that is well worth considering—truth bias. I often work with clients who say something to the effect of, "I like to give people the benefit of the doubt and I feel like I get fooled a lot." If this sounds like you, join the club. Tim Levine's research has made it clear that we are biased toward believing what we hear and experience is true. And this is actually a good thing.[15]

Levine asserts that we tend to believe that another person's communication is honest. Yes, we all get fooled occasionally. However, we receive the truth the vast majority of the time, so we are biased toward believing what we are told is true. In his book *Duped*, Levine goes well beyond discussing truth bias and shares an avalanche of research that supports his Truth Default Theory. Essentially, he contends that most of the time, most people walk around in a Truth Default State, where they passively presume honesty before considering deceit. Levine states that people typically operate in this Truth Default State until they experience a trigger that creates suspicion and kicks them out of it.

Understanding that we all normally walk around assuming others are telling the truth (Truth Default State) and that we are more likely to accept what we are told to be true (truth bias) is helpful in several ways. First, it is beneficial to know that this is how we experience the world around us most of the time. Second, it is important to consider when you may be interacting with someone who may be motivated to deceive you. Anytime you believe these motivations may exist, alertness should be heightened to expose your counterparts' potential attempts at manipulation.

The final opportunity that can make or break a relationship is the way an observer reacts. It is easy for observers to filter their observations through their expectations as well as their moral and ethical standards. Any perceived offense to these standards typically drives how we respond to the offender. In these situations, we do not respond to solve a problem or obtain the truth—we respond to right a perceived moral wrong and reassert our power.

THE DISCONNECT

Leaders possess the ability to hand down consequences to their subordinates. As a result, leadership titles often motivate subordinate communicators to be less honest, timely, and thorough with the information they provide. And who can blame them? Considering that leaders often feel entitled to "perfect" information, this conflict in motivation often causes perceived moral and ethical slights.

Falling into this entitlement trap causes leaders to make a series of mistakes. Two common response mistakes that observers make when they believe they are being misled, is to either attack or ignore their counterparts. They may attack by immediately asking interrogative questions, expressing doubt, and insulting or threatening their counterparts. They may ignore them by refusing to respond, using an intermediary (which sometimes is a great idea) or defaulting to passive-aggressive behavior. Both attacking and ignoring behaviors reinforce out-group perceptions, justify our counterpart's decisions to manipulate information, and defend the positions they've already taken.

> The worst mistake an observer can make is to call someone a liar.

Perhaps the worst mistake an observer can make is to call someone a liar. Norman Anderson famously asked one hundred participants to assign likeability ratings to 555 personality trait words. The results tell a clear story. Four of the top ten most-liked words relate to honesty: sincere (1), honest (2), truthful (5), and trustworthy (6). Six of the ten most disliked words related to dishonesty: untrustworthy (545), deceitful (546), dishonorable (547), untruthful (550), dishonest, (551), phony (554), and liar (555).[16]

Everyone likes being thought of as honest. No one likes being called a liar—most especially liars. More often than not, calling someone a liar forces them to double down on their lie. Admitting to their lie, or changing their story, violates their self-image and presents consequences. The best choice they are left with is to "die with the lie" and ride it out as long as possible in hopes that their accuser either comes to believe them or drops the issue.

Observers often attack liars because being lied to offends their moral sensibilities. These attacks aren't aimed at learning the truth, erasing fears, or healing relationships. They are most often aimed at avenging the moral slight, or winning a one-sided moral argument. As we will illustrate in the next chapter, lying is often a pragmatic choice, not a moral choice.

Dr. Marshall Goldsmith is a *New York Times* best-selling author and has been ranked the number one leadership thinker in the world. Several years ago, he and I spoke at the same conference. I took the time to attend his session and I enjoyed hearing his thoughts on leadership. When he concluded his session, he asked the attendees if they had any questions. A woman in the front row raised her hand and asked him, "What is the biggest lesson you've learned about the CEOs you've coached?" Without missing a beat, he immediately responded, "They win too much. They have to win; they have to get their way, even when they don't have the best idea, or it hurts the relationship." I saw many people in the audience nod their head as they recalled a leader who fit that description.

The following week, I played principal for a day at my local middle school in support of our education foundation. That morning, the actual principal and I spent some time walking the halls together. As we were walking through the eighth-grade wing, we heard a student and a teacher having a bit of an argument in the hall. As we approached them, we could hear the student attempting to talk over the teacher, and the teacher shutting him down. It certainly sounded like neither one was willing to let the issue go and walk away. When we walked around the corner, they both looked at us and quickly re-entered the classroom.

Once they were back inside their room, the principal stopped walking, shook his head, and said, "Do you know how much easier my life would be if both my teachers and my students didn't have to get the last word every single time?" I laughed, told him the lesson I learned from Dr. Goldsmith, and marveled at the fact that both CEOs and eighth graders suffer from an unproductive need to always win.

> When we listen to win, or for opportunities to demonstrate our intelligence, we will likely satisfy our egos, but our relationships will suffer a death by last word.

The goals and expectations we take into any interaction dictate what we observe, how we interpret it, how we react and respond, and how we evaluate the outcome. When we listen to win, or for opportunities to demonstrate our intelligence, we will likely satisfy our egos, but our relationships will suffer a death by last word.

LISTENING FOR SOLUTIONS

In many ways, listening equates to problem solving. The Disciplined Listening Method requires us to sort through a myriad of variables within dynamic environments as we evaluate our observations and seek solutions.

In their book *Think Like a Freak,* Steven Levitt and Stephen Dubner lay out a series of behaviors to become better problem solvers.[17] These behaviors apply to improving our observation and evaluation processes as well:

- Change your goals from a problem-focused mindset, "I don't want to deal with his attitude," to a solution-focused mindset, "I want to use this conversation to earn his commitment."

- Neutralize your expectations. Evolve from "I know he's going to lie to me," to "He's going to need to protect his self-image."
- Update your incentives, or what you experience as rewards for your communications. Switch from, "She needs to recognize my authority," to "I want to reduce the stress of our relationship over the long term." Recalibrating the direction of your mind's eye improves your results.

Another approach they recommend is redefining your problem. As my father used to say, "You can raise the bridge or lower the water." All too often, we slap unproductive labels on problems that evoke our emotions and limit our alternative production. My Brazilian Jiu Jitsu game improved drastically when I stopped thinking, "I have to get this guy off of me." Trying to push bigger, stronger opponents off of me never proved to be productive. However, shifting my mindset to, "I need to improve my position," catapulted my game forward. I stopped trying to move large opponents off of me, and started moving myself out from under them. This approach proved much easier and more effective.

If you aren't learning you aren't listening.

Levitt and Dubner also discuss the importance of being "relentlessly curious and relatively unbiased."[18] Listening equals learning. To put it bluntly, if you aren't learning you aren't listening. Anytime we fall into a validation mentality, we stop learning. Intentionally working to maintain a learning mentality keeps us open to new ideas, perspectives, and alternatives. It also helps us minimize our egos, moral judgments, and competitive impulses.

A big part of remaining curious is seeking feedback. Not the flattering kind, but rather the uncomfortable kind. Ask your counterparts for honest feedback about your communication style, and intentionally work to improve it. Don't worry, the more the feedback hurts, the more valuable it is.

We can't solve problems that we don't know we have. The goal of this chapter was to highlight some of the most pressing obstacles that inhibit our strategic observation efforts. The remainder of this book will introduce skills, perspectives, and techniques to avoid and overcome these pitfalls. We will start by exploring why we should let go of our burning desire to catch people lying.

CHAPTER FOUR

LETTING GO OF LIES

MY WIFE WAS ABLE to attend one of my presentations when she was pregnant with our son. It was a local engagement and she and I both knew a few people in the audience. At the conclusion of the session, one of the audience members raised her hand, looked back at my wife, returned her gaze to me, and said, "Your poor child won't ever be able to lie to you," which drew a fair amount of laughter from the crowd. I waited for the laughter to die down and replied, "I believe you have this all wrong." She paused in shock as I continued, "Children are going to lie. They always have and they always will. Nothing I can say to my son will stop him from lying." After the woman in the audience nodded her head in agreement, I said, "My wife and I have a bigger challenge. If we constantly catch our son lying, he isn't going to stop lying. He is going to hone his skills until he becomes much more proficient in his craft. Our challenge isn't to catch our son lying, it is to raise him with our moral and ethical values while not raising the world's greatest liar." The audience found my explanation humorous, and absolutely true.

OUR LYING BONES

The concept of lying likely precedes spoken language. We start lying early and many of us may be at our lying-best when we are young. Vasudevi Reddy heads the Department of Psychology at the University of Portsmouth. Her research suggests infants learn to deceive their parents before they learn how to speak.[1] The research also challenges the traditional view that children begin lying between the ages of two and four years old, which coincides with the development of their theory of mind (their ability to begin understanding the emotions, ideas, and perspectives of other people). Common lies from toddlers include denying doing something wrong, blaming someone else, making an excuse for their actions, falsely claiming to have completed a task, and falsely claiming to have permission to do something.[2]

Let's also not overlook that as parents, one of our most important jobs is to teach our children how to tell polite social lies. Kang Lee, a psychologist at the University of Toronto, sees the emergence of this behavior in toddlers as a reassuring sign that their cognitive growth is on track.[3] I celebrated my son's first lie. As part of our morning routine, he and I usually had breakfast together. One morning, at barely two and a half years old, he decided he wanted to eat his breakfast in the living room while watching television, something he wasn't allowed to do. On this particular morning, my wife walked into the kitchen and he immediately looked up at her, picked up his plate, and said, "Mommy, Daddy told me I could take my muffins into the living room." Then, he got up and walked into the living room. My wife looked at me stunned, and I laughed uncontrollably. Honestly, I was happy he had developed to the point where he learned he could manipulate the situation to his advantage, and I gladly allowed him to eat his muffins in the living room that morning. We recognized the developmental milestone, let him have the win, and corrected his behavior the next morning. The lie was so innocent (and so very entertaining) that there was no need to risk harming the future of our open communication by calling him on it in the moment.

Despite the fact that we've all been lying since we were in diapers, people are often obsessed with identifying and eradicating dishonesty. People are convinced that if they can just catch anyone in the act of lying, they will be at an advantage. The truth, ironically, is that is often not the case.

HISTORY OF THE HUNT

Focusing on catching people lying creates unhealthy emotions that are typically driven by our need to protect our self-image and maintain our superior moral and ethical beliefs. Humans have been fascinated with catching people lying and obtaining the truth for thousands of years. While the allure of catching people lying has no doubt led to crimes being solved, wars being thwarted, and con artists exposed, it has also resulted in innocent people being imprisoned and executed, ruined relationships, and the creation of unhealthy myths. A look back at the progression of deception detecting techniques quickly exposes both the motivations behind, and the risks associated with, these efforts.

Humans' attempts at deception detection range from comedic, to tragic, to well-intentioned, to scientific. One of the earliest lie detector tests, dating back to 1000 BCE China, is the rice test.[4] Suspects would have their mouths filled with dry rice and then asked to spit it out. The thinking was that an innocent person would be able to generate the saliva necessary to make the rice moist and sticky. However, a guilty person would not be able to produce saliva and the rice would be spit out dry. They reasoned innocent people would not be nervous enough to stop producing saliva as well—despite being detained and held against their will, which is honestly a good enough reason for dry mouth.

Another early deception detecting technique involved equine participation, and dates back to approximately 500 BCE India.[5] The suspects were told that a sacred donkey possessed the power to determine suspects' innocence or guilt based on how they pulled the donkey's tail. One by one, the suspects were asked to enter the tent and pull the donkey's tail. What the suspects didn't know was that the donkey's tail had been covered in soot; the theory was that innocent people would pull the donkey's tail without hesitation and exit with soot on their hands. Guilty subjects who were convinced of the donkey's mystic powers would enter the tent and return with clean hands, as they were too scared to pull the donkey's tail and risk exposing their guilt. I'm assuming these ancient investigators had methods for ensuring that word of this ploy wouldn't spread throughout their population.

The Roman Empire had the "Mouth of Truth."[6] It was a large marble carving of a disc-shaped mouth and face. Allegedly, when people touched it, it had the power to tell the difference between who was honest and who was dishonest.

Deception detecting techniques took a turn for the worse as the centuries wore on. People were forced to retrieve rocks from vats of boiling water, carry hot irons or walk over hot coals, suffer through flames, eat terrible things, get thrown off cliffs, and submitted to other unconscionable acts. The thought process at the time was that the prosecutor's God of choice would spare innocent people death and/or significant injury. However, the guilty would either die, or worse, suffer gruesome injury and subsequent punishment. Historians will never be able to accurately chronicle all the innocent people who suffered and died during these times.

Cesare Lombrosso created what many consider to be the first modern deception detecting device in 1881.[7] He was a criminologist and physician and was motivated to measure changes in peoples' blood pressure while they were answering questions. Lombrosso's Glove, as it was called, took blood pressure measurements and printed them on a chart for evaluation. Dr. William Marston built on Dr. Lombrosso's work and completed a device in 1921 that was capable of measuring changes in suspects' blood pressure and breath rates. These early machines quickly evolved to become what we currently refer to as the polygraph machine. John Larson and Leonard Keele are often credited with designing the first polygraph machine which they referred to as the "Cardio-Pneumo Psychograph." This machine simultaneously measured changes in a suspect's respiratory rate, blood pressure, and galvanic skin changes. Continued technological advances have improved the kind and number of measurements these machines are capable of making.

While technological advances have improved the ability of polygraph machines to detect changes in suspects' autonomic nervous systems, they aren't able to pinpoint the reason for these changes with complete accuracy. Additionally, some examiners do a terrific job, while others struggle and impact or incorrectly interpret results. In consequence, the Employee Polygraph Protection Act became law in 1988 and bans most private sector organizations in the United States from requiring their employees to take a polygraph exam as either a pre-employment requirement or during their employment.[8] Furthermore, polygraph exam results are rarely admissible in court proceedings in the United States.

These legal precedents don't erase the fact the polygraph machines, and skilled polygraphers, are effective tools in certain contexts. In fact, the polygraph machine initiated a cottage industry. Numerous companies have dedicated themselves to building the perfect lie detection device. Inventions include voice stress analyzers, eye scanning machines, touch screens that measure the pulses in people's thumbs, and deception detecting robots. Perhaps the most accurate device is an fMRI machine that can track the changes in a person's brain function while they are connected. Other techniques that have been utilized in truth-seeking are narcoanalysis (truth serum drugs), hypnosis, and statement analysis.

THE HUMAN TOUCH

Even with all the available technology, nothing replaces a well-trained investigator who possesses a high level of situational awareness and arrives with a toolbox full of inquiry techniques. Over the last fifty-plus years, some of the most notorious techniques have been referred to as "the third-degree" and "enhanced interrogation techniques."

In reality, these techniques usually are not used in actual interrogations. These were often methods that interrogators used to reduce their suspects' resistance prior to interrogating them (asking them questions). These techniques, along with other confrontational-style interrogation techniques, are also more likely to elicit false confessions because they motivate people to say whatever is necessary to make the discomfort go away, not to tell the truth.

> People are often surprised by what others tell them when they are respectful of each other.

The best interrogators enter into their conversations focused on obtaining the truth, not obtaining a confession or catching their suspects lying. The most successful leaders and sales professionals approach their conversations the same way and prioritize problem solving over assigning blame. Thankfully, the research over the last twenty-plus years has consistently shown that, in most contexts, rapport-based interrogation techniques are the most effective. People are often surprised by what others tell them when they are respectful of each other. Non-confrontational inter-rogation techniques including the Wicklander-Zulawski Method, the Cognitive Interview, the Strategic Use of Evidence approach, the PEACE model, and others, all demonstrate the effectiveness of rapport-based strategies. As a general rule, it doesn't pay to act like a jerk when you need someone to share sensitive information with you.   9/23

LIE TO SURVIVE

Our collective obsession with detecting deception underscores a potentially uncomfortable fact—deception is a necessary compo-nent of our daily lives. Without lying, our pre-human ancestors may not have lived long enough for human beings to evolve into the species we know today. According to an oft-cited research study led by Bella DePaulo, adults tell an average of one to two lies a day.[9] Curtis Honts, a former polygrapher and professor at Boise State, is quoted as saying that adults lie in roughly 25 percent of their daily conversations. Robert Feldman, a psychol-ogist at the University of Massachusetts at Amherst, found that 60 percent of the participants in his study couldn't complete a ten-minute conversation without lying.[10] Jerald Jellison, a for-mer professor at the University of Southern California, suggests adults may hear as many as two hundred lies a day.[11] To make matters worse, the widely traditional research-based belief is that we have roughly a 54 percent chance at accurately detecting deception in our conversations.

As always, understanding the potential application of these statistics requires more context. First, let's define lying and decep-tion to set the standard for our examination. Tim Levine defines deception as intentionally, knowingly, or purposely misleading another person. He defines lying as a subtype of deception that involves stating outright falsehoods that are not signaled as false to the receiver.[12]

Lies can be separated into two general categories: pro-social and self-serving. Pro-social lies are told with the intention of benefiting others. They include altruistic lies, which serve to benefit the receiver at the cost of the liar, and white lies, which are typically trivial. Believe it or not, multiple research studies have demonstrated that pro-social lies actually increase trust because people often value benevolence over honesty in many situations.[13] Self-serving lies are the lies that upset people the most. These lies are most often told to benefit the liar, usually at the cost of the receiver.

Let's pause to consider the fact that we all have lied, we all love and trust people who have lied to us, and we all likely work with people who have lied to us. Which leads me to the following question: If we are all liars who love and work with liars, why are we so obsessed with catching people lying?

UNDERSTANDING WHY

In the majority of contexts, knowing that someone lied is inconsequential. It will likely only serve to upset you, lead to judgment, and distract you from the greater goals of the conversation. Understanding why and how they lied can help you work your way to the truth.

In Pamela Meyer's book *Lie Spotting*, she outlines four offensive and five defensive motives as to why people lie.[14]

- Obtain a reward
- Gain an advantage

- Create a positive impression
- Exercise power

- Avoid punishment or embarrassment
- Protect someone else from punishment
- Protect yourself or someone else from harm
- Remove yourself from an awkward situation
- Maintain privacy

Timothy Levine from the University of Alabama at Birmingham also identifies ten reasons why people may lie:[15]

1. To cover up a personal transgression
2. Gain an economic advantage
3. Gain a nonmonetary advantage
4. Remain polite
5. For altruistic motives
6. Self-impression management
7. Malice or intent to harm others
8. Humor
9. Avoidance
10. They are pathological liars

Both of these lists are thorough and well-researched. And, in my opinion, they both stop one step short. More often than not, adults lie for one reason—to avoid a real or perceived consequence. Knowing someone lied is rarely important. Focusing on lies is like treating the symptom instead of the disease. What is paramount is understanding what they were hoping to gain or avoid by manipulating the truth, in the context of the situation.

Timothy Levine's research on deception is both thorough and exhaustive. His results are clear. The vast majority of the time, people lie to protect themselves (or someone else). They do not lie to hurt you.[16] Yet despite this fact, people often become furious, disappointed, and offended when they believe they are being lied to. Several years ago, I received a call from one of my CEO clients who literally started the conversation by saying, "I know you told me not to get mad, but I'm pissed that my CFO just lied to me." The CFO's lie didn't make this CEO mad, the CEO's emotional attachment to getting lied to made him mad. Being lied to violated his self-image and moral code, which in turn made him mad at his CFO and completely derailed any opportunity to turn the conversation toward a productive resolution.

> The vast majority of the time, people lie to protect themselves (or someone else). They do not lie to hurt you.

AVOIDING OUR PROBLEMS

According to Levine, lying is the result of a simple decision. People normally default to telling the truth until the truth becomes problematic. Once the truth appears counterproductive to achieving their goals, people deviate from the truth. Once the threat has passed, they return to the truth.[17] That's it.

Most of the time, people lie because they believe (rightfully or not) that it is their best available option at the time. Dan Ariely's research confirms that we are all capable of deception to the degree that we can justify it within our self-image.[18] His research found that, to some degree, we all want to benefit from cheating, and we all want to simultaneously be seen as good people. We can justify our dishonesty based on any combination of the goals we want to achieve, the consequences we are looking to avoid, the people we are communicating with, and the context of the situation. Leaders in all contexts will be well served to remember that when they treat people unfairly, force compliance, have inconsistent standards, and win at the expense of others, they make it much easier for people to justify dishonest actions.

COMMON LIES

When the truth is problematic, and justifications for lying are easy to find, we can expect our counterparts to manipulate the truth. This isn't necessarily malicious or immoral. It is human nature. In fact, there are five ways people can lie during conversations.[19] First, they can deny doing something they actually did. Second, they can intentionally omit information they believe is counterproductive to achieving their goals. Third, they can fabricate a completely untrue story. Fourth, they can exaggerate a story. And fifth, they can minimize details they believe may be problematic. Believe it or not, fabricating stories, or telling bold-faced lies, is the least common method for lying. Most liars prefer to keep as much of the truth as possible in their lies. This reduces the stress levels associated with their deceptions, helps them quickly recall information when they are creating their lies, increases the believability of their lies, and it makes it easier for them to recall their lies at a later time.

Some liars are so skilled it can be extremely difficult to catch them in the act. Creative thinkers have a significant advantage navigating problematic moments in their conversations by facilitating the self-serving justification process. Francesca Gino and Dan Ariely found that people who are skilled at divergent thinking and possess high levels of cognitive flexibility are adept at solving difficult problems that require multi-faceted solutions.[20] His work asserts that divergent thinking likely helps people develop ways to bypass moral rules, and cognitive flexibility likely helps people reinterpret information in self-serving ways.

COMMON LIARS

Beyond our creative levels, many of the most successful liars have several traits in common. Albert Vrij identified eighteen traits that good liars possess.[21] The highlights of this list include acting skills, confidence, experience lying, a good memory, rapid and original thinking, and the ability to use emotional camouflage. Lies can be very hard to identify when they are delivered by liars who possess these skills—especially when we are unprepared, distracted, and focusing on the wrong cues. The impact of these skills is significant; no matter what you may have been told in the past, there is no single behavior that consistently indicates truth or deception. It doesn't exist. There is an infinite combination of behaviors that may betray someone's dishonest intentions and these behaviors can change based on the liar, the lie, the recipient of the lie, and the environment the lie is occurring in. It is also critical to reiterate that truthful people often exhibit many of the behaviors commonly associated with liars.

> **There is no single behavior that consistently indicates truth or deception.**

Just because someone looks stressed or nervous doesn't mean they are lying, and just because someone looks comfortable or consistent doesn't mean they are telling the truth. Consider the fact that people aren't usually aware that their counterpart may have motivation to lie to them and they haven't taken the time to identify ground truth (i.e., evidence or other relevant facts) prior to the conversation, and you can see that trying to catch people lying is often a fool's errand.

However, there is good news as well. Since most lies are told to protect liars, not hurt receivers, Timothy Levine's research has found that most lies are told by a few prolific liars.[22] His work found that while many people may lie occasionally, or even rarely, very few people lie often. He also found that the ubiquitous 54 percent accuracy statistic is a result of how the research was conducted, and that some people are terrible liars and easier to identify. It is important to note that recognizing these transparent liars can create a false confidence in observers. In subsequent studies, he demonstrated several important improvements. First, he demonstrated that when communications are truthful, an observer's identification of honest communication skyrockets. Nine of his studies produced an accuracy rate of identifying honest communication over 75 percent of the time, with one study recording accuracy as high as 96 percent.[23]

SEEING THE TRUTH

The good news is, we generally do a great job recognizing the truth when the truth is being communicated. On the flip side, Levine has demonstrated significant statistical improvement on deception detection accuracy as well. First, it is critical to note that his team discovered that 80 percent of lies were identified with the involvement of some sort of evidence.[24] In real life, most lies are discovered after the fact, with the addition of new evidence or added contextual awareness. This fact is sometimes clouded when, in hindsight, we believe we identified the lies in real time.

Levine's team shattered the previous statistical expectation when they were able to replicate deception detection accuracy results with over 90 percent accuracy with both college students (94%) and trained experts (96%).[25] He found five key factors that increased their ability to accurately detect deception at such a high rate.[26] First was their ability to establish ground truth and evaluate the following communication against this ground truth. Second, leveraging their situational familiarity to assess the plausibility of explanations they receive. Third was considering their counterparts' potential motivations to deceive them based on their situational familiarity. Fourth, asking strategic questions that elicit diagnostically valuable answers. And fifth, harnessing the ability to persuade their counterparts to tell the truth. Dr. David Matsumoto and Dr. Edward Geiselman have also led teams that produced research which confirmed that training can increase observers' abilities to determine when they are being misled.[27, 28]

These keys outline a playbook for you anytime you engage in critical conversations where identifying truthful and deceptive responses is important to you. All of these keys will be addressed in detail throughout this book—but not for catching lies. The Disciplined Listening Method is not an interrogation technique, and it is not a lie-catching technique. Disciplined Listeners observe for opportunities to maximize the value of their conversations and relationships. Lie-catching mentalities typically reinforce confirmation biases, limit opportunities to generate unexpected value, create competitive situations, and damage relationships.

Disciplined Listeners observe for opportunities to maximize the value of their conversations and relationships.

EXCHANGING LIES FOR WHYS

If you are committed to gaining more value from your critical conversations, stop trying to catch people lying. As we illustrated in chapter 3, many lie-catching efforts are fueled by unfortunate myths and incorrect stereotypes. Even if you guess correctly, knowing someone lied to you is information with limited value. Start observing for contextually relevant indications of comfort and discomfort. The behavioral shifts we observe during conversations do not indicate that our counterparts are lying or telling the truth. They are indications that our counterparts are experiencing emotional shifts and their comfort levels are either increasing or decreasing. Correctly determining why your counterpart's comfort levels change within the context of your conversation produces tremendously valuable intelligence. Understanding why their emotions are changing allows you to immediately adapt your approach to take advantage of their shifting feelings.

Applying Levine's five keys will increase your ability to protect yourself, achieve your goals, and maximize the value of your conversations by accurately determining why your counterparts' emotions are changing. First, understand when you are engaging in an interaction where someone may be motivated to mislead you. Prior to these engagements, complete as much due diligence as possible to increase your situational familiarity and establish ground truth (or something close to it). During these interactions, evaluate everything you see and hear within the context of the situation, ask powerful questions to elicit diagnostically valuable information, and persuade people to be honest with you.

If you take anything from this chapter, take this—it is okay to be lied to. People lie to us when they feel like it's their last good choice, and we do it too. The lies we receive often also include the hidden codes we need to unlock the truth if we observe carefully

It is okay to be lied to.

enough to identify them. Stop trying to catch people lying. It typically isn't healthy or helpful. Observe for indications of discomfort and capitalize on your counterparts' current fears and motivations.

Now that we have covered the most common mistakes observers fall prey to, and the importance of graduating beyond catching lies, we are going to start exploring how we can improve our situational awareness in preparation for executing the Disciplined Listening Method.

CHAPTER FIVE

THE SITUATIONALLY AWARE OBSERVER

CERTIFIED FORENSIC INTERVIEWERS CONSISTENTLY discuss the importance of circumstance in their observations and actions. It can be too easy to become myopically focused on one detail, or to let our emotional state drive our observations. All too often, we either observe what we want to observe, what we choose to observe, or what we expect to observe. Unknowingly falling prey to these shortcomings leads to both unnecessary conflict and missed opportunities.

> **All too often, we either observe what we want to observe, what we choose to observe, or what we expect to observe.**

THE CORNERSTONE

Situational awareness is the cornerstone of the Disciplined Listening Method. Situational awareness essentially means knowing what is going on around you, and how these events impact your ability to achieve your goals. It is the ability to see trouble from far enough away that you can avoid it, without anyone else realizing the trouble in the first place. This could be physical trouble, such as getting in a car accident or becoming the victim of a robbery, or conversational trouble, like accidentally offending someone, starting an argument, or missing a chance to secure a commitment or business deal.

The opposite of situational awareness is either remaining ignorant of what is going on around you, or thinking, *That looks like it might not end well*, and walking right into the trap. A common example of an anti-situationally aware approach is knowing that what you want to say is inflammatory, but saying it anyway because it makes you feel better.

An example of this occurs when customers cause a problem and blame the salesperson for it. In these situations, sales professionals often have to patiently suffer through the customers' explanation and take the brunt of the blame before solving the problem. Most of the time, simply solving the problem is enough to satisfy their customers and move on, even when the customers are truly at fault. A situationally aware sales professional would end the call by thanking the customer for bringing the issue to their attention and offering to be of further assistance if necessary. An unaware sales professional may end the call by saying something like, "I'm happy to help you today. In the future, if you avoid these two missteps the problem won't repeat itself." It may feel better to be sure the customer knows it was their fault, but it creates a whole new set of unnecessary problems.

Former United States Air Force Chief Scientist and President of SA Technologies, Mica Endsley, is credited as being at the forefront of situational awareness research and education. Her definition of situational awareness is, "the perception of the elements in the environment within a volume of time and space, the comprehension of their meaning and the projection of their status in the near future."[1] This definition speaks to the traditional application of situational awareness that is taught to military personnel, first responders, and other professionals who are likely to experience physical danger. Being situationally aware is a skill everyone can benefit from. Endsley's definition leaves us with a lot to unpack. Let's explore how situational awareness enhances The Disciplined Listening Method.

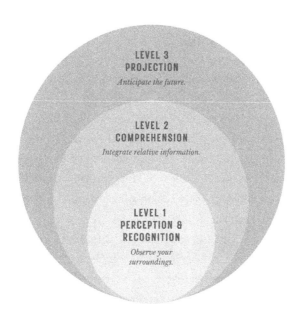

THREE LEVELS OF SITUATIONAL AWARENESS

According to Endsley, there are three levels to situational awareness.[2] Level one, *perception*, involves recognizing all the important information around us. In terms of ensuring our physical safety, this includes recognizing potential threats as well as potential exits. In communication scenarios, this means recognizing the many factors that impact what people think, feel, and say. These observations allow us to form an accurate picture of what everyone in the conversation is truly experiencing. In a 1996 study, Endsley found that 76 percent of situational awareness errors that fighter pilots made could be attributed to errors in perceiving important information.[3] Listeners will be well-served not to overlook any of the factors that may influence how their counterparts are interpreting their conversations.

Level two is *comprehension.* This is the stage where observers combine, restore, and retain information. They integrate the available information and determine what is most relevant in relation to the goals they want to achieve. These assessments position them to prioritize potential alternatives. In the same research study, Endsley found that 20 percent of situational awareness errors involved this stage. It is important to avoid dismissing, overlooking, or explaining away observations that may hold unexpected value.

Level three is *projection.* Endsley refers to this as the highest level of situational awareness—the ability to accurately predict the future. This is the stage where observers project their current understanding and anticipate future events and their implications. Excelling at this stage allows for timely decision making. This is the stage where we choose between the considered alternatives and take action toward securing a better outcome. In communications, this includes a wide range of decisions. Our awareness should encompass the time, day, location, and participants in any important conversation. It should also influence how we structure our message and our tone, volume, speed of delivery, and word choice. It can even influence the patience, understanding, and empathy we show our counterparts.

Endsley states that our situational awareness can be impacted by the dynamic nature of any interaction, where we direct our attention, and the expectations and preconceptions we carry into them. In fact, in the same 1996 study she found that the most common error that fighter pilots made was not attending to the right information when all the necessary information was present.[4] Leaders in all contexts fall prey to the same mistake when they are misled by their biases, expectations, assumptions, and distractions. The information they needed to make the best decision was right in front of them and they missed it because they were either distracted or focusing on the wrong cues.

There is one immediate indication of a failure in situational awareness. We need to stop and reflect anytime we experience a negative outcome and say to ourselves, "I didn't see that coming." Maybe the event or outcome was such a random event that we truly had no warning or ability to anticipate it. Unfortunately, and more often than not, we are presented with indications of the impending calamity and either are unaware of their value, ignore them, or explain them away.

Our conversations almost never occur in a static environment. Our customers' needs, opportunities, and access to our competitors are always changing. Our employees' needs, assumptions, personal lives, and professional goals are constantly in flux. Our families experience even more ever-changing factors. People can quickly change their focus, opinions, goals, and emotional states within a single conversation. Successfully executing situational awareness requires us to limit the negative influences (biases and expectations) and direct our available cognitive resources to the highest priority opportunities.

> Successfully executing situational awareness requires us to limit the negative influences (biases and expectations) and direct our available cognitive resources to the highest priority opportunities.

EYE ON THE PRIZE

Situational awareness and, by extension, the Disciplined Listening Method, are goal-driven exercises. As we've said before, life is a series of solvable problems. We can choose to focus on the problem, or we can choose to focus on the solution. According to Endsley, "In goal-driven processing, attention is directed across the environment in accordance with active goals. The [observer] actively seeks information needed for goal attainment and the goals simultaneously act as a filter in interpreting the information this is perceived."[5]

Goal-focused mindsets help observers identify, prioritize, and integrate information that positions them to make the necessary choices to achieve their goals in a timely manner. In contrast, fear-focused mindsets often prioritize information that confirms our fears and generates self-fulfilling prophecies.

The key is to focus on the correct goals. Let's think back to Bodie's listening approaches.[6] The goal for most task-oriented listeners is to complete the conversation as quickly as possible, just as the goal for most critical listeners is to spot errors in their counterparts' message. In these examples, listeners are prioritizing and integrating information that helps them achieve tactical, self-serving goals, while reducing their situational awareness and eliminating the opportunity to create unexpected value.

Conversely, relational listeners stay tuned into their counterparts' emotions, and analytical listeners focus on capturing the entire message before judging or making decisions. These listeners are prioritizing and integrating information in a manner that helps them achieve goals that they share with their counterparts while increasing their situational awareness, taking the opportunity to create unexpected value.

Steve Kerr, the Head Coach of the Golden State Warriors, offers us one of the best public examples of a situationally aware communications process. Much to the chagrin of many basketball fans, Kerr led his team to the NBA finals five straight years from 2015–2019, winning the championship three of those years.

For those unfamiliar, the NBA finals are a best-of-seven series. The first team to win four games becomes the champion. In 2015, the Warriors exited the floor after Game 3, down two games to one against the Cleveland Cavaliers. After the game, there was a lot of conversation about the Warriors' chances of getting back in the series. Commentators mainly focused on the idea of the Warriors improving their chances by swapping Andrew Bogut for Andre Iguodala in their starting lineup.

The day of Game 4, Steve Kerr was asked twice before the game if he would make the switch. Both times, he told the reporters that he would not. Lo and behold, when the Warriors' starting lineup trotted out, Andrew Bogut was on the bench and Andre Iguodala was on the floor. The Warriors won Game 4 and never looked back. They went on to become champions after winning the series in six games.

Afterwards, Steve Kerr sat at the podium to address the assembled press crew. To no one's surprise, he was asked about the lineup change. His response perfectly represented situational awareness:[7]

"When I was asked today if [Andrew] Bogut was starting, I lied. . . . I figure I have two press conferences on the day of the game. So, I'm asked a lot of strategic questions. . . . If I tell the truth, it's the equivalent of knocking on David Blatt's door and saying 'Hey, this is what we are going to do.'

[Or] I could evade the question, which would start this Twitter phenomenon. Who is going to start for the Warriors? Or I could lie. So I lied. Sorry, but I don't think they hand you the trophy based on morality. They give it to you if you win."

Discussions of morality aside, he perfectly illustrated situational awareness. He was clear about his goal—win the championship. He was keenly aware of his options—tell the truth, equivocate, or lie. He thought through the impact and projected the future based on each of his options. He executed his decisions to change the lineup after lying about it, and he reaped the rewards.

INTERACTION INFLUENCERS

As we expand our situational awareness, engage with our audiences, and evaluate our observations, we need to remain aware that there are six factors consistently impacting our interactions. Any of them can impact how we and our audiences send and receive communications. Additionally, shifts in any of these six factors can alter how messages are communicated and interpreted.

These six factors include:

1. *Speaker* experiences and perspectives

2. *Listener* experiences and perspectives

3. Relationship dynamics

4. Conversation topics

5. Perceived consequences

6. Environment surrounding the conversation

To better understand how these six factors impact our communications, we are going to take a closer look at the variables from both the speaker and listener's perspectives. Both bring all kinds of experiences, assumptions, and expectations into how they express themselves, and how they interpret what they hear. They both bring to the table a plethora of experiences; from previous similar conversations to past interactions with the same person, and even to their current level of physical energy. As they engage in the conversation, the listener runs what is being said through their filter of relevant history and current mood.

For example, everyone in my life is painfully aware that I become an impatient, anxious individual when my blood sugar drops. How I interact with people changes from when I am full, to when I am over-hungry, or *hangry*. My wife always carries protein bars in her purse. If she senses that I am getting close to the line, she silently hands me a snack. As a result of my own experience, I am very respectful of people's mealtimes. I try hard not to schedule a meeting that may force someone to run late for a meal, and I work hard to manage my hunger levels ahead of important engagements so that my physical status does not impact how I'm perceived or what I observe.

THE IMPACT OF RELATIONSHIPS

The relationship between two communicators also has a significant impact on how the message is received. You would not speak to a client the same way you would chat with a friend you've had since elementary school. Think back to the expectations that Margarete Imhof identified in her research; we all behave differently, and have different expectations for others' behavior, in our personal and professional lives.[8]

Relational factors that affect how we express ourselves and understand others include:

- Any working relationship and hierarchy
- Existing group and family dynamics

- Compatibility of personalities
- Any relevant comparison of skill sets
- Any physical attraction or distraction

To further complicate matters, these factors can change during the conversation as ideas and information are exchanged and filtered through multiple lenses by everyone involved in the conversation.

Hierarchical changes are probably the biggest shifts in dynamic in our working lives. When someone ascends to a leadership role, like it or not, their now-subordinates or coworkers perceive them differently. I was recently listening to the *Cleared Hot* podcast and heard the host, Andy Stumpf, discussing getting promoted from an enlisted position to an officer in the Navy with his veteran guest, Jason Tuschen.[8] When Jason referenced his promotion, Andy laughed and said, "Congratulations on your promotion, no one will ever tell you the truth again!" When hierarchy shifts, the perception of power, trust, and priorities shifts with it.

Leaders often believe that being higher up the chain entitles them to more truthful and timely information. They fail to realize that their title, and the potential consequences they can legislate, motivates most people to be less honest with them.

Furthermore, reputations play a significant role. This includes personal, organizational, and abstract reputations. For example, I am cognizant of the fact that professional interrogators are generally thought of poorly, regardless of the ethical standards my peers and I hold ourselves to. As a result, I need to take extra care to avoid taking any negative interactions personally because my counterparts are likely responding to the general reputation of interrogators.

Similarly, sales professionals often express frustration when their prospective customers withhold information from them. Upon further inspection, although the general reputations of sales

our customers

professionals may fall to the level of interrogators, they are very alike. In fact, sales prospects have all been mirandized as well. A lifetime of purchasing experience has taught ~~them~~ that they have the right to remain silent because anything they say will be held against them at the salesperson's very first opportunity.

CONVERSATIONS AND CONSEQUENCES

Potential consequences impact how all parties communicate and evaluate communications. These perceived consequences go beyond getting fired, arrested, or found guilty. They include being believed or disbelieved, feeling disrespected or embarrassed, feeling challenged or ignored, being valued or devalued, or even just being wrong. We all generally prefer to avoid consequences and many times we may look to avoid taking accountability as well. These impulses consistently affect what we say, how we say it, how we react, and how we respond.

The topic of conversation may exacerbate tension, impacting our behaviors and perceptions. Each participant in a conversation might have both rational and emotional attachments to issues being discussed. A leader may feel like they are coaching an employee, while the employee may feel like they are being attacked. A sales professional may feel like they are helping a client, and the client may feel like they are being upsold. A parent may feel like they are listening to their child, while the child feels they are being ignored. As their relevant knowledge and related emotions change, so will their communications and perceptions. It is good practice to recalibrate our perceptions each time the topic of conversation changes.

Your physical appearance and positioning, word choice, tone of voice, demeanor, and perceived motivations can all impact how your audience receives and responds to your communications. It is easy to overlook the fact that how we present ourselves, position ourselves, and behave can all impact how people communicate with us—and in turn, how we interpret their communications and respond.

The first time I traveled to London to teach, I ended up with a free day between engagements. I was speaking with my clients at the end of my first engagement and they asked me what I was doing the following day. When I told them I had the day off, they recommended that I spend the day seeing London and then meet them at Paddington Station in the evening. They had an extra ticket to a Champions League soccer match and wanted me to join them. I couldn't turn it down. The next day, I woke up, had breakfast, and jumped on a big red tour bus, assuming the role of obvious American tourist for the day.

I was told I should see the changing of the guard, so I arrived early. I was fighting through two bulging discs in my lower back at the time, and I decided to relieve some pain by sitting down on the sidewalk, up against a building just across the street while I waited. As I was sitting there, I saw two London police officers look in my direction several times and begin walking my way. I didn't want to make their job any more difficult than necessary so I slowly stood up, smiled and waved, and waited for them to approach me. When they asked what I was doing, I politely told them my name and gave them the whole story. Despite my proactive efforts to ease their concerns, they both looked uneasy. After several tense minutes it finally dawned on me that I was wearing my sunglasses and they couldn't see my face clearly. Once I took my sunglasses off, their demeanor changed completely. We had a quick conversation about that evening's match, and they recommended a pub where I could grab lunch before they walked away. I followed their recommendation, enjoyed a great sandwich with my Guinness, and had a wonderful time at the match. Had I not been aware of the effect my behavior and attire were having on the police officers, the situation could have escalated—and I may have ended up drinking warm water in a London jail cell.

ENVIRONMENTAL FACTORS

Additionally, the surrounding environment's impact on conversations is often overlooked. Choosing the best available location for our important conversations is a critical consideration when obtaining sensitive information. Most people wouldn't plan to have a deep, romantic conversation with their spouse in the middle of a loud sports bar—just like how I've never interrogated anyone in a dark room with a solitary swinging lightbulb overhead.

Distractions ruin connections and impede a leader's ability to influence their counterparts' commitment to sharing information that makes them feel vulnerable. When people are focused on the temperature, lighting, noises, or other people, they are more likely to withhold information than share it.

I, for example, am easily captivated by movement. If something or someone around me moves, it is going to catch my eye. I'm not ignoring my counterpart—I am just drawn to motion. Many people have a hard time paying attention to conversations in large crowds and loud environments. Temperature affects how people behave and evaluate their observations. We think and feel much differently when we are cold, hot, or comfortable. A bright or dark atmosphere definitely affects the mood, and the volume at which our counterparts are speaking also plays a role in influencing our experiences.

We've previously discussed how important it is for people to maintain their self-images. Crowds have a tremendous impact on people. Some individuals clam up and shut down in crowds. Other people will act out in an attempt to garner more attention. When mob mentality sets in, people will act in accordance with the crowd—often in ways they would never act alone. An opposite, and dangerous, potential consequence of crowds is the bystander effect. When this occurs, it can feel almost impossible to take action if others are not.

PHYSICAL ATTRACTION AND DISTRACTION

Existing and shifting interpersonal dynamics can also have a real impact on how people communicate and behave. This reality ties right back into our need to live up (or down) to our self-images. Who's in the room? What is the dynamic between everyone involved?

A prospective client may act entirely differently with you one-on-one than he does in front of his boss. An employee may act very differently with you when it is just the two of you than when her closest coworker is in the room. Your peers may act differently when their goals align with yours and when their goals deviate from yours.

Every parent knows that their kids act differently when their friends, or (gulp) boyfriend or girlfriend are around. My friend Wayne has a funny story about playing catch with his son Greg at the bus stop when Greg was young. They were the first to arrive at the bus stop one morning and decided to play catch. Wayne recalled that Greg was kind of lazy with most of his throws. Then suddenly, Greg started throwing a lot harder. Wayne didn't think much of it—that is, until Greg sailed a throw over Wayne's head. When Wayne turned to chase down the ball, he realized there were now girls at the bus stop. Greg wasn't just playing catch with his dad anymore. He was impressing girls. This was the perfect motivation for Greg's elevated velocity (if not accuracy).

SENSE ALL, QUESTION ALL

In summary, the way toward situational awareness is to sense all, question all, be prepared to deal with anything, and to focus on the next positive steps. Executing the Disciplined Listening Method requires listeners to constantly scan their environment, update their mental models, and adapt to the new intelligence they receive to help them achieve their short-term (this conversation) and long-term (future) goals. This means committing to checking your expectations against your observations, taking other-centered approaches to our communications, and following a process that creates strategic advantages.

Disciplined Listeners are then forced to maintain a learning mentality, while seeking out the hidden value of their conversations. Now that we have begun elevating our situational awareness, it is time to explore what we experience during difficult conversations and how to use these experiences to our advantage.

CHAPTER SIX

THE SEVEN STAGES OF POTENTIALLY CONTENTIOUS CONVERSATIONS

THE DISCIPLINED LISTENING METHOD was born from two important realizations. The first realization is that the very best leaders and the very best interrogators capitalize on the same two core skills—vision and influence.

The second realization is that the cognitive processes that lead employees to commit to saying, "I'll do it," customers to saying, "I'll buy it," and guilty interrogation suspects to truthfully admitting, "I did it," are all essentially identical. We will explore the second realization in this chapter, and the first realization in chapter 12.

Leaders, sales professionals, parents, and interrogators are all tasked with moving their counterparts from resistance to commitment. Thankfully, these conversations are often completed without becoming contentious. However, there is no shortage of combustible elements present in many of these conversations that could ignite with an inadvertent spark.

Avoiding unnecessary conflict requires Disciplined Listeners to take responsibility for how their counterparts experience their interactions. Accepting this responsibility requires us to understand what our audiences are thinking and feeling in real time. After all, it is easier to reach people when we know where they are. There are seven stages that people transition through when they participate in potentially contentious conversations.

The first stage is the *pre-conversation stage*. This includes all the relevant life experiences people bring into their conversations. The second stage is the *arrival and introduction* when both parties meet for the specific conversation. Once the conversation starts, the primary listener will enter the third stage and *begin to listen*. As the primary listener begins to understand where the conversation is going, they enter the fourth stage, *internalization and self-talk*. In the fifth stage, the primary listener *determines what to say and when to speak*. Once the primary listener engages in the conversation, they enter the sixth stage and *choose to continue participating in the conversation*. The seventh and final stage involves any *post-conversation follow-up*.

We all experience these stages through our own lens, which is clouded by our biases, experiences, emotions, and expectations. There will be times when our lens aligns with our counterparts' and there will be other times when our lens conflicts with theirs. The most dangerous occasions occur when we incorrectly assume concurrence when the lenses are in fact not aligned. Understanding the impact of all seven stages will help us identify what we and our counterparts are experiencing throughout our conversations, and why.

STAGE ONE: PRE-CONVERSATION

The pre-conversation stage is often an overlooked stage. It is quite possibly the most powerful stage, because it has the power to set an irrevocable tone for any potentially contentious conversation.

Conversations don't take place in a vacuum. Every discussion you participate in has links to previous conversations and will link to future conversations for all participants. These exchanges are further complicated because your conversations can link to other interactions you weren't involved in and may not be aware of. These may be conversations your counterpart has participated in with friends, family, coworkers, or other authority figures. These may even include discussions you've had that subconsciously impacted your expectations without your realizing it.

Communicators in any leadership capacity can be easily drawn into the assumptions that everything they see and hear during a conversation is directly related to those specific exchanges, and their comprehension is as complete as necessary. The results of these assumptions can range from inconvenient, to unfortunate, to fatal. Parents, leaders, sales professionals, and investigators all find themselves in precarious positions the second they say to themselves, "I've got it all figured out." There are always elements we don't know or understand. Forcing ourselves to maintain a learning mentality is the only way to rise above our short-sighted assumptions. When communicators recognize the tangled webs their conversations weave, they can avoid the metaphorical spiders lurking in the shadows.

Forcing ourselves to maintain a learning mentality is the only way to rise above our short-sighted assumptions.

As we illustrated in the last chapter, all participants carry relevant history into their conversations. How many times have you lost your patience or temper with someone because you carried emotions over from previous experiences? Maybe you had an argument with your spouse, or your boss changed a deadline, or a customer lit you up for a mistake that wasn't yours. Sadly, the next person we talk to often bears the brunt of our emotions in these situations. Our conversations are not just impacted by this immediate contrast—interactions can easily be affected by distant experiences as well.

The pre-conversation stage has four potentially overlapping onsets to consider. The first onset is your counterparts' relevant life experiences prior to meeting you, which are out of your control. The second onset is any relevant experiences between you and your counterparts, which is largely within your ability to control. The third onset is an event that triggers the anticipation of a future conversation—meaning that they prepare for a conversation based on a mistake or revelation they have been a part of and know will need to be discussed. The fourth onset is when the meeting is requested. Failing to account for all these onsets, or even underestimating their power, can result in layers of unnecessary conflict.

THE FOUR ONSETS OF THE
PRE-CONVERSATION STAGE

Relevant Life Experiences

Let us start with addressing how experiences impact the pre-conversation. Growing up, we are all exposed to people in leadership roles—parents, relatives, older siblings, friends, teachers, coaches, counselors, managers, and perhaps even law enforcement. The time, quality, and support we receive from these people varies for each of us; the people who fill these roles spend a lot of time telling us what to do. Our individual interactions with authority figures shape our expectations for how leaders will treat us throughout our lives and offer us a picture of how we should act when we are in leadership roles. Essentially, we are conditioned in how to interact with leaders from an early age.

Leaders and sales professionals are well served to embrace this initial out-group dynamic, as opposed to combating it. It can be tempting to try and convince someone that you are different from the people they've had previous experiences with. Typically, the more we tell someone we are different, the more we reinforce their negative expectations. Let your actions demonstrate your value, not your words.

I tried to keep this in mind as I struggled to learn how to be a good father. Like most kids, my son spent his toddler years alternating between making me extraordinarily proud and testing my patience. Sometimes he made legitimate mistakes, sometimes my instructions weren't clear, and sometimes he would look me right in the face and either lie or do exactly what he wasn't supposed to. No matter how we arrived at our teachable moments, I had to remember that how I handled these situations with him would no doubt have a real impact on how he and I navigate more serious situations later in life.

Relational History

The second onset—relational history—includes many opportunities for leaders to influence how they are perceived. As leaders, we are always on a stage. Our audience is consistently watching, assessing, and categorizing us. This is true with our management staff, employees, people who see us at conferences and networking events, our customers, and anyone else who sees us in action. Whether your audiences have positive or negative expectations for you, they will immediately look to confirm the accuracy of their expectations. They will likely also begin anticipating what their interactions with you will be like.

It is important to remember that there is a reasonable possibility you will have a difficult conversation with anyone in your world, at any moment. How the people around you perceive your treatment of them is going to have a significant impact on the outcomes of these conversations. This starts at the first moment of your very first interaction. Remember, we are capable of judging someone's trustworthiness and categorizing people as fast as 100 milliseconds. The immediate impression you make on someone the first time you meet them sets the standard that they will either expect you to live up or down to in all future interactions.

> The immediate impression you make on someone the first time you meet them sets the standard that they will either expect you to live up or down to in all future interactions.

Considering the long-lasting impact of initial introductions, there are several best practices to adhere to when you meet people for the first time. To the degree that it is culturally appropriate, slow down and be warm and welcoming when you meet others. Show your respect with a firm handshake, look them in the eye, address them by name, and ask them at least one question to demonstrate personal interest. This combination will consistently result in establishing stronger anchor impressions. Appearing rushed, distracted, and aloof will result in negative anchor impressions. As will crushing handshakes, rolling your hand on top of theirs, pulling them toward you, inappropriate touching, and violating their spatial expectations.

There is one nearly effortless thing every leader can do to improve the impressions they create with everyone around them: say hello to every single person you walk past. Simply smiling, nodding, waving, and/or saying hello while preferably saying their name tells them you are aware of their existence, they are valuable, and you care about them.

Think about how great you would feel if you went to a concert and a member of your favorite band looked you right in the eye, said hello, and thanked you for coming to the show. Those five seconds of personal interaction would supercharge your night and cement that band as your favorite.

Leaders commonly lose sight of the fact that they are viewed as "celebrities" in their own organizations and fail to realize how impactful these brief interactions can be. These moments of public acknowledgment become even more important when you see people in hourly or front-line management roles. You only have to ignore someone a few times before you are irrevocably perceived as an arrogant and aloof leader, which will cloud the perception of all of your future communications.

My favorite investigative achievement from my early years in the private sector may be surprising. There was usually a diametrically opposed relationship between the number of dishonest employee cases we resolved and the number of employees who were willing to tell us about people they suspected of participating in dishonest activity. My team and I intentionally combatted this issue by spending time at the start of every shift just walking the floor and talking to employees about their jobs and lives. We congratulated them on any achievements, recognized their promotions, and personally thanked them for any help they provided. This allowed them to view us a regular people with a job to do, not as mini-terminators always on the hunt for the next case. As a result, their tips flowed in. These efforts culminated with my team leading the organization in both dishonest employee cases resolved and employee tips (snitches). That combination had not been previously achieved.

Participation in a Trigger Event

The third onset occurs when a person either participates in an event or obtains knowledge of an event that they believe will trigger a future conversation. People often consider what it may feel like to be questioned immediately after they become aware that they have either participated in, or obtained knowledge of, an event that may be against rules or policies. In these cases, they likely think through several facets of the impending conversation, including who may ask them questions and what questions they may be asked. If they desire to be truthful, they will likely contemplate what information they are willing to share, with whom they may be willing to share it, and under what conditions they will be comfortable sharing it. On the untruthful side, they will likely think through what questions they may be asked and any denials, explanations, or excuses they believe will help their situation.

Meeting Request

The fourth onset for the pre-conversation stage is when the meeting is requested. This could be a formal request provided days or weeks in advance, or it could be the dreaded, "Please come down to my office," or "Please come sit down with your father and me," requests. It is common for people, even for those who've done nothing wrong, to assume negative reasons when they are requested to meet with anyone in a position of authority. This is when people might start thinking, "What is this about?" and be tempted to think through worst-case scenarios.

These four onsets are not exclusive to investigations. They hold true for performance-based conversations, discovery calls with customers, and parent-child interactions. Ignoring the expectations created at each of these onsets puts leaders at a disadvantage before their conversations even start. If our perception of our experiences leads us to believe that someone will not have a lot of value to offer, we likely will not fully engage with them during the conversation. If we believe that a person is likely to start a conflict during our conversation, we are far more likely to start the conflict ourselves because we are bracing for it. Similarly, if we assume that someone will be meek, we will be totally caught off guard if they become assertive or antagonistic. We are better served taking a goal-oriented approach, maintaining a learning mentality, and capitalizing on the opportunities that arise during our conversations.

STAGE TWO: ARRIVALS AND INTRODUCTIONS

With the pre-conversation stage behind us, the second stage of potentially contentious conversations is the introduction at the start of the conversation.

The First Second

As previously stated, we judge people's trustworthiness and intelligence, and categorize them using our existing mental models, within 100 and 500 milliseconds of first meeting them. In the blink of an eye, we decide how trustworthy our counterparts are and we apply any labels to them that we feel are appropriate. Once we make these determinations, we back them up with cognitive biases that quickly make us feel comfortable with our decisions.

With this knowledge in mind, leaders should maximize the first second of every interaction to their advantage with a welcoming introduction. Kindness does not equate to an abdication of power. A warm, kind demeanor at the start of any conversation can be disarming and create unexpected opportunities to build rapport. You can always dial up the heat during the conversation if it becomes necessary—in fact, if you take an incremental approach to turning up the heat, you can often turn it right back down when you no longer need it.

There are precious few scenarios that include a real, strategic benefit to dominating someone when you meet them. Whether they realize it or not, people who resort to these dominating tactics do so because they lack the tools and confidence to approach the conversation any other way. They feel the need to bully their way into control immediately instead of earning their influence as the interaction progresses.

These dominating or controlling tactics reinforce any existing us-versus-them dynamic and magnify the resistance we are likely to encounter. Despite how many leaders and authority figures feel, no one owes them respect. They owe everyone they interact with the opportunity to respect them. So many violent encounters, shouting matches, fractured relationships, and missed opportunities can be directly traced back to one person unnecessarily attempting to impose control over another. You can't unpick a fight.

Diffusing Expectations

Judee Burgoon's Expectation Violation Theory (EVT) illustrates the perfect reason to forgo the old-school controlling approach to introductions. For this explanation, please temporarily suspend any negative connotations you have for the word "violation." Violating an expectation just means that someone expected you to do one thing and you did another. It could be as innocuous as wearing a red shirt instead of a blue shirt or ordering French toast instead of pancakes.

According to EVT, people become more mentally alert when their expectations are violated as they focus on the violator and attempt to interpret the meaning of the violation within the situational context. Additionally, the perception of the violation will be driven by the perception of the violator. Violations are generally viewed more positively when the violator is held in high regard.[1]

Essentially, we can immediately alter the tone of a conversation by violating our counterpart's negative expectations of us. Little gestures like being nice, using their name, asking them how they are doing, allowing them to speak first, and not immediately accusing them of any wrongdoing, can all help diffuse conflict before it starts and adjust the lens through which they view your communication.

This is why I take a strategic and surprising approach every time I call for customer service. I realize that the agents I speak with are likely not treated well by most people they speak with and they're typically not motivated to go out of their way to help people. This is especially problematic if I need their assistance to correct a mistake I've made. As a result, my conversations typically start as follows:

Agent: Thank you for calling Customer Service. My name is Donna. With whom am I speaking today?

Me: Good morning, Donna. How are you?

Agent: (two second pause) Ahh, actually, I'm good. How are you?

Me: I'm well, thank you. My name is Michael Reddington and I'm calling today hoping for some additional assistance with a situation that may be my fault.

Agent: Certainly, Mr. Reddington. How can I help?

This approach violates the agent's potential negative expectations and resets the tone of the call when I speak calmly, use the agent's name, ask how she is doing, and make a self-effacing request. Thankfully, this approach consistently yields the results I require.

EVT reinforces two key takeaways from the first two phases of potentially contentious conversations. First, leaders, parents, sales professionals, and investigators should dedicate time to connect with people prior to any difficult conversation. This will help improve the expectations their audiences have for them during stressful conversations. Second, they should maximize the opening seconds of every interaction to violate any us-versus-them expectations that their audience may have and reset their perceptions for their conversations.

There are several ways to violate these negative expectations. One alternative is to set meetings, invite people to your office, and approach people publicly when you have positive messages to share with them. You can also change how you communicate the need for a meeting by using positive, curious, or goal-oriented language instead of dictating someone's time or schedule. Another alternative is to do nice, unexpected things for your team, customers, or family. It may take time and a number of experiences, but you can absolutely reset how you are perceived.

If you are calling someone to meet you in your office, get out from behind your desk and wait for them at the door. If you are walking toward someone to meet them, be mindful of your pace and posture. Instead of rushing toward them, pace yourself a bit more casually. Also, take yourself off their center line as you approach them. If you approach someone quickly and stand directly in front of them (nose to nose) you may appear more aggressive than you intend. Take half a step to your left and approach them with your right shoulder in line with their right shoulder. This will help limit their defensive response and line you up for an introductory handshake.

The Space Between Us

We can also manage the space between ourselves and our counterparts to our advantage. Anthropologist Dr. Edward T. Hall is credited with defining and publishing how people interact with others based on the distance they maintain during their interactions. According to his research, there are four zones that we position ourselves in while we are interacting with others.[2] The intimate zone is from zero to one and a half feet apart, and is typically reserved for people we have close relationships with. The professional zone is one and a half to four feet apart. Most business conversations are typically conducted in this range. The social zone is from four to ten feet apart, and the public zone is anything beyond ten feet apart. Astute leaders can move in and out of these zones to manage the impressions they create and the connections they make. Business conversations should typically take place with about four feet of spacing between participants. It is also important for leaders to be aware of any size, gender, age, or cultural norms that may make it prudent to expand or reduce the distance between themselves and their counterparts.

The Handshake

Many cultures have a version of a handshake introduction that provides another crucial moment in both establishing or violating the expectations for your conversations. Culturally appropriate handshakes provide a unique opportunity to show interest, demonstrate respect, and set the preferred tone. Here in the United States (and similar Western cultures), a great handshake includes a slight step toward our counterparts, a fully extended arm, good eye contact, a warm facial expression, a respectfully firm grip, and a professional and polite verbal welcoming statement.

Handshakes can hurt relationships as much as they can help. Leaders who crowd their counterparts (stand toe to toe), use a death grip, roll their hand on top of their counterpart's hand, pull their counterpart toward them, demonstrate dominance by grabbing their counterpart's arm with their left hand, maintain too much eye contact, and use authoritarian welcoming statements immediately reinforce any relevant negative expectations their counterpart may possess.

Set Up for Success

The setup of the meeting room can also play a substantial role. When many people envision speaking with an authority figure, they usually picture sitting on the opposite side of a desk from them. This has been largely true, from the kitchen table, to the principal's office, to the police station, to the manager's office. Not only does this setup align with our counterpart's negative expectations, it reinforces unhelpful aspects of us-versus-them relationships. Sitting behind a desk conveys a disparity in power and perceived value. The desk also inhibits our ability to build rapport and make an empathetic connection while limiting the totality of the nonverbal communication we can observe.

An easy way to avoid these negative effects, disrupt your counterpart's negative expectations, and reframe the tone of the conversation is to come out from behind your desk and sit about four feet across from your counterpart in the same style chairs. This setup removes the authoritarian symbolism of the desk, creates the opportunity to make an empathetic connection, and opens up all of their nonverbal communication for your evaluation. As a bonus, the unexpected set up of the room violates their expectations, heightens their focus, and potentially reframes their participation in the conversation. If your counterpart looks at the chairs and then looks at you like you have three heads, calmly say something to the effect of, "I want to be sure everyone knows they have my complete focus," and proceed as planned.

The same dynamics are present when leaders sit at the head of the conference room table. Sitting in a chair at the head of the table is a clear statement to everyone else in the room about who is in charge. It reinforces age-old stereotypes and can reinforce us-versus-them dynamics that can limit the information people are willing to share and how they perceive your communications. Sitting in a chair at the middle of the table removes these stereotypes, reframes your counterparts' perspectives, and violates their expectations.

I was privileged to have the opportunity to teach in Nairobi, Kenya. After my first session, I was approached by one of the attending CEOs who asked me for ideas on how to get his team to open up more during meetings. I asked him to help me understand what his meetings looked and felt like. Sure enough, he described sitting at the head of a long conference table that could seat more than ten people. When I suggested the new seating arrangement, he said, "They will think I lost my marbles." I laughed and replied, "Only at first." We talked through the nuances of the opportunity and he eventually agreed to try it. I was very happy when he emailed me several weeks later to tell me what a difference it made to the atmosphere of his meetings.

Giving Up Ground

Too many times, leaders participate in a range of behaviors that prioritize their comfort, copy what they've seen other leaders do, or they feel it is how leaders are supposed to act. All of these reasons are focused on the leader, not the leader's audience. Anytime we are truly looking to connect with our audience, our behavior and approach should be driven by what our audience needs to experience, not what we want to experience.

A perfect example is a conversation I recently had with a client. I spoke with a manager who was asking for assistance in re-engaging with a subcontractor who had gone radio silent. My client had been having issues with this subcontractor for some time, including several examples of poor-quality work and missed deadlines. These issues culminated in a significant problem that was going to cost someone over $100,000 to fix. When this issue was identified, my client called the owner of the subcontractor and asked him to come to his office to discuss the problem. At the last minute, the subcontractor called and said he couldn't make it. The manager called him back to reschedule the meeting several times and received no further follow-up.

As we were discussing the situation, he told me, "This guy needs to come to my office so we can work this out." This statement was very telling. The manager made his priorities crystal clear. He was focused on getting his subcontractor to come to his office, not resolving the situation. I asked him why the conversation needed to take place in his office and he said, "Because it is our project and our owners should be there too." Got it. This is a common perspective: I am in charge; you need to come to me.

The manager let me work through several follow-up questions. I asked him how he thought this subcontractor felt he was treated by most of the companies he worked with. We both agreed the subcontractor probably felt like the little brother who was always getting beaten up. And now he is being forced to come to the manager's office for the conversation. Again, we agreed that he would likely feel like he was being treated like a child being called to the principal's office. Then I asked him, "Can you blame this guy for ghosting you?" and he said, "Not at all."

We then pivoted the conversation to what to do next. I asked him "What's more important, having the conversation here or resolving the issue?" He replied, "Resolving the issue." So, we discussed options. We talked through the benefits of meeting this guy at the job site, going to the subcontractor's office, or setting a neutral site for the meeting. At the end of the conversation, the manager committed to meeting the subcontractor at the jobsite and scheduling the actual conversation when it was convenient for the subcontractor, either at the subcontractor's office or at a neutral location.

This approach seems very counterintuitive for many leaders. An attitude of entitlement reinforces negative expectations and creates additional barriers to obtaining the truth. If leaders are truly interested in obtaining the truth and inspiring commitments to action, they must consider the benefits of resolving the situation, and their counterpart's fears and motivations when they schedule the meeting.

STAGE THREE: PURPOSEFUL LISTENING

The third stage of potentially contentious conversations starts after the introductions and the perfunctory polite social exchanges are completed, and people begin to purposefully listen to what you are saying. When the real conversation starts, their focus shifts to determining what the conversation is about, what your intentions are, where the conversation is going, what you may ask of them, and what the outcomes may be. They will make these judgments based on their relevant previous experiences, the demeanor of your introduction, their perception of your delivery, and either their fears or aspirations. For example:

- Thieves may be wondering which one of their crimes has been discovered, what evidence has been collected, what the consequences are, what the interviewers' goals are, and how they may be able to talk their way out of it.

- Employees may be replaying the trigger event in their mind, contemplating what other people have told you, wondering if you believe them, worrying about the consequences, and planning what to say when you give them the chance.

- Customers may be ignoring your pitch while convincing themselves they've heard it all before, planning their first question or statement, and thinking about either what their manager will say about the agreement or what other options they have besides doing business with you.

Admittedly, our counterparts' internal dialogue isn't always negative. A victim may be thankful she gets to tell her story. An employee may be hopeful of a promotion, and a customer may be excited to hear more about your product. However, we often underestimate the fearful and self-serving focus of our counterparts' initial internal conversations.

STAGE FOUR: INTERNALIZATION AND SELF-TALK

As soon as your audience believes they have figured out what the conversation is about and where it is going, they graduate to the fourth stage of potentially contentious conversations and begin internalizing the situation and talking to themselves. This internal monologue can quickly take them in many directions. They will likely talk themselves through how they feel about you, the conversation, and the surrounding circumstances. They may begin retracing their steps as they try to remember previous events, or spin their thoughts forward as they try to create new ideas, excuses, or resolutions. They may start weighing their alternatives against the potential rewards and consequences. They may even revisit promises they previously made to themselves about how they would act during this conversation when it inevitably took place.

During this stage, your counterpart is only hearing a portion of what you are saying. They may maintain less eye contact as their internal monologue dominates their attention. They may catch on to changes in your tone, large shifts in your posture or gestures, and some of your words. They certainly aren't receiving your entire message. Leaders can increase the attention they receive by varying their tone and speed of delivery. It may even help to use the occasional short pause to recapture your counterpart's attention.

STAGE FIVE: DETERMINE WHAT TO SAY AND WHEN TO SAY IT

The fifth stage of potentially contentious conversations starts when your counterparts decide what they are willing to say, and when to share it. This is the stage where they start setting rules for themselves and begin to consider the circumstances that will make it appropriate to share information, accept agreements, or allow different outcomes. It might be as straightforward as, "Okay, I'll just tell them," or "I'll just buy it," or "I'll just do it." They may also need to justify their impending actions by telling themselves, "I'll only tell them if I feel like they aren't judging me," or "I'll only tell them if I won't get in too much trouble," or "I'll only buy it if I believe he's not trying to take advantage of me," or "I'll do it, but only if I get some kind of reward."

The greatest illustration of this occurred in maybe the most famous interview conducted by past teammates of mine. My former coworker Chris was part of a team investigating a significant theft ring at a large distribution center. The first man Chris was scheduled to interview walked into the room, looked around, and said, "I don't think I've done nothing wrong," as he walked around to the opposite side of the table from Chris. Chris asked the gentleman to come back and sit in front of him, which he reluctantly did. In retrospect, what happened next was wildly entertaining.

First, the subject asked Chris if he was a lawyer, which was unexpected. As Chris started the conversation, the subject leaned back, turned his body away from Chris, and stared at him suspiciously. Chris started the interview by attempting to establish the subject's behavioral baseline by asking him to verify his personal information. When Chris asked him to verify his address the subject asked, "Where I'm living at or where I stay?" He then appeared to forget his address. When Chris asked him what his job title was, the subject took a lengthy pause before mumbling, "I'm not quite sure." He also couldn't remember his salary.

Given the subject's apparently evasive answers and nervous demeanor, Chris began to think that this guy was possibly involved in the theft ring. Chris continued the conversation by telling his subject that he was there to help investigate some issues at the distribution center. Upon hearing this, his subject started laughing, sat up straight, turned toward Chris and said, "Great, I can relax now." Chris was understandably surprised by this. Before he could say anything, the subject said, "I thought you were here about my child support, man. I can relax now." Chris composed himself, capitalized on this new revelation, and during the ensuing interview he was able to establish that his subject wasn't involved in any of the theft.

This subject was well aware that he wasn't paying child support, had braced himself for his inevitable arrest and interrogation, and had apparently promised himself that he wouldn't say anything to help the investigators. He spent the first several minutes of the conversation evaluating the situation, and Chris, and had said nothing to dissuade him from his previous determinations. Once Chris told him the conversation was about a work-related issue, the subject completely dropped his guard, and decided to fully participate in the interview with Chris.

However, just because they've joined the conversation, doesn't mean they will stay involved.

STAGE SIX: CONTINUED PARTICIPATION IN THE CONVERSATION

The sixth stage of potentially contentious conversations is their decision to continue participating in the conversation. Their continued participation is directly related to how they feel they are being treated and what they believe the potential outcomes are.

Occasionally, an interrogation suspect will come right out and tell the truth because they feel guilty and their actions have been weighing on them. Those are good days. More often than not, interrogation suspects tell the truth when they believe the truth is either already known, or will be known shortly, and they have the chance to save face and put their own spin on the story.[3] It is generally much harder to obtain the truth if an interrogator attempts to force the suspect to admit fault at the first admission. It is exponentially harder to encourage someone to tell the truth if the interrogator attempts to force the suspect to admit their previous statements were lies.

Your counterpart will likely continue to participate in the conversation with you as long as they are feeling respected and an undesirable outcome hasn't already been predetermined. If at any point during the conversation your counterpart feels disrespected, repeatedly disbelieved, ignored, or helpless, they are likely to shut down. They may stay in the room with you, but they are done contributing meaningfully to the conversation.

I came perilously close to falling victim to this reaction during an interrogation. I was requested to take over a stalled investigation into two men who were abusing a third man at work. First, I spoke with the victim whose story was clearly both true and heartbreaking. The abuse began escalating when the two suspects accused him of being a snitch—which he wasn't.

I was asked to interview both men eight weeks after they were originally interrogated and denied any wrongdoing. After assessing both suspects, I made the decision to interview the secondary suspect first because, as the project manager, he was the higher ranking of the two. My theory was that I could use his position to work backward from the project to the abuse and then get him to snitch on the primary antagonist. Admittedly, this was a risky approach considering the abuse allegedly started with the two suspects accusing the victim of snitching.

When I spoke with the secondary suspect, the initial conversation went very well. In fact, when he described the incident that started the whole situation he said, "You could say that was the start of their holy war." That was a very powerful description.

After almost forty-five minutes, it appeared that he was on the verge of confessing. He paused and asked me if I knew the victim. I reflexively answered, "I've spoken with lots of people here," because professional investigators are all trained to protect victims during their interviews. We don't want to say or do anything that will create additional exposure for the victims of any crime.

My answer backfired immediately. The suspect said, "Well, I guess I can take that to mean whatever I want," crossed both his arms and legs, and turned away from me. He interpreted my response as a slap in the face. This perceived violation of the bond he felt we had established told him that I expected him to share information with me, but I wasn't going to share information with him. His body language told me that he was done sharing information if this was a one-sided deal. With about one second to salvage the conversation I said, "Yes, I apologize. I have spoken with him. I just didn't want to create the impression that he was the only person I've spoken with." Thankfully, the suspect accepted my reply, forgave my misstep, and went on to confess his participation in the abuse and (ironically) snitch on the primary aggressor.

STAGE SEVEN: POST-CONVERSATION FOLLOW-UP

The final stage of potentially contentious conversations is the post-conversation follow-up. Although this stage may not appear to be part of the actual conversation, it most certainly is. You can exhibit all of the attentive listening behaviors during the conversation, but failing to follow up inadvertently renders them meaningless; the one and only way to prove to someone that you listened is to give them tangible evidence by following up after the conversation. We have iterative relationships with nearly everyone we interact with. Make no mistake, the end of your conversation (and the interviewing follow-up communication) actually serves as the start of your next conversation. If we don't follow through on our commitments, check in to see how they are doing, circle back to close any open topics, or even reference something they said in future conversations, they won't believe that we listened to them.

This stage can simultaneously go in several different directions. Our audiences will be waiting and watching, evaluating our behavior, and judging our follow-up actions or lack thereof. They may also use this time as an opportunity to collect their thoughts and re-engage with us to discuss additional information, ideas, or alternatives they didn't consider during our conversation. Your audience could very well walk away committed to outcomes and actions you both agreed upon. Or they could walk away feeling like they were forced to comply with your requests, and either refuse to take the actions or apply the minimum required efforts to avoid another conversation. They can also use this stage as an opportunity to take any concerns they have (valid or not) to an audience they feel is supportive in an attempt to reaffirm their perspective.

While we have explored these stages from our counterparts' perspectives, we must realize that we will also experience these stages. Our experiences and expectations will cloud our perceptions and influence what we hear and say. We will either cement our expectations at the introduction, or potentially form new ones. Once our counterparts start speaking, we will evaluate their messages until we reach a point where we need to determine how we feel and what we say or do next. At this point, we will cycle through the internalization and self-talk stage, choose what to say, and decide how long to continue participating in the conversation.

From a Disciplined Listening perspective, each of these seven stages are very important to understand. Connecting with our audiences requires us to accurately comprehend the perspectives and expectations they bring into our conversations, as well as where they are cognitively and emotionally throughout the conversation. We can't reach people if we don't know where they are.

Diligent efforts can turn the first two stages to our advantage. Stages three through six will be rinse and repeat for the duration of your conversations. Your audiences may travel that cycle many times as their perception, the topics, your delivery, the potential outcomes, and their emotions change. The follow-up stage is where leaders have the chance to cement or ruin their credibility and agreements.

We can't reach people if we don't know where they are.

Disciplined Listeners work hard to account for their audience's perspectives, fears, and motivations throughout the conversations. Acknowledging that our counterparts may be motivated to withhold information, lie, feel defensive, and seem antagonistic helps Disciplined Listeners separate people, messages, and emotions within the context of their conversations.

In the next chapter, will explore the impact of the core behaviors that Disciplined Listeners consistently exhibit during their strategically valuable conversations.

CHAPTER SEVEN

THE DISCIPLINED
LISTENING METHOD

MY JOB AS A Certified Forensic Interviewer was to connect with victims, witnesses, suspects, and clients in a wide variety of investigations to obtain the truth with morally, legally, and ethically sound techniques. Perhaps surprisingly, I was expected to use my interviews and interrogations as tools to improve morale, trust, and productivity within the organizations that hired me.

Each person I spoke with had life experiences and perspectives that I could never fully understand. Many of them came in with ideas, emotions, opinions, or had taken actions with which I strongly disagreed. However, the more offended I felt, the more important it was to put my emotions in my back pocket and find authentic ways to connect with my subjects.

To add an additional degree of difficulty, as a traveling interrogator, the interview settings were often out of my control. Choosing where to conduct the interviews often came down to picking the best of the bad options.

Over time, accounting for these challenges while I prepared for my investigative interviews consistently led me to a riddle I needed to solve: *How do I create the experience my subject needs to*

commit to sharing the truth when our emotions and goals conflict,
and the environment is largely out of my control?

The answers I arrived at formed the pillars of what became the Disciplined Listening Method and will be outlined in detail throughout the remainder of this book.

The Disciplined Listening Method assumes that the process of listening is cyclical. What we say and how we behave impacts how people communicate with us. The information we receive from our audiences and how we interpret it influences our responses, and the cycle continues.

The Disciplined Listening Method addresses how to prepare for, engage with, and observe our audiences. Essentially, Disciplined Listeners understand the potential value of any given interaction and study the totality of their communication experiences for opportunities they can leverage to enhance relationships and improve results. To this end, Disciplined Listeners consistently exhibit seven core behaviors. They:

1. **Understand** how every interaction impacts their ability to achieve their long- and short-term goals.

2. **Leverage** their perceived weaknesses to develop their communication strategies.

3. **Allow** the conversation to come to them.

4. **Identify** strategic intelligence by evaluating the totality of their counterparts' verbal and nonverbal communications within the context of the situation.

5. **Adapt** their communication strategies to immediately integrate the new intelligence they acquire.

6. **Encourage** their counterparts to always protect their self-images.

7. **Develop** trust equity through post-conversation follow-up.

FIRST CORE BEHAVIOR: KEEPING OUR GOALS IN MIND

The first core behavior of the Disciplined Listening Method defines the reason for listening and determines the accuracy and application of the remaining six core behaviors. It's like Stephen Covey said, "Begin with the end in mind."[1] I'm assuming most people wouldn't jump onto a sailboat off the coast of Ft. Lauderdale, cut it loose from the dock, unfurl the sails, and just head east without a destination or a planned route of travel. Skills such as assessing the currents, understanding changing weather patterns, and reading navigational charts offer little value if you don't know where you are going. Choosing which environmental factors to react to either becomes random, or worse, dependent on the challenge you're immediately confronted with and independent of any desired destination. Either scenario could likely cause your vessel to travel in unnecessary directions, get lost, and eventually become listless. The destination gives your sailing skills value, just as your communication goals give your listening skills value.

 There is a direct relationship between the amount of effort we commit to listening and the amount of value we receive from any interaction. Anytime we perceive that a person won't know, won't listen, or won't have the information we need, we won't give our full effort. Similarly, if we believe that the topic of conversation isn't worthy or can't be influenced, we won't dedicate our full attention to the conversation. Listeners perform better, stay more engaged, and increase both the thoroughness and accuracy of their evaluations when they believe they have a good reason to listen. Defining their reason for

> Listeners perform better, stay more engaged, and increase both the thoroughness and accuracy of their evaluations when they believe they have a good reason to listen.

listening is the first and potentially most important core behavior of the Disciplined Listening Method.

Clearly identifying how any conversation can help them achieve their long- and short-term goals creates several advantages for Disciplined Listeners. First, it reframes the expectations listeners carry into conversations and the value listeners believe they can gain during their conversations. Reframing and focusing on the potential value of the conversation allows Disciplined Listeners to compartmentalize their emotions, ignore distractions, and motivate themselves to remain present. Knowing what they are working to achieve helps them remain above these negative influences.

A second advantage is elevating the listeners' focus to think beyond the moment. It is easy for listeners to focus on their short-term, tactical goals. Think about how many times you've entered into a conversation thinking, *I need to wrap this up as soon as possible*; *I need to hurry up and get to my next meeting*; *I just need him to be clear about my expectations*; or *I need to make sure she knows this can never happen again*. These are all short-term, tactical goals that focus on what you are feeling and wanting in that exact moment. They are almost always focused on relieving your discomfort or inconvenience, and not connecting with your counterparts.

Focusing on our long-term goals cultivates significantly more value from any conversation. This approach allows us to reframe our discomforts and inconveniences as investments in a greater cause. Conversations graduate from being unnecessary wastes of time and become opportunistic tools toward greater achievements. We can accomplish this by reframing the statements in the previous paragraph to, *I need to maximize the time I have available*, and *I need to make sure he understands this process well enough to teach it to someone else*.

One example of this approach in action is an exercise we facilitate early on in our sales training programs. We start the exercise by asking the group what their big, strategic goals are at various stages of the sales process. The conversation almost invariably proceeds as follows:

Question: What is your big, strategic goal making cold calls or at the initial customer introduction?

Answer: To schedule a meeting to learn more about them and see if they are a good fit for us.

Question: What is your big strategic goal during your discovery meetings?

Answer: Identify their pain and learn the details I need to schedule a demo.

Question: What is your big strategic goal during your demos?

Answer: Get them to see the value so I can send them a proposal.

Question: What is your big strategic goal when you present your proposal?

Answer: Get them to accept it and sign the contract.

Question: What is your big strategic goal once they've signed the contract?

Answer: Deliver on what we committed to and keep them happy.

The sales teams we work with often get a little frustrated when we point out that every one of these goals is a short-term, inward-focused, tactical goal. At each phase in the process, we often find that sales professionals are focused on getting what they think they need—information—to move onto the next step. They are not focused on what they *actually* need—intelligence—to impact the larger strategic picture from the first interaction.

There is a significant difference between information and intelligence. People often fall into a check-the-box mentality when they listen for information. They've already decided how they want a conversation to end, so they listen for a few key pieces of information they can use to set up the conclusion they're expecting.

Listeners identify intelligence when they are guided by their long-term, strategic goals and they focus on creating opportunities to demonstrate value—not arrive at predetermined destinations. Intelligence may be hidden in someone's tone, word choice, pace, and body language. It may also be hidden in off-the-cuff statements, sidebars, and seemingly unimportant conversations. This intelligence holds the key to creating new value.

As the sales training exercise continues, we brainstorm long-term, strategic goals until we arrive at "turn our customers into our best sales representatives." This is a strategic goal. We want to interact with our customers in a manner that causes them to want to recommend us, brag about us, and create new opportunities with us both within their organization and their networks. Keeping this goal in mind from our very first interaction increases our opportunity of achieving it.

This feat is accomplished by providing unexpected and unsolicited value during every step of the process. If we are only listening for the information necessary to get to the next step, we won't be able to identify the intelligence necessary to surprise customers and add the value required for our customers to eventually sell on our behalf. Our mind's eye simply won't be open to the opportunities.

We are beholden to our mind's eye. We go wherever it directs us. We can choose to focus on the painful or unfortunate nature of what is right in front of us, or we can choose to focus on the opportunities our current discomfort can lead us to. Focusing on our immediate discomfort will almost assuredly bring our fears to life. Focusing on the opportunities we can create will bring us closer to achieving them.

Target Fixation

As an example, I had the opportunity to take a motorcycle training course inspired by the training completed by motorcycle police officers. These officers are among the most capable riders on the planet and what they can do with fully packed machines weighing roughly a thousand pounds is astounding. Walking out onto the course the first morning was like wading into a sea of orange road cones. These cones were placed just wide enough for the Harley Davidson Road Kings to fit between and featured an indeterminable number of tight turns leading in all directions at various angles. As we walked the course, the head instructor told us that as we navigated the course we needed to look where we were going, not at the cones. He promised us that looking at the cones would result in our machines rolling straight into them. He then smiled and told us we needed to immediately stop and pick up any cone we knocked over. I heard him loud and clear, trusting his advice.

Later that morning, I entered the course for the first time and approached the initial ninety-degree turn. I downshifted, feathered the brakes, attempted to set my torque, looked right at the cones in front of me, and thought, *Don't hit those cones.* Just like the instructor had promised, I plowed right into the cones. I stopped, picked them up, and earned the opportunity to enjoy my instructor's vulgarity-laced reminder of what I did wrong from all the way across the parking lot.

I had two simple choices: "see cone, hit cone," or "see exit, hit exit," and I chose wrong. When target fixation sets in, we end up riding, speaking, or listening our way right into the problem we are looking to avoid.

> When target fixation sets in, we end up riding, speaking, or listening our way right into the problem we are looking to avoid.

Intelligent Listening

The third and perhaps largest advantage that this goal-oriented mindset creates is allowing listeners to observe for intelligence, not information. Intelligence is information with greater potential value and application. When listeners focus on obtaining information, they often find themselves in a check-the-box mentality. They listen and may ask for specific information that fits within their preexisting expectations. They feel good about what they "heard," but they are very limited with what they can do with it.

When Disciplined Listeners focus on obtaining intelligence, they look and listen beyond the face value of their observations. They increase their attention levels and situational awareness to study the nuances of their audience's communications and identify unexpected opportunities to achieve their goals. The only way listeners can separate information from intelligence is by understanding the goals their conversations can help them achieve *before* engaging their counterparts. This approach creates new opportunities to strengthen relationships and rapport, makes it easier for others to take accountability, and generates larger customer commitments.

Knowing that you benefit from identifying the goals of a conversation seems like an obvious and potentially unnecessary place to start. Unfortunately, too many people bounce in and out of their conversations without taking a moment to understand where these conversations can lead them. This impulsive approach can result in missed opportunities and unnecessary conflicts that we may not realize until it is too late. All too often I hear leaders, sales professionals, and even parents believe they can rely on their observation skills, wit, or ability to navigate a conversation while they're involved in it. Not only does this lack of intention limit their options for success, it also opens the door for their emotional shifts to play an unhealthy role in their conversations.

SECOND CORE BEHAVIOR: LEVERAGING PERCEIVED WEAKNESSES

Once Disciplined Listeners are clear on how a conversation can lead them closer to achieving their long- and short-term goals, they apply the second core behavior of the Disciplined Listening Method—leveraging their perceived weaknesses to develop their communication strategies. It can be easy and even natural for leaders, sales professionals, investigators, and parents to feel entitled to information. One of the biggest communication mistakes a person with any level of power can make is to assume that their counterparts owe them the truth because of their position, title, or perceived power.

The exact opposite is most often true. People owe it to themselves to protect themselves from those who may have power over them. Power often equates to the ability to punish. The more powerful a listener is in title, influence, position, or contextual control, the more fearful a speaker will likely be of the consequences the listener may enforce.

Everyone has the right to share or not share information with you, in a manner that protects their own interests. Our self-protection or self-preservation instinct is one of the most powerful

influences on our communications, especially with people in positions of authority. This isn't dishonesty, it's human nature. Leveraging your perceived weaknesses to develop your communication strategies protects you from falling into the entitlement trap.

As a professional interrogator, the nature of the job meant sitting down and speaking with people who had little to no interest in speaking with me. Most victims, witnesses, suspects, and clients were hesitant to speak openly about incidents under investigation. They all faced real and perceived consequences, which motivated them to withhold, or at least slightly manipulate, the information I needed to obtain.

To make matters more difficult, my former teammates and I were regularly requested to resolve lingering, mismanaged investigations that were void of evidence. It was common for such cases to involve multiple suspects who had already declared their innocence during previous interviews. An honest assessment of these investigations led me to an inconvenient conclusion: our subjects had no reason to tell us the truth.

The honest subjects had already been unnecessarily burdened by the investigation and the dishonest subjects were 99 percent of the way to escaping accountability for their actions. Either way, they likely believed (maybe accurately) that openly participating in another interview would only make their experiences worse. I had the choice to either deny or embrace this reality.

It is too easy for leaders in any context to fall into the perceived strength trap and become overconfident, attempt to project their strengths onto their audience, and fail to accurately account for potential hurdles they may need to clear. Embracing the fact that the deck was stacked against me caused me to realize that the key to my success was hiding within my perceived weaknesses. This realization was liberating for me and unlocked a new strategic approach that I continue to apply to every interview, negotiation, coaching session, sales meeting, and critical parenting conversation by inverting the strategic framework I used.

Most people who have taken any business course in school, attended any business-related seminars, or found themselves stuck in at least one strategic planning session have been exposed to the "SWOT" analysis.[2] This universally accepted process was created to help people expand their strategic thinking at both the business and individual level. Practitioners are taught to execute the process in the order that the acronym outlines.

Strengths

Weaknesses

Opportunities

Threats

However, this traditional approach to the process increases the probability of practitioners falling prey to their own biases, limiting their perspectives, and misjudging potential obstacles. A careful review of this approach exposes its flaws. First, "S" is for strengths. Starting the process by highlighting our perceived strengths triggers our biases. People and organizations are predisposed to overvalue their perceived strengths. In their book *The Challenger Sale*, Matthew Dixon and Brent Adamson point out that one research study showed the market only perceived 14 percent of self-selected company differentiating factors as truly differential.[3] Initially overvaluing our perceived strengths clouds the rest of the evaluation process.

"W" is for weakness. Relating to how we might inflate our own strengths, we also tend to downplay our weaknesses. They are uncomfortable to admit, especially publicly. This tendency to minimize our weaknesses is exaggerated when they are immediately juxtaposed to our strengths. Once any trait lands on the strengths list, we can't possibly include it on the weakness list.

Third, "O" is for opportunity. The problem here is that practitioners may only examine the opportunities they believe are currently on the table. This limits their ability to consider opportunities that may be presently unavailable, but not outside of their ability to generate.

Finally, the "T" stands for threats. When external threats are considered last, they become an afterthought and may not be thoroughly considered. Especially if they conflict with or reduce the strengths and opportunities previously listed. Overlooking potential threats in the planning stages can cause significant issues during conversations.

The logic behind the SWOT analysis can be maximized, and the bias driven limitations reduced, by reorganizing the order of operations. Disciplined Listeners embrace the WTSO approach.

Weaknesses

Threats

Strengths

Opportunities

The first two steps require leaders in all contexts to have a painfully honest conversation and document all the internal weaknesses and external threats that may thwart their efforts. If an idea seems like it could be a weakness or threat but you're not sure, it should definitely make the list. If this conversation doesn't make you at least a little uncomfortable, then you're probably not being honest enough.

Documenting your weaknesses and threats first allows you to take an evolved approach to examining your strengths. The original analysis requires practitioners to ask themselves, "What are my strengths?" The WTSO model positions practitioners to ask themselves, "How can I leverage my weaknesses and threats to maximize the perception of my strengths?"

> Documenting your weaknesses and threats first allows you to take an evolved approach to examining your strengths.

Your actual strengths aren't as important as how your audience perceives them. Embracing our weaknesses and threats creates a new opportunity to examine how we can apply our strengths in a manner that reframes our audiences' perspectives and increases our ability to influence them toward our desired outcome.

Finally, WTSO practitioners graduate from focusing on the opportunities they believe are currently on the table and ask themselves, "What new opportunities does this approach open up for me?" This pivots a leader's attention from where they are now to where they want to be, and how they can get there. Not in spite of their weaknesses and threats, but because of them.

Starting with the Opposite

Many people have been taught to prepare for potentially contentious conversations by asking themselves, "Why should they commit to what I want them to?" The goal of answering this question is to identify our audiences' motivations so that we can capitalize on them. Unfortunately, answering that question forces us to transpose our perspective onto our audience and make dangerous assumptions based on how *we* view the situation. Truly putting yourself in someone else's shoes isn't as easy as it sounds. Especially if you have opposing views, interests, emotions, or experiences.

As a card-carrying, flag-waving, hill-defending WTSO practitioner, I ask myself the opposite question when I prepare for any significant conversation: *"Why shouldn't they commit to what I want them to do?"* I kick off my preparation by thoughtfully considering all the reasons my audience may not want to commit to what I want them to based on their perspective, experiences, and interests. We are all predisposed to prefer our own ideas and protect our own interests.[4] This is especially true when communicators in any leadership capacity are communicating with anyone in a perceived subordinate role. The most effective first step we can take to achieving commitments during potentially contentious conversations is to embrace these facts and build our strategies around them.

Once I've answered the first question, I ask myself its sister question: *"Why haven't they already committed to what I want them to do?"* The answer to this question will fall into one of two broad categories. Either they weren't previously aware this was an option for them, or they don't see the value. Breaking down the details and understanding why they either weren't aware or don't see the value, positions you to formulate your communication approach to resonate with your audience.

Answering these questions provides several important benefits. First, they get us as close as possible to truly putting ourselves in someone else's shoes. Second, it forces us to limit the destructive powers of our egos and helps us avoid falling into the entitlement trap. Third, it significantly increases the level of empathy we feel toward our audiences, whether we like what we learn or not.

The next question I ask myself is *"What do they need to experience before choosing to commit to what I need them to?"* It can be tempting to ask yourself, *"What do I need to say to convince them to do what I need them to?"* However, this question focuses on you, not your counterpart, and is predicated on convincing your counterpart. The process of convincing reliably requires people to stake themselves to positions you will later have to move them away from so they can accept your idea. Focusing on what your counterparts need to experience during your conversation increases your opportunities to help them save face, protect their self-images, feel respected, reduce their resistance, and take idea ownership for committing to your desired actions.

Moving Toward the Goal

With my fourth and final preparation question, I pivot and use the answers from the previous three questions to frame my communication approach: *"What is my goal and how will everything I say and do help me achieve it?"* At this point, I will look at all the intelligence within the answers to the previous three questions, and I'll consider as many aspects of the impending interaction as possible. These include the logistics (day, time, location), modality (in person, phone call, video call, email, etc.), participants, key points I'd like to make, key questions I'd like to ask, and the most effective order to present these points and questions.

I leveraged this approach when I was tasked with identifying the person responsible for stealing two firearms. Two months prior to my involvement in the investigation, a Bureau of Alcohol, Tobacco, Firearms and Explosives (ATF) auditing team visited a gun store and found two handguns were missing from their inventory, and were unable to identify the thief. The case was handed to the local police department and their detective was also unable to obtain any admissions. Two months later, I was asked to interview five employees who had access to the missing firearms in one last attempt to resolve the investigation.

My preliminary investigation identified a primary suspect. Of the five employees who had access to the missing guns, he was the only part-time employee, employed at the location for less than one year, and the only employee who was a twice-convicted felon.

The list of reasons this suspect shouldn't have told me the truth was very long. A few top-line considerations included that he had been previously interrogated many times for multiple crimes, he knew the consequences for telling the truth, he had a family to support, and after two months, he had to believe he had already gotten away with the theft. He likely hadn't told the truth because he didn't want to go back to jail, disappoint his family, and lose his job.

My success or failure hinged on my ability to use these truths to my advantage. I carefully thought through my attire, demeanor, word choice, and the location of the interview to ensure I didn't impose unnecessary authority. I also selected a non-confrontational interrogation approach that would allow him to save face and choose an excuse to blame his actions on. I even scripted out my initial monologue to ensure my word choice and illustrative examples were likely to help him convince himself I knew about his actions, I wasn't judging him, and that it was okay for him to tell me the truth.

Thankfully, these preparation efforts paid off. When he confessed to stealing both guns, he told me, "It's just like you said, the opportunity was there, and I could use the money." He went on to provide me with a hand-drawn map to where one of the handguns was hidden in his basement as well as the name, phone number, address, and turn-by-turn directions to the home of the man he gave the second handgun to.

The first two core behaviors of the Disciplined Listening Method result in conversational game plans that allow communicators to maximize their listening and influencing opportunities.

THIRD CORE BEHAVIOR: ALLOW THE CONVERSATIONS TO COME TO YOU

The third core behavior allows Disciplined Listeners to put their plans into action. Many leaders don't list patience as one of their top qualities. It has been my experience that they often describe themselves as "Type A" personalities—intense, fast-paced, task-oriented, or results-oriented.[5] We've already covered the dangers associated with time- and results-focused listening approaches. Remember to ask yourself which is more important: satisfying your self-image and committing yourself to a "Type A" approach, or obtaining the information you need, when you need it? If obtaining the information isn't important, go ahead and force your perceived default personality on your audience. If obtaining the information is important, leaders will be well served to be patient and allow conversations to come to them.

Two of the leading interrogation techniques in the United States take diametrically opposing approaches. One approach requires interrogators to directly accuse their suspects of the crimes they're suspected of committing at the outset of the interrogation. The other approach requires interrogators to execute a ten-to-fifteen-minute educational monologue prior to issuing their first soft accusation. When students see both techniques outlined next to each other, they typically assume the direct approach obtains admissions quicker because the interrogator cuts right to the chase.

However, the direct approach puts people on the defensive, creates a competitive environment, increases their resistance, and creates more obstacles for the interrogator to navigate. The educational approach allows interrogators to reframe their suspects' perspectives and reduce their resistance prior to posing their soft accusations.

On average, interrogators who use this patient approach obtain the first admission in under twenty minutes, whereas interrogators who directly accuse their suspects right out of the gate typically need at least forty-five minutes to obtain the first admission. Slow is smooth and smooth is fast. When we rush to secure what we want, we can create additional, unnecessary problems. When our approach is patient and intentional, we are more likely to experience less stress and more success.

Disciplined Listeners patiently observe for strategic value. The more they encourage their counterparts to share, the more they observe, the more they learn, and the more intelligence they acquire. The patient approach also positions them to have their questions answered before having to ask.

> When we rush to secure what we want, we can create additional, unnecessary problems. When our approach is patient and intentional, we are more likely to experience less stress and more success.

Many leaders participate in conversations and ask questions that force their audiences to think through their responses as they are sharing them. When people think and talk at the same time, the most valuable intelligence will likely be toward the end of their answer, not the beginning. When people initiate their responses, they often build up to the real meat and value of their answers as the conversation goes on. If leaders don't patiently wait for that value to come to them, they will miss it all together.

It turns out Isaac Newton's third law of motion has limited applicability.[6] Sure, in nature every action creates an equal and opposite reaction, but this couldn't be further from the truth in interpersonal communication. Metaphorically speaking, if someone feels pushed, they aren't going to push back equally. They will push back harder. This escalated response will no doubt result in the original offender pushing back and escalating the situation even further, and the interaction can spiral out of control. These *your counterparts*

harmful escalations can easily be avoided. If you don't push your counterparts, they don't feel the need to push back. If they don't feel the need to push back and assert control, you're in control. As long as you know where you want to be at the end of the conversation, you can let them start the conversation wherever they want and use their contributions to guide the conversation toward the results you need while allowing them to believe they've been in the driver's seat the entire time.

In the aforementioned workplace abuse case, I chose to speak with the secondary suspect first because, as the project manager, he was the higher-ranking of the two. Both suspects had previously been interviewed, denied any wrongdoing, and likely felt confident that there was no substantiating evidence of their victim's accusations. If I spoke with the primary suspect first, my options would have been limited and I may have had to address the accusations much earlier than I wanted, potentially provoking strong denials.

Interviewing the project manager first allowed me to focus the conversation on the project, not the accusations. I started the conversation by asking him to help me understand his role with the company. After he educated me on his responsibilities as a project manager, I asked him what projects he had been leading recently. Sure enough, his list included the project that involved the abuse allegations.

Next, I asked him a few questions about one of the other projects he mentioned to avoid sparking a defensive response. After we discussed the non-related project, I transitioned to the project in question. We patiently worked our way from the start of the project into issues that caused delays. During the conversation, the suspect mentioned the primary suspect's name and the victim's name without me having to ask for them. This persuasive path finally led him to share his previously mentioned assessment, "I guess you could say that was the start of their holy war," which was the perfect transition point for me to switch to the interrogation where the suspect confessed and snitched on the primary suspect.

If I had started the conversation by directly accusing my suspect, directly referring to the victim's statements, or even asking the suspect what he knew about the investigation, I almost certainly would've received strong denials. Working in reverse from the project to the confession allowed me to build credibility, avoid sparking defensive responses, lead my suspect to believe the truth was already known, and obtain the truth without receiving a single denial.

When Schedules Get in the Way

Admittedly, our daily responsibilities may make this patient approach more challenging to adopt. Many leaders look at their calendar as an obstacle course. They see days packed with meetings and calls from start to finish, think about what these meetings entail, ruminate about what they will miss while trapped in these meetings, stress over what they will still need to do after the meetings are over, and then resolve to complete their meetings as fast as possible. However natural this mindset may be, it is the opposite of being in the moment. Instead of intently observing the entirety of what your audiences communicate, you focus on where you need to be next, or what else you could be doing, and catch only a portion of the message. Again, when we focus on time over quality, quality suffers.

> When we focus on time over quality, quality suffers.

Many companies went from smooth sailing to utter chaos, seemingly overnight, when the COVID-19 pandemic struck in 2020. The adverse impacts of the pandemic were widespread. Within businesses, human resources teams were besieged from all sides. They were tasked with maintaining morale, communicating health and safety guidelines, constantly updating policies in an ever-changing environment, creating work-from-home programs, and leading workforce reduction efforts, all while maintaining their normal responsibilities. While some people took advantage of the pandemic to go back to school, learn guitar, or lose weight, HR executives were treading water as fast as they could.

This tenuous balance was made evident when one of my HR executive clients called me with an issue with her payroll coordinator. She was overwhelmed while preparing and facilitating strategic initiatives with her team, who were all working remotely. Her payroll coordinator had become increasingly disgruntled throughout the pandemic and decided to retire early. She initially gave three months' notice. However, with one month remaining, she emailed my client and said that she was no longer able to, and therefore no longer would, process payroll. As timing would have it, the payroll coordinator sent the email on the Friday before a payroll Monday.

Nothing is more important than making sure employees are paid on time, especially during an economic crisis when many are struggling to support their families. It would have been easy for this HR executive to either send a response email or pick up the phone, and say something along the lines of, "Yes, you are. That is your job. If you don't do it, we will terminate you and you won't have the opportunity to retire." In fact, many people might nod their heads and think that is an appropriate way to react—especially in a high-stress, time-sensitive environment.

Thankfully, this is not the path my client chose. We briefly discussed the situation, allowing her to vent her frustration, refocus her thinking, and arrive at the course she wanted to take. Her idea was to call her payroll coordinator, express concern, and ask why she could no longer process payroll.

This turned out to be the perfect approach. During the phone call, the HR executive learned that her payroll coordinator was experiencing difficulty remotely accessing the programs she needed to process payroll after moving into a new home. Her original emails didn't mention these details. She was already disgruntled, knew her days at the company were quickly coming to an end, and determined that a short and direct email was appropriate.

In reality, it wasn't that she did not want to ensure that five thousand employees got paid during an economic crisis. She simply did not have the access to complete the tasks. Once my client heard this, she immediately relayed the message to her IT department, and they had the issue fixed within a few hours. Everyone got paid, no one got fired, and maybe most importantly, the HR executive didn't spend the entire weekend running payroll herself.

React reflectively, not reflexively.

This situation likely would have ended differently if my client had reacted promptly and emotionally to the initial email. Instead, she was aware enough to react reflectively, not reflexively. Yes, this was a serious and time-sensitive issue, but realistically there was no difference between responding within a few seconds or a few hours. She realized this, applied a situationally aware approach, considered her goals, thought her options through, and acted in a way that she believed was most likely to get the results she needed. She chose a multifaceted and thoughtful approach, not one that would simply make her feel better.

Path of Least Resistance

Many of the interrogations I conducted were non-custodial. The subjects I spoke with were not under arrest, they were free to leave anytime they wanted, and they weren't compelled to speak with me if they didn't want to. The United States Supreme Court has ruled that non-custodial interrogations must conclude within a reasonable amount of time considering the totality of circumstances. This slightly ambiguous statement leaves plenty of room for interpretation from everyone involved including investigators, interview subjects, human resources personnel, attorneys, and judges. As a result, the teams I worked with erred on the side of caution and operated with the understanding that we had roughly sixty minutes to get the first acknowledgment of wrongdoing. If after sixty minutes, we had yet to obtain any acknowledgment of wrongdoing and lacked any credible evidence that indicated the subject's guilt, we would begin to transition out of the conversation while leaving the door open for potential follow-up interviews. When we obtained the first acknowledgment of wrongdoing inside sixty minutes, we would commit the necessary time to obtain all the relevant information related to the investigation.

These rules of engagement leave interrogators with two potential mindsets: either "If this subject was involved, I have to beat the clock and get the first admission in under sixty minutes." Or "I have to connect with this subject in a manner that makes them want to tell me the truth."

When interrogators focus on the ticking clock, they are more likely to establish insufficient levels of rapport, incorrectly evaluate their subject's reactions, rush to make accusations, and jeopardize the investigation. However, when interrogators patiently allow the conversation to come to them, they create the opportunity to maximize all sixty available minutes. This approach allows them to educate their subjects, reframe their subjects' perception, and deliver accusations after the requisite bonds have been established and their subjects are prepared to truthfully respond. There is a strong tie between the success that interrogators achieve and whether they are focusing on the clock or establishing the necessary relationship with their subjects.

Next time you are flying across the country, grab a window seat and look down at the rivers you fly over. Note that none of them flow in a straight line from their source to their outlet. Rivers follow the path of least resistance. They flow in one direction until the terrain becomes too difficult to cut through, then they change direction. The direct path is the path of most resistance, for rivers and for conversations. Disciplined Listeners know this and patiently allow their conversations to come to them so they can ebb and flow as necessary while maximizing their observations, collecting intelligence, and solidifying relationships.

FOURTH CORE BEHAVIOR: EVALUATE VERBAL AND NONVERBAL COMMUNICATION

Once Disciplined Listeners allow the conversation to come to them, they create the opportunity to execute the fourth core behavior of the Disciplined Listening Method—accurately evaluating their counterparts' verbal and nonverbal communication within the context of the conversation. This skill set is often marketed as a shortcut, and this couldn't be further from the truth. Accurately identifying what your counterparts are thinking and feeling in real time is not nearly as straightforward as people would have you believe.

Listeners who excel at this have several other building blocks in place. First, they have to be clear on their goals so they know what to observe, and understand the potential value of their observations. Second, they have to maintain a very high level of situational awareness. The behaviors we observe can mean many different things depending on the context in which they are displayed. It is precisely their situational awareness that allows Disciplined Listeners to comprehend what actually triggered any behavioral change, what emotional shift the behavior may represent, and the new opportunities this emotional shift creates. Finally, Disciplined Listeners must be patient while comparing and contrasting observations over time to double-check the accuracy of their evaluations and consider other alternatives.

In short, the quality of your preparation and the depth of your situational awareness will increase the accuracy of your observations. Furthermore, Disciplined Listeners do not focus on catching their counterparts lying. That path is fraught with peril, plays into dangerous biases, and jeopardizes relationships. Disciplined Listeners observe the totality of their counterparts' communications for indications of comfort and discomfort within the context of the conversation. They capitalize on these fluctuating comfort levels by determining how the most

> The quality of your preparation and the depth of your situational awareness will increase the accuracy of your observations.

likely causes of these emotional shifts may impact their ability to achieve their goals. We will be going in depth into how to identify these behavior shifts, specific behaviors to look and listen for, and their potential values in the next four chapters.

FIFTH CORE BEHAVIOR: ADAPT YOUR CONVERSATIONAL APPROACH BASED ON GATHERED INTELLIGENCE

Observing behavior shifts is half the battle. The other half is the fifth core behavior of the Disciplined Listening Method—adapting your conversational approach based on the intelligence you observe. Strong preparation efforts can significantly reduce the variables we need to address during our conversations. All the preparation and consideration in the world can't possibly prepare us for every variable that may arise during our conversations. Disciplined Listeners don't stay married to suboptimal plans when their counterparts' communications create new opportunities. They allow their observations to guide them toward the best path to achieve their goals.

Disciplined Listeners essentially have three options for applying the intelligence they observe. They can apply it immediately, they can put it in their pocket and wait for a better opportunity to use it, or they permanently file it away. Honestly, all three choices have contextually appropriate applications. Applying your observations immediately and confronting your audiences with what you've heard or seen is most often not the best decision. This tactic usually creates greater, more unnecessary resistance. Putting your observations in your back pocket and waiting or creating an opportunity to use them to your advantage, is the best course of action the vast majority of the time. Observers who are clear on their goals make the correct choice more consistently.

> Disciplined Listeners don't stay married to suboptimal plans when their counterparts' communications create new opportunities.

Knowledge as Trivia

I'm assuming most readers have heard the phrase, "knowledge is power." It certainly is a catchy phrase. It is also false. Instead, knowledge is trivia. Yes, it is important to gather and retain as much relevant knowledge as we can. However, the real power lies in our ability to successfully apply our knowledge within the context of the situations we find ourselves in. If we can't use what we know to our advantage at the most advantageous times, our knowledge is useless.

Our ability to successfully apply our knowledge hinges on several factors. The first factor is our knowledge base; how prepared we are, how much relevant information we have retained, and how familiar we are with the context of our conversations.

The second factor is our ability to accurately identify our audience's motivations, fears, and intentions through our observations in real time. The third factor again goes back to our level of situational awareness. How quickly we can tie our goals, previous knowledge, and current observations together to adapt our communication plans and redirect the conversation to where we need it to go.

SIXTH CORE BEHAVIOR: PROTECT YOUR COUNTERPARTS' SELF-IMAGES

Disciplined Listeners adapt their approach based on the intelligence they observe with one goal in mind—encouraging their counterparts to always protect their self-images. This sixth core behavior of the Disciplined Listening Method is the most important to exhibit during the conversation. Disciplined Listeners know that causing their counterparts to feel judged, demeaned, or embarrassed on any level will quickly eliminate any opportunities to obtain sensitive information. They go out of their way to allow their counterparts to protect their self-images throughout their conversations, especially when they are asked to share sensitive information.

Leaders in all capacities have four opportunities to encourage their counterparts to save face and protect their self-images during potentially contentious conversations. The first opportunity involves the setting of the meeting. Disciplined Listeners are careful to extend meeting invitations (formal or informal) and choose meeting locations that will not increase their counterparts' defensive responses. You can pretty much kiss the opportunity to obtain the truth goodbye if people are embarrassed or angry before the conversation even starts based on how you extended the invitation and where the conversation is taking place.

I was thrilled when a detective at my local police department gave me a tour of his facility. Not only was it cool to see all the technological advances that law enforcement has at their disposal, but it also gave me an unexpected opportunity to learn his perspective. During our tour, he led me to the interrogation rooms. I was happy to see that they were not set up like every episode of *Law and Order*. Instead, they were set up like any normal office would be. Each room featured a round table with padded chairs. This is a much more comfortable, normal environment that is much less likely to create additional resistance. The fact that they didn't feel like interrogation rooms makes the interrogators' job much easier.

As we were walking away, the detective pointed at the signs next to each interrogation room door, smiled, and said, "Don't worry, we are going to change these too." Each room was labeled "Interrogation Room 1, 2, 3, 4, etc." He knew that the verbiage on the signs erased the benefits of how the rooms were set up. The rooms were specifically designed to make suspects feel that they weren't being interrogated, but the signs they saw as they entered these rooms explicitly reminded them that they were going to be interrogated. Ordering new signs that read "Office" or "Meeting Room" or any other similar title can solve that problem immediately.

The second opportunity is how leaders discuss and inquire about sensitive issues. The tone, word choice, speed of delivery, nonverbal behavior, and perceived intentions leaders display work to either convey an empathetic mindset or a judgmental mindset. The intricacy of this delivery is important. Leaders often think they are demonstrating empathy while their audiences are perceiving judgment.

The most common mistake leaders might make in these situations is conveying a parental approach. This approach is often perceived as controlling or authoritative. Authoritative statements assume hierarchy; direct assumptions convey judgment. Another common mistake is asking questions that feel like accusations. Here are a few examples:

Authority	Judgment	Accusations
What I need you to do . . . What you need to do . . .	I'm sure you're thinking . . . You look scared . . . I know you must feel disappointed . . .	Did you . . . Why didn't you . . . Do you . . .

One quick example was discussed during a candidate interviewing training program that I was facilitating. During the module that focused on increasing one's influence, a hiring manager asked me why a candidate got upset when he asked if the candidate had experience in a specific area. I followed up by asking the hiring manager how he asked the question. He said, "Do you have experience with . . ."

Imagine being a candidate for a management position, with over ten years' experience, a résumé that you believe clearly outlines this experience, and then being asked, "Do you have experience . . ." This can be offensive for any number of reasons. It could be, as the executive on the call asserted, that the candidate is offended because you clearly didn't take the time to review their résumé prior to the conversation. It could also be that they believe the question is beneath them based on their experience. They can also be offended because they feel the question is actually an accusation that they don't have the experience.

The hiring manager had never thought to consider these unintended consequences. He was just asking a direct question, to get a quick answer in an effort to save time. Once again, time remains undefeated in its fight against quality. Far more productive alternatives to asking that same question are:

- "Please walk me through your experience with . . ."
- "What has been your most challenging experience with . . ."
- "Based on your experience, what is your preferred approach to . . ."

All of these options allow candidates to protect their self-image while sharing important information with their interviewers.

The third opportunity is how they demonstrate they are listening. Vulnerable people are constantly looking for any clues that indicate they are being judged for any part of their message or behavior. They are particularly focused on this during the introduction, when they begin to listen and determine their level of participation. Disciplined Listeners execute high levels of self-control and suppress any verbal or nonverbal behavioral leakage that may signal judgment to their audience. They consciously choose to exhibit understanding and appreciation, even in the face of information or ideas they disagree with.

The fourth opportunity to encourage your audiences to save face lies within your response to their statements. Leaders, parents, investigators, and even sales professionals are easily seduced by the need to hold people accountable. Falling victim to this temptation causes them to interrupt their counterparts, immediately point out inaccuracies or inconsistencies, express doubt, or shoot down excuses. Every one of these responses conveys judgment and authority, and directly assaults our counterparts' self-image.

Disciplined Listeners don't view these issues as affronts to their authority or intelligence. They embrace these issues as gateways to new paths that their counterparts have chosen, to obtain the truth and arrive at accountability. The acceptance of responsibility should be where we get off the train at the end of our trip, not where we start. It is nearly always easier and more productive to lead our counterparts to accepting responsibility at the end of the conversation than at the beginning.

Chapter 12 is dedicated to exploring the concepts of encouraging our audiences to save face and protect their self-images in greater detail.

SEVENTH CORE BEHAVIOR: FOLLOWING UP AFTER THE CONVERSATION

The seventh and final core behavior of the Disciplined Listening Method is following up after the conversation. If I had a dime for every time my father said, "Michael Garrett, actions speak louder than words," I would be the world's richest man. Actions such as maintaining eye contact, smiling and nodding, and summarizing what we hear can definitely make people feel like you listened during the conversation. However, the only way to unequivocally prove that we listened to someone is through our follow-up conversations and actions.

You can apply all the traditional attentive listening skills you want while someone is talking to you, but if you don't take tangible action based on what you heard, they will not believe that you listened to them because they don't have any evidence. Disciplined Listeners know that commitments to real change are solidified after the conversation is over.

Disciplined Listeners know that commitments to real change are solidified after the conversation is over.

Listening is a cyclical process. We can only observe what people share, and they are far more willing to share much more truthful information when they trust you. Disciplined Listeners develop trust equity through post-conversation follow-up. They understand that every conversation they participate in today is linked to future, and potentially more difficult, conversations down the road.

Trust and vulnerability are synonymous. For someone to truly trust you, they must be comfortable feeling vulnerable in front of you. Few things will make people feel worse than demonstrating vulnerability during a conversation and feeling like it was all for naught. Failing to follow up on our important conversations can lead your counterparts to feel embarrassed, devalued, and taken advantage of. All these emotions will breed resentment and create long-term problems for your organizations, families, and relationships.

This last core behavior brings the Disciplined Listening Method full circle by validating your audience's participation in the conversation, demonstrating you listened, and moving the initiative forward. This can be done by working a topic you discussed into a future conversation, visibly taking the actions you committed to, offering them support in actions they've committed to, or even simply touching base. It is important to check on how they are feeling after your conversation has been completed. Failing to follow up after any important conversation is like your favorite football team driving the ball inside their opponent's five-yard line, fumbling, and watching their opponent return it ninety-seven yards in the opposite direction for the game-winning score. Please don't work so hard for so long and throw it all away in the end.

To summarize, Disciplined Listeners build stronger relationships, achieve greater results, and create unexpected advantages by consistently executing a series of seven behaviors in all their critical business and personal conversations. They prepare for their conversations by clarifying the long- and short-term goals their conversations can help them achieve. They also leverage their perceived weaknesses to truly empathize with their counterparts and create strategic advantages. Once they engage with their audiences, they stay patient and allow their conversations to come to them, which increases the amount of intelligence they acquire through their observations. This approach also opens up new opportunities to adapt and apply what they've learned, all while encouraging their counterparts to protect their self-images. Finally, they dedicate the time to prove that they listened, and solidify commitments by following up after their conversations.

The first six chapters of this book illustrated the power and necessity of applying the Disciplined Listening Method. This chapter outlined the seven core behaviors involved in Disciplined Listening. The following six chapters will cover how to increase the power and accuracy of your observations, what to specifically look and listen for, and how to activate the truths you discover.

CHAPTER EIGHT

OBSERVE LIKE AN INTERROGATOR

READING BODY LANGUAGE IS rarely, if ever, the shortcut it is often portrayed to be. It is easy to be fooled by someone's body language. It is easy to fool ourselves with our interpretations of someone's body language. To further complicate the process, the meaning of similar shifts in body language can change as stimuli change over time. Disciplined Listeners increase the power and accuracy of their observations by withholding judgment and separating the message from the messenger and their own emotions.

Observable shifts in verbal and nonverbal communication are rarely definitive. In fact, these shifts are often referred to as clues, cues, hot spots, or red flags. These observable behavior shifts are just one piece of a much larger puzzle that must be completed before we understand the entire picture. My preferred term for these behavior shifts is "alert signals" because they alert us to an emotional shift that our counterpart is experiencing. It is our job as Disciplined Listeners to determine the likely trigger and meaning of these shifts, within the totality of circumstances surrounding the conversation. This is another reason why developing a high level of situational awareness is paramount.

Developing the skills necessary to accurately evaluate your audience's real-time communication opens up many advantages and opportunities. This skill helps observers identify their counterparts' hidden intentions, fears, emotional shifts, and preferred alternatives in real-time. Successful execution of these efforts requires leaders to dedicate the extra effort, quiet their mind, and remain cognizant of the context of the situation. When Disciplined Listeners evaluate communication they understand, perhaps above all else, that context is king. As we discussed in chapter 5, there are a myriad of factors, both seen and unseen, that impact how people display communication behaviors and how observers interpret these behaviors.

Context is king.

There is a high likelihood that you've once participated in a personal or professional conversation where you witnessed your counterpart's behavior change, believed that he or she lied to you, and validated your assessment later on. As we mentioned, we often mistake what is focal for what is causal.[1] It wasn't your counterpart's behavior that led you to believe he or she was lying, it was the context of the situation in which you witnessed the behavior change. That behavior took on a specific meaning to you because of when it happened in the conversation and what you were talking about. Furthermore, the actual dishonesty was likely later confirmed by corroborating evidence.

The first three core behaviors of the Disciplined Listening Method are designed to enhance observers' contextual awareness. Pinpointing the goals a conversation can help you achieve frames your perspective and highlights the value you can gain through your observations. This is also the step that allows you to separate information from intelligence during the conversation and identify the valuable nuances you may otherwise miss.

When we leverage our perceived weaknesses, it forces us to calibrate our conversation with our goals. Strategically addressing both the location and our approach prior to the conversation positions us to glean extra value from our observations. Everything we say or do needs to reflect an intentional effort to get us at least one step closer to the truth.

When most people think of interrogations, they picture a dark room with basic metal chairs, a matching metal desk, and the ubiquitous swinging lightbulb hanging over the table. Admittedly, this makes for great theater. However, this is the exact opposite of the environment we want to create. Why would we want to make someone feel especially uncomfortable and potentially helpless if we need them to change their mind and commit to sharing sensitive information with us? Based on years of industry experience, I can't think of a good reason.

The most common fear that holds people back from change is not failure—it's embarrassment. Failing isn't the problem. The problem is what other people (including the person we see in the mirror) think and feel about us when we fail. Furthermore, the number one reason why most adults lie is to avoid a perceived consequence. Anytime we need to discuss potentially sensitive topics with someone, we want to choose an environment that is not likely to increase their feelings of embarrassment or judgment, or remind them of any potential consequences.

> **The most common fear that holds people back from change is not failure—it's embarrassment.**

Interrogators are required to simultaneously do two things to increase the accuracy of their observations. They must limit the number of variables that can impact the conversation, and they must increase their focus. Achieving these tactical objectives starts with setting up the physical environment in which the conversation will occur. This approach holds true for critical business and personal conversations as well.

LOCATION, LOCATION, LOCATION

The first decision is selecting the location itself. In a business context, this often means choosing the best available office, conference room, or public location. Access, privacy, space, décor, and the physical setup of the room are all important factors. Questions to consider include:

- Can all parties find the room easily enough?
- Is the location private enough to reduce distractions, interruptions, and unwanted observers?
- Will the room provide all the preferred amenities?
- Is there a reasonable amount of space for everyone?
- Is the décor appropriate?
- Is the physical setup of the room conducive for the goals we are looking to achieve?
- Does the room avoid any unnecessary reminders of power or punishment?

Answering each one of these questions is critical before setting up an important meeting.

Inside the room, Disciplined Listeners come out from behind their desks and set their chairs up approximately four feet from their counterparts.[2] This removes all physical barriers, creates a perception of equality, and allows them to observe 100 percent of their counterparts' communication during their conversations.

Choosing the location is another application for the first core behavior of the Disciplined Listening Method—knowing how this conversation can get you closer to achieving your goals. A common mistake leaders make in this thought process is prioritizing conversational control over desired outcomes. It can be easy for any leader to feel like a conversation needs to happen in their office, or their location, at a time that is most beneficial to them. Remember, if you need people to share sensitive information with you, you are not in control of the conversation. If you force people to adapt for your convenience, you could easily be creating unnecessary resistance. If the person, topic, or goal is important enough, the best move is likely meeting your counterpart when and where it is best for them.

> **If you need people to share sensitive information with you, you are not in control of the conversation.**

Sometimes this means meeting them in their office, choosing a neutral setting, or selecting a public location for the meeting. There can be power in meeting your counterparts at their office or a location of their choosing. This gesture alone can signal the respect, value, and trust necessary to move the conversation forward. If you have to meet them in your building, consider finding a neutral room. The manager's office is often equated to the principal's office or the police station. The location alone can create additional barriers to achieving new commitments.

MAKING IT WORK

As a contract interrogator, I worked very hard to avoid interviewing anyone in a manager's office or the HR office whenever possible. As hard as we worked to choose the perfect interview location, our hands were often tied. Anytime I was forced to use an office with a window, I made sure to position the chairs so my subjects faced away from it. If I had no choice but to use a very small, cramped office, I would make a joke about it when my subjects walked in to hopefully alleviate any stress the room size created. If my subjects and I had to walk to another location I tried to maintain consistent small talk to keep their mind from focusing on potential consequences while we transitioned locations. Despite my best efforts, I occasionally found myself conducting interviews in suboptimal settings like fire escape stairwells, warehouses, restaurants, and rooms that were under construction.

My most memorable interview location mishap occurred in Miami, Florida. I flew in the day before the interviews were scheduled and scouted out the physical location where the incidents were alleged to have occurred and where I would be conducting the interviews. There were no good options. I ended up selecting an outdoor location at the far end of a terrace on the third floor of the complex. The advantages of the location were that it was fairly isolated on this campus, the suites attached to the terrace were empty (and unfortunately off limits), and there were two patio chairs and a patio couch already positioned at the end of the walkway. The disadvantages were that it would be a long walk to get there with my subjects, it was outside and would be impacted by any weather changes, and I had no way of keeping anyone else from walking into our conversation. I figured there was no good reason for anyone else to be all the way down the end of that terrace, so I settled on using this location.

I arrived early the next morning and positioned the three chairs so my chair was facing the terrace, my subject's chair was facing me with the trees providing a decent backdrop, and I positioned the couch several feet behind (and to the left) of my subject's chair so that the neutral witness who was required to observe the conversation would be out of sight and out of mind.

The walk from my subject's office to the interview location

wasn't nearly as uncomfortable as it could've been and the conversation got off to a great start. Luckily for me it was still spring in Miami, so the heat and humidity weren't bad. However, the sun was shining bright and the wind was blowing pretty hard. This caused my subject to continuously squint, blink, move the hair that blew in her face, and adjust her head to compensate for her blowing hair. All these actions rendered most of my observations of her face useless.

Even so, we worked our way through the interview portion of the conversation and transitioned into the interrogation. I was three quarters of the way through the process of setting up my first accusation when some movement caught my eye in the background. Thankfully, I was well prepared for the conversation and I was able to put my mouth on autopilot while I tried to determine who was approaching us with my peripheral vision. I didn't want my subject to see me searching the scene behind her, as that would certainly result in diverting her attention at a pivotal moment in the conversation.

Thankfully, a gust of wind blew, my subject dipped her head to fix her hair, and I was able to look down the walkway and identify the intruder. I could not believe what I saw—a woman, shoving fist-fulls of popcorn in her mouth from a giant bucket, walking right toward us. I'm serious. My subject, my witness, and I were sitting in the only three chairs at the end of a third-floor terrace with no occupied suites in sight. I had no idea why this woman was on this terrace to begin with, and I certainly couldn't explain why she was approaching, with popcorn, when the only three seats were obviously in use. This conversation wasn't meant for public entertainment.

My only choice was to ignore her, hoping that she'd realize she was approaching a private meeting and decided to turn around. To my complete disbelief she walked right up to us, stood behind my witness, looked at all three of us sitting there, and then sat down on the couch next to the witness. It was like I was living on another planet!

I managed to stay completely locked in on my subject and prayed that the woman would hurry up and leave without catching my subject's attention. As I was talking to my subject, I saw my witness shrugging her shoulders and nodding toward our popcorn-crunching intruder. Finally, after what seemed like an eternity, my witness discreetly asked this woman to leave. The woman responded by shaking her head no and shoveling more popcorn in her mouth. Thank God for small miracles, my subject still had no idea this woman was there.

My witness stayed calm and asked her to leave again. This time the woman stood up, stuffed a few more kernels in her mouth and defiantly said, "Fine, I'll go." My subject's head flew around in time to see the woman start to walk away before returning her gaze to me with eyes full of shock. I shrugged my shoulders and continued on with my monologue as if nothing had happened.

Unfortunately, something had most definitely happened. It was enough to shake my subject from her previous mindset and forced me to retrace my steps in an effort to lead my subject back to where I needed her to be. Thankfully, we were able to obtain enough of the truth to resolve the investigation, but not in the level of detail we desired. I'll never know the true impact of our interruption, but I'm confident it was significant.

Public meetings have become the norm over the last decade. Meetings in coffee shops, restaurants, bars, and other locations are increasingly prevalent. While you may not have control over these environments, you do have the ability to influence them. Whenever possible, choose or request a table that limits distractions and provides you with reasonable privacy. Be mindful of the most traveled walking routes through the location: proximity to televisions, speakers, fans, restrooms, and the kitchen. Additionally, take note of your surroundings. Be aware of anything going on around you that may temporarily capture your counterparts' attention. These will be important factors to consider when evaluating your counterparts' behavioral changes.

It is also easy to fall into the trap of thinking that we can't influence the room setup when we are in our counterparts' location. You still have options. You can arrive early and potentially create the opportunity to choose your seat first, or maybe even rearrange the setup of the room. One of my favorite techniques is to leave my notebook or laptop in the seat that I want to sit in and then wait for my counterparts by the door. You can even distribute drinks or support materials prior to your counterparts' arrival to influence where people will sit in the room. There is almost always an opportunity if you look hard enough.

POSITION TO PERSUADE

This was the case for me when I revisited a technique I first used in a negotiation training seminar. During the second day of the seminar, participants were broken up into groups of three. Each member of the group randomly drew a card that designated them as either player A, B, or C. Player A had the strongest position, player B had an almost as strong position, and player C had the worst position by a wide margin. The goal of the role-playing session was to maximize your position in the final agreement. Of course, I drew the player C card.

It was obvious from the start that the best way for players A and B to maximize their positions was to cut me out entirely. This was a role-play scenario with no real-world consequences and they were total strangers, so relational-based strategies wouldn't work.

To make matters worse, I was sitting on the far-left-hand side of the group. If they wanted to cut me out, they didn't even have to talk to me.

As soon as the professor said "go," I stood up, picked up my chair, and walked over to where players A and B were sitting. I placed my chair between them, just off the center line. We were now sitting in a triangle formation with player A on my left and player B on my right. My new placement necessitated my role in the conversation and created the opportunity for me to direct the conversational traffic.

As the "negotiations" continued, I was able to use my body position, gestures, and tone not only to participate in the conversation, but to lead it. When time was up, the professor asked everyone to end their "negotiations" and report their final agreements. When all the agreements were tallied, I ended up with the second highest percentage of the agreement among all the C-players in the exercise. Unfortunately, I never identified the person who did better than me to find out how he or she did it.

A year later, I got to use the same technique in a real negotiation. To make a very long and intricate story short, I worked for a small company with a large and excellent reputation. We had partnered with a large company via one individual relationship, to essentially operate as an extension of their organization throughout the United States. From our perspective, this was an important relationship that opened a lot of doors from which we were previously precluded. We didn't generate a lot of revenue from the partnership but the opportunities were more important than the dollars.

They did not benefit at all from the partnership. Yes, it looked good for both companies to partner together. And yes, their local offices around the country occasionally made a few extra dollars. However, the agreement created a series of accounting challenges on their end and the inconvenience far outweighed any financial benefit they were receiving. Frankly, we needed them, they didn't need us.

We were able to keep the agreement in place for several years until a new vice president took on oversight of the group that we partnered with, questioned the agreement, and decided to terminate it. Honestly, I couldn't blame him. I also couldn't afford to let it happen. They were open to talking through the situation and their director (our relationship contact) and their new vice president (VP) agreed to meet with me.

I arrived twenty minutes early for the meeting. While I was waiting, I spotted the conference room I assumed the meeting would occur in. It featured all glass walls and a long, rectangular table that could easily sit twenty people. Not at all optimal for what I was trying to achieve.

After several minutes, the director came into the lobby, greeted me, and walked me inside where we met the VP. He began walking and was clearly leading us to the same conference room I had seen earlier. As we were walking down the hall, I positioned myself on the left side of my counterparts because I knew we would have to turn left to get to the conference room. This move naturally put me in the pole position, and I arrived at the conference room door first.

Upon arrival I opened the door, looked at the VP, said "please," and motioned him past. I followed him as he walked past me, reached back to hold the door for the director and said "thank you." This positioned me behind the VP and in front of the director as we walked toward the table.

The VP didn't sit at the head of the table. He sat in the first seat on the side of the table closest to the door. I'm sure they assumed I would sit across from him and the director would sit next to him. Instead, I calmly put my hand on the back of the seat next to the VP and smiled at the director. This allowed me to sit in the second chair and the director to sit in the third chair. We were now sitting side-by-side at one end of the long table in this big conference room, with me in the middle.

While this may seem like an uncomfortable setup, it created a big opportunity for me. I knew coming in that the VP wanted to end the agreement. I also knew the director was open to trying to save it or he never would've called me in the first place. By positioning myself between them in their conference room, I had taken the position necessary to control the conversation and made it more difficult for the VP to influence the director. As a bonus, I allowed for the potential perception that the director and I were on the same page because we were seated next to each other.

I started the conversation by thanking them for sharing their time with me and acknowledging that they certainly didn't need to maintain our agreement if they didn't want to. Simultaneously, I slid my chair backward so they could see each other, and I could direct traffic. They turned their chairs toward me, and we quickly found ourselves discussing the issues and opportunities with the current agreement.

The conversation couldn't have gone much better for me. At the end of the meeting, they agreed to continue our agreement as long as we made a few small billing adjustments on our end. Deal.

The agreement held for another six months before the VP decided enough was enough and terminated it. Again, I can't blame him. That extra six months gave us the opportunity to find another partner. It was a seamless transition that still stands in place today.

PATIENCE PREVAILS

The third core behavior of the Disciplined Listening Method—allow the conversation to come to you—is important because Disciplined Listeners observe the totality of their counterparts' communications within the context of the situation, and they understand the more their counterparts share, the more they have to evaluate.

There is one more preparation technique that Disciplined Listeners apply to add both value and accuracy to their observations. Perhaps the best way to protect yourself from being fooled or misled during any conversation is to gather as much relevant information as you can prior to engaging in the conversation. Investigators refer to this as establishing ground truth. The goal is to gather enough facts to arrive at an objective picture of what has happened or likely will happen—and keep this information to yourself during the conversation. Remember, knowledge alone doesn't create power. Successfully applying knowledge creates power.

Successfully applying knowledge creates power.

One way to apply knowledge is by actually keeping it to yourself and comparing what people tell you to what you already know. This allows us to internally fact-check our counterparts in real time, generate appropriate questions, and increase the accuracy of our observations. Top interrogators don't try to catch their subjects lying—they give their subjects every opportunity to tell the truth. They only conclude their subjects are lying when they've clearly been unable to verify that their subjects are telling the truth. Withholding what they know is a key step in this process.

Gathering as much relevant information as possible, and keeping it to ourselves, is like playing poker. Your counterparts don't know what you know and can't adjust their message to match it. Not declaring your knowledge also increases your confidence and takes away the opportunity for your counterparts to stake themselves to a position they will need to defend. This approach can be applied in business, investigations, and your personal life. Which I do, often.

My wife and I had our son about three years after moving into our house. When we moved in, we knew we would have to replace the upstairs carpet. This project jumped to the top of our priority list when we found out she was pregnant. I did a little research on the options and process, reached out to several companies, and scheduled the initial consultations.

The night before the first company was set to visit my house, I was thinking through what information I needed to know to protect myself, my house, and my money throughout the process. I figured the best place to start was to know the exact square footage of the carpeted area of my second floor. After spending a little time with my tape measure and the calculator on my phone, I was confident I had the square footage correct within a few feet.

The next morning, their representative arrived and laser measured my floor with an application on his iPad. When he was done, he showed me a picture of what was a perfect representation of my second floor. After seeing the picture, he told me that I would need to purchase twice the square footage in carpet than what I had measured. I simply replied, "Really?" and looked at him quietly. After a few seconds he said, "Well, I guess if we moved these two seams it would save you some money." It certainly would. That cut the overage by more than half.

Now I was onto him. He definitely appeared to be trying to take advantage of me and sell me more carpet than I needed. But I wanted to be sure. After he moved the seams, I said, "Thank you. Quick question, what was the total square footage your computer calculated?" He shuffled his feet, looked away, looked back at me, and said, "Ah, well, it doesn't really tell me that." I calmly let it go and we wrapped up our conversation. He told me that the information would be submitted by the end of the day and left.

You may be wondering, why would I let someone lie to me about facts that I know to be true, and not call him on it right then and there? The first rule of being lied to is don't get accusatory. Clearly, he thought lying was in his best interest at that moment. He was not lying to hurt me. He was lying to help himself. In this instance, I decided to wait patiently and let the situation come to me.

Two days later, I got a call from the store telling me that my measurements were in and I could come down and speak with the consultant. I drove over, let the guy pull up my file, and listened to his whole speech about what I needed. When he was done, he asked me if I had any questions. I said, "One. Please confirm for me what the square footage of my second floor is." He said, "No problem, it's right here," as he flipped the page and showed me the number. My measurements were only one foot off. Checkmate.

After looking at the number I said, "Thank you. I appreciate your time, but unfortunately we can't move forward on this project together," and I turned around and started walking out the door. Clearly shocked, he said, "Wait, why?" I turned around and told him how the representative measured my floor and how he answered my questions. When I finished, I said I couldn't work with a company that would send someone into my house and intentionally mislead me. He then asked the single most predictable follow-up question ever: "What can I do to make this right?" I asked him for his ideas, and by the time we were done I locked in a 10 percent discount on the carpet I wanted, the top-quality padding for the price of the lowest quality padding, free installation, and free removal of my old carpet. I saved over a thousand dollars by establishing ground truth (the square footage of my second floor), staying patient, not confronting a liar, and allowing the conversation to come to me. Whereas if I had accused the initial representative of lying to me, I would've likely started an argument and certainly limited my opportunity to get the discounts.

PLAN FOR SUCCESS

The biggest thing Disciplined Listeners do to maximize their observations is limit their internal monologue. *Talking is the most important part of listening.* Yes, you read that correctly. Our brains aren't nearly as good at multitasking as we want to believe they are. We can only truly listen to one conversation at a time. If you are talking to yourself while someone else is talking to you, your internal monologue always wins. You will prioritize listening to what you're telling yourself over what your counterpart has to share. Worse yet, you hear just enough that it feels like you received their full message.

Our internal conversations tend to focus on what we want to say, how we feel, and our assumptions about what our counterparts are saying. We get lost in our own minds as we think about our next statement or question, which often defends what we already think or believe. We also get lost in our emotions, especially our negative emotions. Few things set off our internal monologue as quickly as our feelings, when our ideas or beliefs are being challenged or misunderstood. We also love to assume we know what our counterparts are going to say next and what their intentions are.

People love to talk about "staying present in the moment." Getting sidetracked by our internal monologue may be the fastest way to kick ourselves out of the moment. We all talk to ourselves; it's normal. It's typically not harmful if we are taking quick mental notes while staying engaged as opposed to leading ourselves into a full, emotional conversation. Disciplined Listeners quickly catch themselves, shut down their internal monologue, and refocus on their audiences. We literally can't listen to someone else if we are talking to ourselves.

Disciplined Listeners create game plans for their strategically valuable conversations. They clarify the goals they're looking to achieve, the illustrations they want to make, the questions they want to ask, and the potential resolutions or agreements they are willing to accept. This preparation drastically reduces the variables they have to address during their conversations, reduces their inner monologue, and helps keep their emotions in check. This reduction in cognitive workload allows Disciplined Listeners to increase their contextual awareness throughout their conversations.

LISTENING IS LEARNING

Limiting our internal monologue helps us avoid another potentially disastrous trap—believing we have it all figured out. Like Joe Strummer said, the future is unwritten. One of the most dangerous moments in any conversation is the moment we believe we know it all, because we stop listening to learn and we start listening to confirm. Disciplined Listeners work hard to maintain a learning mentality in every interaction.

There is always something we don't know or a perspective we have not yet considered. I'll never forget receiving a call from a client who literally said he was "desperate" for help resolving an investigation that his team was unable to wrap up. I agreed to take the case and met him and his team later that week. We all sat around a conference room table and I asked them to bring me up to speed on the investigation. The investigator opened his folder, smiled at me, and said, "Okay, we've got it all figured out . . ."

My eyes widened with confusion. If they had it all figured out, why was I there? They should've wrapped this investigation up weeks ago. This example of diagnosis bias is one of many that I experienced in both my investigative and business careers. I strongly believe this biased belief of having everything figured out is one of the biggest contributors to both false confessions and guilty suspects evading detection. Investigators convince themselves they know exactly what happened and act accordingly. They stop investigating to learn and only investigate to validate what they already believe. If they observe something that doesn't fit their narrative, they ignore it, rationalize it away, or challenge it because they don't believe it could be true.

Business leaders and sales professionals fall into this same trap all the time. I have heard many clients say, "We know exactly what our customers are looking for." I have also heard too many leaders say, "I've got it figured out," right before a coaching conversation or negotiation. The most entertaining moment for me is the shock on their faces when they realize they do not have it all figured out.

> Force yourself to accept that you do not have all the information you need and you will be surprised with the additional intelligence you observe.

The next time you catch yourself saying, "I've got it all figured out," stop. Think about the situation again and reset your mind's eye. Ask yourself, "What may I be missing?" There is always more to the story than we can see. Force yourself to accept that you do not have all the information you need and you will be surprised with the additional intelligence you observe.

THE STRATEGIC PROCESS

Disciplined Listeners strive to understand what their audiences are thinking and feeling during their conversations. There is no single word or behavior that will magically unlock this information. As we stated earlier, observing for strategic intelligence is a process, not an easy button. Specifically, it is a four-step process. First, they must establish their audience's behavioral baseline. Once the baseline has been established, they need to observe groups of behaviors that simultaneously shift away from this behavioral baseline, identify the trigger that caused the behavior shifts, and evaluate everything they saw and heard within the context of the situation.[3]

Again, Disciplined Listeners do not try to catch people lying. This mindset is riddled with biases, damages relationships, and is fraught with peril. Knowing that someone lied is more likely to make you mad than it is to add real value to the conversation. However, understanding what someone is thinking or feeling at any given moment can provide significant strategic value. To this end, Disciplined Listeners observe (listen and look) for indications of comfort and discomfort. Understanding when and likely why your counterpart's comfort levels change creates real advantages in real time.

Establish the Behavioral Baseline

The first step, establishing the behavioral baseline, is extremely important. Similar to the scientific method, we are establishing the control before we begin testing variables. We cannot reliably know what someone looks and sounds like when they are uncomfortable in the conversation, until we know what they look and sound like when they are comfortable in the conversation.

You should establish your counterparts' behavioral baseline at the very beginning of your strategically valuable conversations.

This is typically done by asking them a few questions they should be comfortable answering. In a perfect world, these should be questions you already know the answer to. If you are interviewing a job candidate, or conducting an investigative interview, you can ask them to verify their contact information. In many business contexts, you can ask your counterparts about their commute, their breakfast, last night's game, and even the weather if you have to. The key is to ask a few (three to five) questions that your counterparts are almost certain to be comfortable answering. While your counterparts answer these questions, ask yourself, "What do they look, act, and sound like when they are providing truthful information?" The answer to this question becomes your counterparts' behavioral baseline for future comparison.

Another great opportunity for establishing a behavioral baseline occurs when your counterparts are trying to build rapport with you. Many sales professionals, negotiators, and investigators are taught to build rapport at the start of their conversations. You can use this to your advantage. Simply answer their questions in a way that inspires them to respond in kind, or ask them follow-up questions. If their goal is to demonstrate common ground with you, they will almost certainly reciprocate with answers of their own.

A situational example might be when you are out looking to purchase a car. The salesperson is trained to build rapport with their customer. Instead of ignoring them, lean into it. Ask the salesperson questions like, "When was the last time you had a day off?" "How late are you here today?" "What time is your lunch break?" and, "If we can't make a deal today, when is your next shift?" They will feel like they are winning and building rapport. Meanwhile, you will be establishing a clear behavioral baseline before they may choose to mislead you about the vehicles you want to buy.

Recognize Behavioral Shifts

With the behavioral baseline established, we can transition our attention to recognizing behavioral shifts. One school of thought stresses listening for changes in someone's voice, word choice, and verbal delivery. Another school of thought believes we should focus on evaluating someone's nonverbal behavior. A third school of thought believes both of these approaches are too difficult, and proposes that we only rely on the facts we acquire before and after our conversations to drive our decisions and interpretations.

The Disciplined Listening Method makes it possible to evaluate both your counterparts' verbal communication and their nonverbal communication in real time. Simultaneously, the method trains us to limit our distractions and focus our mind's eye. Knowing our goals, creating a game plan, and gathering relevant facts prior to the conversation drastically reduce the variables we need to address during the conversation. This level of awareness also helps focus our attention during conversations.

Allowing the conversation to come to us and limiting our internal monologue provides us with much more communication to evaluate and helps us withhold judgment, while also increasing our situational awareness. Additionally, we avoid the temptation to look for lies and focus on identifying indications of shifts in comfort and discomfort levels. All these actions prime us to be much more accurate with our observations and interpretations.

Evaluating the totality of everything you see and hear requires you not to get locked into one specific body part or behavior. Disciplined Listeners maintain appropriate levels of eye contact during their conversations while observing the rest of their counterparts' behaviors with their peripheral vision. This allows them to observe any body shifts—movements in their counterparts' arms and hands or movements in their counterparts' legs and feet—all while remaining engaged in the conversation.

Identify the Trigger of the Change

As you recognize shifts in your counterparts' verbal and nonverbal behaviors, please remember this: *when a behavior changes is much more important than what behavior changes.* After establishing the behavioral baseline and observing groups of behaviors, the next step is identifying the trigger that caused the behavioral change. These triggers, or stimuli, are the strongest clues to the true meaning of the behavioral shifts. Did they react to something you said? Did their behavior change as a result of something they said? Was there a change in the surrounding environment that caused their behavior to change?

WHEN a behavior changes is much more important than WHAT behavior changes.

It is foolish to guess the meaning of any behavioral shift without considering the trigger that caused it. The vast majority of verbal and nonverbal behavioral shifts are the result of a change in our counterparts' emotions. The stronger their emotional change, the more behavior leaks out for us to observe.[4] Behavior clusters illustrate these emotional changes.

Evaluate Using Context

The final step is to evaluate everything you saw and heard within the context of the situation. This ties directly back to our situational awareness lessons in chapter 5. Factors such as their life history, their relationship with you, the potential consequences of the conversation, the topics of discussion, and the physical environment, all play a role in potentially impacting behavioral shifts.

Alone, behavioral shifts carry no reliable meaning. Identifying what likely triggered the behavioral shift and evaluating the observed behavioral shift within the context of the situation leads astute observers to the most likely meaning behind the behaviors.

Disciplined Listeners complete this four-step evaluation process by asking themselves the payoff question: *"Why did their behavior change like it did, on time to that trigger, in the context of this situation?"* Once the payoff question is answered, they activate their observations by answering the strategic value question: *"How does this information help me achieve my goals?"*

This contextual awareness is what separates accurate assessments from wild guesses. Disciplined Listeners can further narrow their evaluation context and significantly increase the accuracy of their observations by providing their audiences with what I call a *Suggestive Series* of alternatives. Essentially, they provide their counterparts with a list of three to five options and observe how their counterparts react to each option.

This is a technique that great servers use at restaurants when they list the specials or wine choices. You may have had a server tell you the specials for the evening are lobster, filet mignon, swordfish, and duck. They are watching your reaction to each item on the list. When they mention swordfish and see you smile, or maybe nod your head or look at your spouse, they immediately follow up and tell you how great the swordfish is or how many other customers have ordered it. They may even tell you it's their favorite dish. This isn't a lucky guess; they read your behavior and reacted accordingly to motivate your decision.

Throughout my career, I commonly interrogated people who were suspected of committing pattern crimes. Very few criminals steal, embezzle, commit fraud, harass, or discriminate one time. Many criminals offend multiple times in multiple ways. Instead of telling these suspects what I believed they did, I would give them a short list of crimes people commit, ways people can steal, or methods people can use to commit fraud or embezzlement. I would watch their reaction to each item on the list. If I listed five ways a person could commit fraud and my suspect only appeared to react nervously to one of them, there was a pretty good chance they had committed that type of fraud. It wasn't a guarantee. There was a chance they could look nervous because they'd been previously accused or knew someone else who had committed that type of fraud. I still had to conduct the interrogation and find corroborating evidence. However, the fact that it was the only item in the series that appeared to make them nervous was an alert signal that helped me focus my attention and questions during my interrogations.

ANTICIPATING OBJECTIONS

One of the biggest myths in sales is the idea that you can't know what your customers' objections are until they tell you. This idea is both wrong and dangerous because once customers declare their objections, they may feel forced to defend them. Sales professionals who do their homework, create strong game plans, and maintain their situational awareness can get a very good idea of what their customers' objections may be by using a *suggestive series* of potential concerns. For example, the sales professional may say, "At this point in the conversation, we often find that our customers may still be concerned with the project timeline, the total cost, the value to their end users, or even how this partnership may impact existing relationships." If the customer reacts nonverbally to "valuing their end users," the sales professional can be reasonably confident that this is their top potential objection at the moment. Now they can transition to educating their customer on the value of the agreement without forcing their customer to either ask for it or declare their objection.

Leaders often struggle to inspire employees to take accountability for their actions. This typically happens because they attempt to get their employees to admit fault at the beginning of the conversation. Remember, people are highly motivated to protect their self-images, especially when consequences may be on the line. Leaders can short-circuit this roadblock by providing their employees with a *suggestive series* of reasonable excuses as to why the employee has failed to meet expectations.

For example, they may say, "We know that sometimes our team members' production may drop because they feel overwhelmed with all they're being asked to do, or because they have multiple managers asking them to focus on different priorities. We have seen occasions where customers' demands impact their performance, and we know there are times when family stressors or other issues outside of work can impact people's performance." If the employee reacts nonverbally to "multiple managers asking them to focus on different priorities," they likely just alerted the leader to the excuse on which they are willing to blame their lack of performance. Leaders would be wise to follow up and ask them what priorities they have been asked to focus on, unpack their employee's excuses, and move for accountability at the end of the conversation.

UNETHICAL APPLICATIONS

The Disciplined Listening Method involves strategic, ethical observation and persuasion techniques. There are unfortunately unethical applications as well. Perhaps the most common unethical application occurs when con artists and other criminals employ a similar technique called "cold reading." They approach their marks and start the conversation by mentioning topics or experiences that are common across the human experience. When they observe a behavioral hit to one of the topics they mentioned, they dive deeper and provide a secondary list with a new range of common experiences that fit under this umbrella. It only takes three or four of these lists before the mark feels like they have real similarities with the con artist—making them prime targets.

OPPORTUNITIES IN THE FOLLOW-UP

The observation process doesn't end when the conversation ends. Disciplined Listeners take the information they acquire during conversations and look for opportunities to either validate or invalidate it after the conversation. Tim Levine's research is clear that most lies are discovered after the fact.[5] It is also true that most people get fooled because they don't take the time to validate the information they've received after the conversation.

> The observation process doesn't end when the conversation ends.

This is another major contributor to people getting wrongly convicted based on false confessions. The investigators were almost certainly unable to secure the proper evidence and the case rests entirely on the suspect's confession. After receiving the confession, the investigators and prosecution team fail to search for new or additional evidence that would either contradict or validate the confession. They just take the confession at face value and base their entire case on it. Had they taken the time to find objective evidence that corroborated or conflicted with the suspect's statement, they would have most likely learned that the suspect was innocent and dropped their case. This is why many HR executives are vigilant about collecting the necessary documentation before deciding to terminate an employee.

Leaders will be well served to avoid falling into this decision-making trap as well. Do not take the information you receive at face value, especially during a high-stakes conversation. Like Ronald Reagan said, "Trust, but verify."[6] Take the time to educate yourself, learn the necessary information, and search for available evidence that either substantiates or disproves what you have learned.

There is no doubt this observation approach requires more time, awareness, and effort—and it's worth it. The perfect time to apply this approach is when the outcome of a conversation is important to you, and your counterpart could be reasonably motivated to withhold or manipulate the information they share with you. This approach is even more important if you believe the odds of receiving the information you need or achieving the outcome you desire are stacked against you. Observing like an interrogator does not mean assuming a cynical or biased approach. It simply means increasing your situational awareness to understand and account for any present risk factors that may inhibit your ability to achieve your goals.

Now that we have introduced the Disciplined Listening Method and the approach necessary to increase the value of our observations, the next three chapters will outline specific non-verbal and verbal behavioral shifts Disciplined Listeners identify during their high-value interactions.

CHAPTER NINE

EXAMINE THE FACE

MOST OF US RELY heavily on our counterparts' faces for clues to how they truly feel when they talk to us and react to what we say. This focus on the face is natural, given our cultural communication expectations and the volume of messaging that comes from our mouths, eyes, and facial muscles. However, focusing too much on our counterparts' faces during conversations provides us with many opportunities to mislead ourselves as well.

> **Disciplined Listeners strive to evaluate the totality of their counterparts' communication with the context of the situation.**

As we explore the observable components of communication, we will separate nonverbal and verbal communication for illustrative purposes. Considering the large amount of attention we give to our counterparts' faces, we will pay special attention to the face first.

It is important to reinforce the fact that no single behavior is consistently indicative of truth or deception (see the *Othello* and *Brokaw* errors).[1] Disciplined Listeners strive to evaluate the totality of their counterparts' communication with the context of the situation. Context is king. Our goal is to understand what people are likely thinking and feeling, as well as their motivations and concerns, in order to create the unanticipated value in our conversations that solidifies commitments and relationships.

For the purpose of this discussion, our operational definition of nonverbal communication, or body language as it is often referred to, are the messages a person's body or behavior exhibit, excluding spoken words and other speech attributes.[2] We will discuss observational opportunities related to spoken words and speech attributes in the verbal communications chapter.

Much of our verbal and nonverbal communication is intentional, but not all. Paul Ekman has illustrated that a greater proportion of our nonverbal behavior is unintentional.[3] Nonverbal communication is also less controllable than verbal communication. The nonverbal communication we observe represents either a conscious decision to display the behavior, or a subconscious behavioral leakage resulting from an internal emotional shift. To this point, the stronger an emotional shift is, the more corresponding behavior will leak out for Disciplined Listeners to observe. Both conscious and subconscious behavioral displays provide astute observers with plenty of intelligence.

David Matsumoto believes the face is arguably the most prominent nonverbal communication channel.[4] After all, we have forty-three muscles in our face and we are capable of making over ten thousand facial expressions.[5] Some of these expressions are biologically hardwired within all of us, while others are learned through cultural experiences. He states that emotions are one of the most important signals the face displays because they can give observers insight into a person's emotional state, intentions, motivations, personality, trustworthiness, and credibility. Emotions provide all this intelligence because they are immediate, automatic, involuntary, and unconscious reactions to events that people find important. We would be rendered incapable of making rapid decisions without our emotions. Knowing what emotion someone is feeling, and identifying the event that triggered the emotion, alerts observers to why the event is important to their counterpart. If an event was important enough to your audience to create an emotional response, that event should be important to you as well.

This is where Disciplined Listeners elevate themselves beyond both active listeners and lie catchers. The goal of most active listeners is to appear attentive and convince their counterparts that they are engaged. The goal of most lie catchers is to identify when someone is lying to them so as to convince their counterparts to tell the truth while the lie catchers disengage or feel morally superior.

Disciplined Listeners are motivated to access the potential value hidden in their relationships and conversations. They

If an event was important enough to your audience to create an emotional response, that event should be important to you as well.

unlock this value by observing for strategic intelligence, understanding what their counterparts are likely thinking and feeling (and why), and adapting their approach to integrate their new intelligence and achieve their goals.

According to Matsumoto, humans are born with a core set of emotions that are biologically innate and genetically encoded.[6] These emotions allow us to appraise events and situations in reliable and predictable ways. These biological emotions are caused when we experience a trigger event.

They motivate us to evaluate the trigger event, prime the body for action in response to the trigger event, channel our attention and thoughts, generate unique feelings, and produce unique nonverbal behaviors. Matsumoto states the two keys to understanding what to do about your counterparts' emotions are knowing what triggered the emotional change and what the emotion's function is. In fact, Matsumoto's research has shown that spontaneous expressions of emotion from both blind and sighted people look similar.[7]

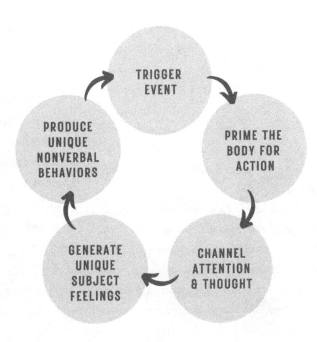

THE SEVEN CORE EMOTIONS

Research shows that all humans share seven core emotions. These emotions are *happiness, sadness, anger, disgust, fear, surprise*, and *contempt*. Every human being displays these emotions the same way on their face. As David Matsumoto states, recognizing them isn't enough. Understanding what triggered your counterparts to feel an emotion, and the function of the emotional shift within the context of the situation, is necessary to determine the proper response.

Happiness is triggered by goal attainment. According to David Matsumoto, Mark G. Frank, and Hyi Sung Hwang's *Nonverbal Communication Science and Applications,* the function of happiness is to ensure future motivation toward goals and to facilitate goal-directed behaviors. We often smile at people when they please us, encouraging them to continue their pleasing behaviors. Science has identified over fifty smiles that can indicate a wide range of feelings from happiness to fear, as well as fake smiles. The real smile is often referred to as the Duchenne smile, after its discoverer.[8] Duchenne de Boulogne combined his fascination with both facial expressions and electrocution to stimulate faces and pinpoint specific expressions. The Duchenne smile involves both lip corners and cheeks raising as well as crow's feet and narrowing eyes. A great way to differentiate real smiles from fake smiles is to look for movement in your counterparts' eyes, not their mouths. Fake smiles will often feature raised lip corners and cheeks. However, the crow's feet and narrowing eyes will be missing.

Sadness is triggered by the loss of valuable objects. These objects can range from people, to material objects, to feelings, expectations, and beyond. Sadness functions to shut down our mind and body to recoup our resources and signal for help. Sadness is expressed by raising the inner corner of our eyebrows, raising the cheeks, drooping the upper eyelids, and down-turning the lip corners.

Anger, the opposite of happiness, is triggered by goal obstruction. Anger functions to remove obstacles and prepare to fight. Anger is displayed through lowering of the eyebrows and glaring eyes.

Disgust is elicited when we come into contact with rotten and offensive objects. We can be disgusted by objects such as food or bugs, graphic pictures or injuries, people, and ideas. Disgust functions to eliminate these offensive objects and ideas. It can be displayed by either wrinkling the nose or raising the upper lip, which causes an upside-down "U" to form around the nose.

Fear is triggered by perceived threats to our physical or psychological safety. Fear functions to help us avoid these threats and is displayed through the raising and narrowing of the eyebrows, raising of the eyelids, large visible white space above the eyes, and horizontal stretching of the lips. When people show fear, it may appear as if they are mouthing the letter "E."

Surprise is often the briefest emotion and typically segues into other emotions. It is triggered by sudden or novel objects and functions to orient people toward the surprising object and process more information about it. People may be surprised by objects, events, ideas, behaviors, and other people. It is displayed through the raising of the eyebrows and eyelids and dropping of the jaw. When people are surprised, it may look like they are mouthing the letter "O."

Contempt is triggered by feelings of moral superiority. This typically occurs when we perceive actions, words, behaviors, or ideas to be morally beneath us. Contempt functions to assert our moral superiority, displayed by only raising one lip corner or appearing to smile with one side of the mouth.

EVALUATING OUR EMOTIONS

There are likely an infinite number of contextual motivations and proper responses for each of these seven emotions. I will provide a few examples to illustrate how understanding the triggers and functions of emotions can inform our best responses. If you offer an alternative and your counterpart immediately produces a

Duchenne smile, it is likely your alternative helps them achieve their goals and you should proceed. If you are talking with someone and they appear sad, it may be productive to offer them the support they need before continuing toward your goals. If you say something and your counterpart flashes anger on their face, it would be a good idea to immediately de-escalate the situation. If someone shows fear in response to one of your ideas, it should be helpful to minimize the perceived threat the idea presents to them. If someone appears surprised, register the trigger and pay close attention to the next emotion they show before determining your best response. If someone declares their moral superiority by displaying contempt toward you, it may be beneficial to further explain your idea, or let the moment pass and readdress the issue at a more opportune time.

> Disciplined Listeners add depth to their evaluations when they pinpoint the motivations behind the facial expressions of emotion they observe.

Disciplined Listeners add depth to their evaluations when they pinpoint the motivations behind the facial expressions of emotion they observe. We express our emotions when we display what we are truly feeling with no modifications, amplify our emotions when we exaggerate our expressions to display more than what we are feeling, de-amplify our emotions when we reduce the intensity of our expressions and display less, and neutralize our emotions to show no emotion whatsoever. We qualify our emotions when we pair the expression of the emotion we are feeling with another expression (often a smile). We mask our emotions when we outwardly display an emotion we are not feeling to disguise the emotion we are truly feeling. We simulate an emotion when we show an expression of an emotion we don't actually feel.[9]

Disciplined Listeners who identify the trigger that causes an expression of emotion, the function of the emotion, and the reason the emotion is being displayed, will be rewarded with an accurate understanding of what their counterparts are most likely feeling and why.

ADDITIONAL ITERATIONS ON CATEGORIES OF EMOTIONS

Interestingly, several research teams have taken updated looks at this universal set of emotions. A research team from the University of Glasgow, led by Rachel Jack, completed a series of research that claims we only have four universal core emotions.[10] They contend that our emotional displays include both biologically and socially specific purposes. The formation of our emotional displays informs us what we are feeling, and the completion of our expressions informs our counterparts what we are feeling. As a result, they believe our four core emotions are *happiness, sadness, fear/ surprise*, and *anger/disgust*.

Paul Ekman has previously written about what he refers to as blended emotions as well.[11] Blended emotions are simultaneous facial displays of multiple emotions. A research team from Ohio State University, led by Aleix Martinez, has developed this concept further. They believe our universal expressions of emotion can be separated into twenty-one categories.[12] They start with six core emotions (excluding contempt) and add on fifteen compound emotions. A few examples of these compound emotions include happily surprised, sadly fearful, sadly surprised, fearfully angry, angrily surprised, and angrily disgusted. Recognizing blended, or compound emotions helps paint a much clearer picture of what someone is feeling and why within the context of our conversations, and the best way to respond.

MICRO-EXPRESSIONS VS.
MACRO-EXPRESSIONS

Despite Paul Ekman's vast research contributions, he is most associated with the concept of micro-expressions. Ekman and his research teams have perhaps done more than any other group to forward the research in facial displays of emotion. Ekman labels displays of single, truly felt emotions as macro-expressions.[13] These fully felt emotional displays typically last from .05 to four seconds. The longer someone holds an emotional expression beyond four seconds, the more likely they are not truly feeling that emotion. Other clues to recognizing potentially false displays of emotion include asymmetry (only appearing on one side of the face), timing, and congruency. Facial expressions of emotion that aren't displayed immediately alongside the correct corresponding words or behaviors could indicate false emotional displays. Essentially, fake displays of emotion can be difficult to display at the right time and in coordination with the right words and behaviors.

Micro-expressions are fully displayed emotional expressions that are displayed for less than .05 seconds and can be displayed in as fast as .67 miliseconds.[14] David Matsumoto explains that micro-expressions are likely signs of emotions that people wish to conceal. A third category of facial expressions of emotions are subtle expressions. These are low intensity, not fully formed expressions of emotion that occur when someone is starting to feel an emotion, or when a person is trying to cover up their emotion but are unable to. Subtle emotions are the brief displays we see before people stop themselves from fully revealing how they feel.

The controversy surrounding micro-expressions generally involves two questions. Can they be recognized, and are they really indicative of deception? I'll answer the first question emphatically—yes. Matsumoto's team has proven that, with training, we are capable of seeing these fleeting expressions of emotion in real time.[15] I'll double down on his team's findings and state that, from my personal experience, once you've been trained to see them, it becomes difficult to not see them. I would like to share a word of caution when you are observing for micro-expressions: *don't miss the forest because you are looking for a specific tree.* Your counterparts' faces, bodies, and words are fountains of intelligence. If you focus too much on micro-expressions, you run the risk of missing other, potentially more obvious clues to your counterparts' emotional shifts. Like all other behaviors, micro-expressions should be observed and evaluated within the totality of your counterparts' communications.

The second question has produced the most debate. Matsumoto's team has replicated research that correlates micro-expressions to deception, and additional research has correlated subtle expressions to deception as well. Others disagree, as is the nature of research.

My position is that it doesn't matter. We have consistently stated that the Disciplined Listening Method is not about catching people lying. The fourth core behavior of the Disciplined Listening Method is evaluating the totality of our counterparts' communications within the context of the situation. Knowing the emotions our counterparts are feeling, being reasonably confident you recognize the trigger that caused the emotions, the function the emotions serve, and whether our counterparts want us to see their emotions, all provide us with significant intelligence. When we realize that our counterparts are trying to conceal an emotional shift from us, we should immediately work to determine why, and seek to understand how their motivations impact our opportunity to achieve our goals. Increasing our situational awareness and limiting our internal monologue helps us build this puzzle in real time.

INTELLIGENCE IN THE EYES

While recognizing the value facial expressions of emotion provide is a critical component of strategic observation, we can't overlook the intelligence lurking within our counterparts' eyes. However, we also need to reiterate the intelligence our counterparts' eyes do *not* provide. There is absolutely no link between gaze aversion and dishonesty. People can break eye contact for any number of reasons. Honest people may feel stressed telling the truth and dishonest people may feel no stress lying. Another common myth is that people lie when they either look to the left or to the right. Again, this has been scientifically proven untrue beyond debate. There is no link between which way we look and whether or not we are lying. With that being said, accurately following your counterparts' eye movements while they are developing ideas and considering answers can be wildly informative for Disciplined Listeners.

Understanding how people assemble their answers to your questions starts with understanding how memory works. The process of memory involves three stages: encoding, storage, and retrieval.[16] The encoding stage involves perceiving and representing an event in our mind. As Edward Geiselman writes, the mental record of an event is not an exact replica of an event. Rather, it reflects a web of interactions between the event, the surrounding context, the observers' mood and thoughts at the time, and general knowledge of related experiences.[17] As we experience daily life, we rarely realize that an event is important enough to remember, nor do we consider that we may be asked to recall specific details of an event at a later time. As such, accessing detailed memories can be difficult.

Geiselman is clear that we don't store our memories like movie clips or photos.[18] Our memories are stored in pieces and scattered throughout our brain. He also alerts us to the fact that these stored mental records can be altered when they come into contact with other stored information and can become harder to retrieve.

The final stage, retrieval, may well be the most difficult stage. This stage requires people to sort through the billions of facts we are capable of storing. The process of searching through all our stored memories can be overwhelming, create errors, and even cause people to give up trying.

Our eyes are directly tied to our memory retrieval process, and they will rotate toward the areas of the brain necessary to pull our past experiences from our mind. Our eyes will rotate up when we are accessing our memories through our visual channel, to the side when we access our audio channel, and down when we access our emotional communication channel. Recognizing your counterparts' preferred communication channel can help you improve rapport and increase how your questions resonate with them. If someone appears visually dominant, you can use visual language such as, "Do you see what I'm saying?" or "When was the last time you saw . . . ?" If someone appears audio dominant, you can use audio language such as, "Do you hear what I'm saying?" or "When was the last time you heard . . . ?" If someone appears to be emotionally dominant, you can use emotional language such as, "Do you understand what I'm saying?" or "When was the last time you experienced . . . ?"

The side-to-side movement of our eyes is where the most common incorrect stereotypes come into play. It has long been assumed that when people look to the left, they are accessing the recall center of their brain and therefore telling the truth because they are recalling real events. The same assumption contends that

> Recognizing your counterparts' preferred communication channel can help you improve rapport and increase how your questions resonate with them.

when people look to the right they must be lying because they are accessing the creative parts of their brain and making up their answer. Unless of course you are left-handed, then the popular assumption is you look to the right to recall the truth, and the left to create lies. While these assumptions may seem intuitive to some, they are absolutely false.

Let's take a minute to bust these myths. First, Tim Levine's research is clear. When people lie, they love to include as much truth as possible to increase plausibility and ease both the generation and recollection processes associated with lying.[19] For many people, lying starts with recalling the truth, and then adjusting it as necessary to avoid unwanted consequences. Please also keep in mind that people may look to their recall side as they access lies they've previously told.

People also access the creative side of their brains for many reasons. Their eyes may rotate in that direction if they have to do math or integrate memories. They may access their creative side in an attempt to answer a novel question or formulate a guess. People will even rotate their eyes to their creative side as a verification mechanism, after accessing their recall side, and before verbalizing their thoughts.

In 2009, I had the opportunity to partner with Bobby Masano, a decorated federal investigator, on a research study to cut through these assumptions and get to the truth. We created a nine-question interview. Each question was simple, straightforward, written to be stress-free, and scripted to elicit either a recall or a create response from our research subjects. We noted our observations during the interviews and compared our notes to the videos of our interviews to ensure consistency.

After interviewing hundreds of participants, the results of our study were clearly contradictory to "conventional wisdom."[20] We found that 71 percent of our interview participants looked up and to their left when they recalled a previous true event. We found that 21 percent of participants looked up and to their right to recall a previous true event. Additionally, we found that 3 percent of our interview population didn't move their eyes to recall previous true events. They de-focused their eyes and stared straight ahead. Finally, we found that 5 percent of our interview population did not display consistent recall behavior. Their eyes moved in different directions and did not follow a consistent pattern. We did observe that this final 5 percent of participants had other behaviors associated with their recall efforts including licking their lips, closing their eyes, placing their hand on their chin, and rubbing their hands.

As a bonus, we tracked the left-handed participants in our studies. Research shows that roughly 10 percent of our population is left-handed.[21] In our study, 9.6 percent of our participants were left-handed, which is statistically consistent with our global population. When we extrapolated our left-handed participants, we found that 77 percent of them looked to the *left* to recall previous true events. This finding officially nails the coffin shut on the idea that left and right-handed people look in opposite directions to recall information.

Now that we have killed the myths associated with evaluating eye accessing cues, let's discuss how to observe eye movements correctly and gather strategic intelligence. As we stated in chapter 8, the first step in accurately evaluating our counterparts' communications is establishing their behavioral baseline. If you want to evaluate your counterparts' eye-accessing cues, you have to establish their recall side. When you ask your baseline establishing questions, be sure to include a couple questions which should cause your counterparts to pause and recall the information they need to answer you. Take a mental note of which way their eyes rotate when they recall information. Once you've established their recall side, you know their create side will be the opposite.

As the conversation progresses, track where your counterparts' eyes rotate as they develop their thoughts and answers to the questions you ask. Do not assume they are telling the truth when their eyes go to their recall side or their create side. Evaluate their eye movements in conjunction with their facial expressions, body movements, and any verbal clues such as exhales, inhales, ahhs, ums, errs, and similar utterances. Remember, single-factor decisions are dangerous. The more intelligence we have to evaluate, the more accurate our judgments are likely to be.

As an example, let's say you ask your counterparts a question and see their eyes access their recall processes, while their facial expressions express doubt. Then their eyes roll across to their create side, one shoulder shrugs, and they deliver their answer with a questioning tone. In this scenario, you can be confident they couldn't find the exact information they were looking for and they aren't confident in their answer.

A second example: you ask your counterparts a question and they look up to their recall side, visualizing the memory. While their eyes are up and to their recall side, they furrow their eyebrows, slightly shake their head as if they are saying "no," and then look down and to their recall side. This likely indicates they are unsure of the initial information they accessed and they're now having an internal conversation as they attempt to sort out the situation. Now they nod their head from side-to-side as if they are considering several alternatives, their eyes roll back up to their recall side, then bounce over to their create side as they nod their head and answer with a confident tone. This process indicates they most likely considered several alternatives, settled on the one they liked best, quickly verified their decision, and shared it with you. Capturing this intelligence is far more productive than simply (and erroneously) assuming they lied to you.

I taught these concepts often, but in 2011 they were put

to the test. I was leading a three-day session at the Federal Law Enforcement Training Center in Glynco, Georgia, and called a few students to the front of the room to demonstrate how effective questions can cause people's eyes to rotate to either side, even when they are actively trying to stop themselves from doing it. We worked through a few volunteers, got a bunch of laughs, and clearly demonstrated the value of accurately understanding and evaluating our counterparts' eye movements.

Just when I thought the exercise was over, several students asked if blindness significantly affected these motions. Coincidentally, we had a blind student in the class and, out of curiosity, he insisted on coming up front and participating in the exercise. This gentleman was born blind. His eyes never functioned properly and were a milk-white color with no fully-formed pupils. He came up front, sat down facing the class, declared he was ready, and I started asking him questions. Like clockwork, his eyes started rotating up and to the right and up and to the left as he generated his answers. Throughout his life he had used his operating senses to create mental pictures, and he was accessing these mental pictures with his eyes to help gather his answers. It was a powerful lesson for the entire group, and I was grateful for his participation.

The eyes often provide other indications of emotional shifts as well. Our blink rates often change when we are under stress. The blink rate may increase, or the eyes may get frozen in a blink-free stare depending on the context of the situation. Our pupils dilate when we are emotionally stirred. Admittedly, recognizing pupil dilation can be very difficult in real time. People may roll their eyes when they are displeased and close their eyes when they are concentrating heavily, experiencing significant emotional shifts, or even attempting to shield themselves from an emotion or issue. People's eyes may tear up when they are emotionally overwhelmed, or when they are pretending to be emotionally overwhelmed.

OTHER FACIAL INDICATORS

Other areas of our faces provide plenty of strategic intelligence as well. People often flare their nostrils or clench their jaw when they are upset. People will also lick, bite, or purse their lips as their emotions fluctuate. People may yawn to release stress. This is sometimes comically referred to as the silent scream. Of course, people yawn when they are tired as well. They may also let out a burst of laughter when they are nervous, which is sometimes referred to as the gallows laugh.

People will inhale to take in the energy they will need to emphatically respond. Often, the deeper the inhale, the more emphatic the response will be. Moving in the opposite direction, people will often exhale as they capitulate and decide to share sensitive information. If they made an emotional decision to share sensitive information, their exhale may be accompanied by a downward eye movement, a dropped head, and drooping shoulders. People's mouths will often become dry and potentially make a clicking sound when their stress levels rise. This was the premise behind the Chinese rice test.[22] People with fair skin pigmentation may blush, or their skin may look flush or appear to have a rash if their emotions shift quickly. Our foreheads are often very expressive and useful for differentiating between real and fake expressions of emotions because, according to Ekman, our foreheads contain reliable muscles that we can't use to display unfelt emotions.[23] It is worth noting that drug and alcohol use, plastic surgery, injuries, medical conditions, and other factors can impact displays of facial expressions and reduce our ability to accurately evaluate them.

Years ago, I was teaching an interrogation class and had a student tell me that he makes his interrogation suspects spit out their gum prior to starting an interrogation. When I asked him why, he said it was because he found their gum chewing to be disrespectful. I immediately coached him against this for several reasons.

First, forcing someone to spit out their gum creates an adversarial, parent/child relationship prior to the interrogation even starting. This will almost certainly be counterproductive to establishing rapport and encouraging suspects to protect their self-images. Second, he was forcing his suspects to discard a source of intelligence. If his suspects started chewing their gum faster or slower, it may be the result of an emotional shift. As observers, we shouldn't be removing observation opportunities from the equation, especially if it risks fracturing the relationship.

People will also bring their hands to their face as their comfort levels ebb and flow. They may play with their hair, scratch their nose or cheeks, rub or tug their ears, scratch their neck, or rub their lips. People may even face-palm themselves if they are embarrassed or in a state of disbelief. Please remember that these behaviors may also be a result of any number of emotional shifts, or even because your counterparts actually have an itch. As always, context is king and situational awareness is paramount.

Paul Ekman has documented that the face is very expressive, communicative, and offers the most nonverbal communication.[24] This is great news for astute observers because we all pay so much attention to people's faces when they are communicating with us. The level of intelligence that observers can gain from accurately evaluating their counterparts' facial expressions and eye movements is massive, as long as observers can avoid the myths, establish a behavioral baseline, and evaluate everything they hear and see within the context of the situation. The accuracy of our facial evaluations is solidified and expanded when we compare it with the remainder of our counterparts' body language and the verbal components of their communication. We will tie all three elements together in the next two chapters to position leaders to ascertain what their counterparts are likely thinking and feeling in all of their important conversations.

CHAPTER TEN

ANALYZE THE BODY

MY FRIEND JOHN IS a highly regarded professor who teaches forensic accounting. I've been fortunate to partner with him on several projects over the years. One year, he devised an interesting plan to run an experiment with his students to show them how people's behavior changes when they aren't being completely honest.

He asked students to volunteer for mock interviews, which he would film and later show to the class. He told his volunteers that the mock interviews were for a fictitious test-grading position and the students were to pretend that they were late for the interview because they had a flat tire. Each video followed the same plotline. The student would come into John's office and sit down. John would greet them and establish their truthful and comfortable behavioral baseline by asking a handful of harmless questions such as what year student they were, what their major was, where they lived on (or near) campus, and what they did for work. He would then ask them why they were late for the meeting and every student dutifully replied, "I'm sorry, I had a flat tire."

From there, John inquired about how the students got the flat tires, for which they weren't prepared. Every student struggled to create their stories on the fly, keep the details straight, and occasionally even provide logical answers. The laughter in the classroom reached a crescendo when John asked one student, "Which tire went flat?" and the student replied, "The back, rear tire." My role was to sit in the back of the class, observe the students, critique the videos, and then provide any final insight to the class at the conclusion of each interview.

John saved the most interesting video for last. A young man walked into John's office and took a seat. He had a big smile as he talked with John and appeared to be an easy-going, friendly guy. After they exchanged their initial pleasantries, John asked his behavioral baseline questions. The student calmly and quickly told John that he was a junior, an accounting major, lived nearby off campus, and played football. Then John asked him what he did for work over the summer and the student's behavior fell apart. He took a long pause, looked down at the floor, adjusted his position in his seat, rubbed his hands together and gave John a hesitant and evasive answer. He never specifically told John what his summer job was. John clearly knew this was coming and had intentionally saved this video for last. After the student "answered" the summer job question, John tapped me on the shoulder, shrugged his shoulders, and whispered, "Why?" I didn't want to interrupt the video or disturb the class, so I wrote a quick message on a piece of paper, folded it in half, and asked him not to open it until we spoke with the student after class.

Trying to keep a college student in the classroom after the bell rings isn't an easy task. We finished critiquing the video just as the bell rang and I asked the student if he would stick around for a minute, and he agreed. I thanked him for participating in the experiment and told him that I knew it took a lot of guts to be vulnerable in front of the class like that. Then I told him I had one quick question for him: "Over the summer, did you work construction for your dad or uncle?" His eyes popped out of his head and he replied, "It was my friend's dad. How did you know?" I smiled and said, "Lucky guess." Then I asked, "How many years has he been paying you under the table?" The student's eyes darted from me to John, before returning to me as he tried to find the right answer. I let him off the hook and said, "Don't worry, it's nice getting paid under the table when we're young. Enjoy it while you can." He let out a sigh of relief and said, "Thanks, man," shook my hand, and walked out of the classroom.

Once he was gone, I pointed at the note in John's shirt pocket and told him to open it. John shook his head and smiled when he read, "He worked construction and got paid under the table." John asked me how I knew, and I said, "Do the math. He is a good kid in a forensic accounting class where he is learning how to catch people committing fraud at work. He's also a big strong dude that lives out in the country. Big, strong country kids often do construction or farm work over the summer and get paid under the table for it. Your question made him nervous because he didn't want to tell his forensic accounting professor that he and his friend's dad were breaking employment laws." John laughed and invited me to lunch.

CATCHING THE LIE, MISSING THE POINT

We have all likely heard the phrase, "It's not what they say. It's how they say it." There is a lot of truth in that statement. Disciplined Listeners know in addition to what people say, and how they say it, it is critical to recognize how people react to what you say as well.

Paul Ekman believes the reason why people do so poorly in judging deceit is that they rely too much on what people say and ignore discrepancies between the expressive behaviors and what is said.[1] I'll put a slight spin on Ekman's idea and say that one of the reasons observers often fail to capture the potential value of their counterparts' communications is because they don't evaluate the totality of what they see and hear within the context of the situation. They get fixated on one aspect of their counterparts' communication and miss the rest.

According to David Matsumoto, varying research studies state that nonverbal communication constitutes 65–95 percent of the messages our counterparts communicate.[2] Yes, their words and speech attributes are important and we will discuss those in the next chapter. But ignoring the vast majority of any communication we observe, especially in strategically valuable conversations, is irresponsible.

Perhaps the most famous research findings on this subject belong to Albert Mehrabian.[3] In his book *Silent Messages*, he shares that nonverbal communication represents 55 percent of our communication, tone of voice represents 38 percent of our communication, and the actual words we speak represent only 7 percent of our communication when we are discussing our feelings and attitudes. Two of the most common critiques of Mehrabian's results I hear from my clients refer to the specificity of his percentages and their applicability to conversations not involving expressions of feelings or attitudes.

Considering our cultural and individual differences, the specific percentages likely aren't as important as the range they represent. When people convey their feelings and attitudes, we can assume that roughly 55–65 percent of their message will be delivered through their nonverbal communication, 30–40 percent will be communicated through their tone of voice, and less than 10 percent of their message will be communicated through the actual words they speak. As David Matsumoto previously illustrated, the words we speak are not always consciously selected.

Furthermore, many of the words we speak can have multiple potential meanings, which allows speakers to leverage strategic ambiguity and listeners to misperceive the intention and meaning of the statements they hear.

Evaluating communication for potential value involves observing for congruency between your counterparts' spoken words, tone of voice, and nonverbal communication. If all three sources are congruent, there is a larger likelihood that their message is authentic, or that they are at least comfortable communicating it. The greater the incongruency, the more uncomfortable they likely are communicating the message. Determining the source of their discomfort requires Disciplined Listeners to leverage their situational awareness, ask additional questions, and look for corroborating "evidence" after the conversation.

In regard to the second critique of Mehrabian's research, I would like to ask you this: When was the last time you participated in a conversation that didn't involve any expressions of feeling or attitudes? I'm assuming the answer is rarely. It should be an enormous red flag if you speak with someone who controls their emotions so well that they never leak any indications of their feelings or attitudes, unless you are speaking with someone who has been diagnosed with a condition that impairs their emotional communication.

Your counterparts will provide you with observable intelligence from two primary sources: the behaviors and words they consciously choose to share, and the nonverbal behavior and speech attributes that subconsciously leak out. Observing and comparing both sources provides observers with much more accurate conclusions as to what their counterparts are likely thinking and feeling.

As Disciplined Listeners, we are not trying to catch people lying; we are observing, in part, to identify when and why

214   The Disciplined Listening Method

someone's emotions change. Regardless of the specific percentages, Mehrabian's research gives us a very important point of consideration. If our counterparts subconsciously leak how they truly feel or think, it is likely it will be through their nonverbal communication or their tone of voice.

THE RELATIONSHIP BETWEEN NONVERBAL BEHAVIOR AND VERBAL COMMUNICATION

Paul Ekman laid out the six ways nonverbal behavior relates to verbal communication.[4] He states that nonverbal communication can:

1. be substituted for verbal communication (a head nod instead of saying, "Yes")
2. repeat verbal communication (a head shake while saying, "No")
3. contradict verbal communication (nodding the head "yes," while saying, "No")
4. complement verbal communication (a person may flop into a chair while saying, "I'm tired")
5. accent verbal communication (pound their fist into their hand while they say, "This is important")
6. regulate verbal communication to help keep it within cultural expectations

Recognizing the relationship between your counterparts' nonverbal and verbal communication will leave you with a far more educated evaluation than simply listening to the words. If you observe someone make an affirmative statement while nodding their head yes and speaking with a confident tone of voice, you can be more confident that they at least believe what they are saying. Conversely, if you hear someone make an affirmative statement while they shake their head no, and speak with a questioning tone, you can be more confident that they aren't completely sure. Pay attention to the timing of accenting nonverbal behavior. If someone giving a motivational speech says, "We can do this together," they should emphasize the word *together*. If they pound their right fist into the palm of their left hand as they say, "Together," they probably mean what they are saying (or they are well rehearsed). If they pound their right fist into the palm of their left hand several seconds after saying the word *together*, it is less likely that they mean what they are saying.

PULLING IT ALL TOGETHER

Before we dive into exploring specific nonverbal communication behaviors, it is important to share a few reminders. I cannot say it enough—there is no single behavior that consistently indicates truth or deception. Disciplined Listeners strive to evaluate the totality of what they see and hear, within the context of the situation, before assigning meaning and value to their observations. Single-factor decisions are dangerous. The more behavioral shifts you can observe, the more valid your observations will be.

> **The more behavioral shifts you can observe, the more valid your observations will be.**

As you observe your counterparts' communications, you want to be on alert for any behavior shifts that don't appear normal for your counterpart, the topic of conversation, or the context of the situation, and appear to either contradict or be out of time with your counterparts' statements. Remember, *when* behaviors change is more important than *what* behaviors change. You must withhold judgment when you make these observations. Allow the conversation to come to you. There can be any number of explanations for these behavior shifts. The more you learn about your counterpart and increase your familiarity with the situation, the more accurate your evaluations will be over time.

Observing nonverbal communication means considering everything your counterparts do. This includes how they dress, how they walk, how they sit or stand when communicating, how they position and orient themselves toward others and their physical environment, where their attention appears to be drawn, and any accessories they may have with them (food, drinks, phone, computer, vehicle, etc.). It is often also worth noting their physical condition. Do they appear to be calm, composed, collected, and healthy? Or do they appear to be rushed, disheveled, injured, or in rough physical condition?

All of these observations can help you gather intelligence about your counterparts. Assessing the potential meaning and value of these factors is different than profiling. Profiling is judging or stereotyping someone, often based solely on one factor such as race, gender, or age, whereas Disciplined Listeners observe these nonverbal elements without judging. Our intent is to gather intelligence that will help us ethically add value to our relationships and achieve our goals.

Shoulders and Torso

As we work our way down from the head and face, we evaluate the shoulders and torso. There are three primary shoulder behaviors to observe for. The first is the orientation of the shoulders. When people are engaged with one another, their shoulders should be parallel. If your counterparts experience an emotional shift that makes them feel defensive, embarrassed, vulnerable, or threatened, they may turn their shoulders perpendicular to yours. The second is the height of the shoulders. If someone slumps their shoulder, it may be an indication that they are sad, submissive, or giving in. If someone carries their shoulders high, they may be projecting confidence or power.

The third shoulder behavior is the shrug. When people are unsure of something, they typically shrug both of their shoulders, shake their head, extend their arms from their body, and turn their palms to the sky. Correlating shrugs to the message your counterparts share can produce a wealth of intelligence. If your counterpart sounds confident telling you a message, and shrugs their shoulders while they share it, they are likely less confident than they are projecting. Asymmetric shrugs can also be revealing. A full shrug involves both shoulders. If you are observing your counterpart and they shrug one shoulder while presenting a confident message, they are likely less confident. The opposite is often true as well. If someone presents you with a message that lacks confidence and they shrug one shoulder, they may be more confident than they are letting on.

The torso and abdomen present observational opportunities as well. We have already busted the crossed-arms myth. If someone crosses their arms, it is likely a signal of either physical comfort or emotional vulnerability. You will need to evaluate the totality of the rest of their behavior within the context of the conversation to determine the most likely meaning of their arms crossing, like their respiration patterns, for example.

When people experience stress, their breathing patterns often change. Assuming your counterparts enter the conversation with a normal, relaxed respiration rhythm, take notice if they start breathing heavily or holding their breath. People are more likely to breathe heavily if they are surprised by a stressful stimulus, and are more likely to hold their breath anticipating a stressful stimulus. It is also worth observing changes in the directions they might lean and shift toward in their posture.

Remember that these shifts could be caused by physical discomfort, an uncomfortable chair, or even hearing issues. They can also be caused by shifts in emotions and stress levels. Use your situational awareness to determine their most likely trigger when you see them.

Arms and Hands

Our arms and hands are sources of a tremendous amount of both conscious and subconscious intelligence. When people aren't feeling high levels of stress, their hand and arm movements are smooth and comfortable. As our stress levels rise, it becomes harder to maintain our fine motor control, and our hand and arm movements may take on a ratcheting appearance.

A common example of this occurs when two people are out on a first date. They both may be having a great time and enjoying their conversation over a few beverages. Both people likely don't have to look at their glasses as they pick up and put down their drinks. Then, one of them asks a question that causes the other to experience a momentary spike in stress levels. The suddenly stressed-out individual reaches for their glass to take a quick sip of their drink . . . and knocks it over. They didn't have any issue picking up their glass previously. Now that their stress levels have risen, their arm muscles tense up and their hand doesn't reach quite as far as it did before, knocking the glass over instead of picking it up.

Our hand and arm movements can be separated into three categories: illustrators, emblems, and manipulators.[5] *Illustrators* are gestures that add value to what a person says and can be culturally specific. Illustrating is often referred to as talking with our hands. Everyone illustrates when they speak. Our individual volume and frequency of illustration is culturally driven. Examples of illustrators include someone pointing left when they say "turn left" and someone holding their hands in front of their body as they say, "It was this big."

There are two primary observation opportunities with illustrators. The first one, as with all observable behaviors, is timing and congruency. It is worth noting an illustrator that happens out of time with the word that it is supposed to emphasize, and if an illustrator does not match the word it is meant to emphasize. These could be indications of at least a partially manufactured message, or maybe an indication that someone has become distracted.

The second opportunity is when people temporarily stop illustrating. You want to register when your counterparts appear to be illustrating within their norm, stop illustrating, and then start illustrating again. Pay extra attention to what they say and don't say, when their illustrators go quiet. If your counterparts are talking and illustrating at the same time, that is generally an indication that the topics of discussion don't present them with appreciable levels of stress.

If at some point during the conversation they stop illustrating, it can indicate their stress levels have spiked and their brain is conserving energy and resources while paying extra attention to the words the mouth shares. Once this stress has passed, the hands can return to illustrating as normal. When this occurs, don't just pay attention to what they do say, pay attention to what they don't say. This temporary termination of their illustrators can indicate they are choosing their words carefully, and actively managing the messages they are communicating.

The second category includes *emblems*, which are behaviors that replace words. Again, these can be very culturally specific. The thumbs-up gesture can mean "good job" in Western cultures and some vulgar variation of "up yours" in several Mediterranean and Asian cultures. Examples of emblems include the aforementioned thumbs up and shrugging shoulders, clapping hands, clenched fists, shaking or nodding heads, and many more. As always, timing and congruency are very important when evaluating emblems. Any emblems that don't appear to occur on time or congruent with the spoken message should be recognized.

Another observational opportunity is recognizing partially suppressed emblems. Partially suppressed emblems often represent subconsciously leaked behavior that belie what our counterparts are truly feeling. The asymmetric shrug is the quintessential example of a partially suppressed emblem. In that scenario, your counterpart doesn't want you to know that they are either more or less confident than they are appearing to be, but their single shoulder shrug reveals their true confidence level.

The third category, *manipulators*, represents a created job to avoid eye contact. Across cultures, people believe that breaking eye contact is associated with discomfort and (incorrectly) lying. As a result, most people don't simply look away when their stress levels spike. They give themselves a reason to look away. These reasons are often manifested as jobs for their hands that they can observe. A few examples include when people look down and watch themselves play with their wedding ring, rub their fingers on their coffee cups, rub their fingers over their watches, pick (real or imaginary) lint off their shirts, or look down at their pens. As with all behaviors, *when* these manipulators occur is an important clue. Someone may really be interested in the time, wearing a new ring, or have lint on their shirt. If these behaviors happen at random times, they can have a wide range of meanings. If these behaviors occur on time to stressful stimuli, they can be an indication of your counterparts' spiking stress levels. Their facial expressions, words, and corresponding body language will provide additional clues to the actual emotions they are feeling.

The Handshake

Handshakes provide another great opportunity to assess your counterparts' communications. Again, it is important to note that cultural expectations vary widely. When I meet someone and we shake hands, I take note of the distance they keep, if they step toward me, look me in the eye, the words they use, and of course the strength of their grip. While these observations may not be definitive, they often provide indications as to my counterpart's confidence level, personality, and aggressiveness.

I personally appreciate it when someone exposes their desire to dominate me by shaking my hand with a crushing grip, pulling me toward them, rolling their hand on top to assert dominance, or placing their left hand on my elbow or shoulder to assert dominance. Let me be clear—I would *never* coach anyone to do this, but some people feel compelled to. When people shake my hand this way, they expose their attitude and intentions, immediately relinquishing the strategic advantage to me. Once I know their mindset and approach, I can adapt mine in any number of ways to apply this gained knowledge.

My most memorable example of this occurring in an interrogation happened when I had to interrogate a director of consumer marketing for a national retail organization. He was in the process of being promoted to vice president when rumors surfaced that he was committing fraud and embezzling money. There was no hard evidence and the promotion process was already in motion. I was told quite clearly that if he confessed, he would be terminated. If he didn't, he would be promoted to vice president. Just another day at the office.

My client warned me the suspect was six feet, four inches tall and weighed over two hundred and fifty pounds. They said he had recently lost a ton of weight and had become considerably more arrogant. They prepared me for the fact that he liked to use his size to try to bully and intimidate people.

It's always nice when people come as advertised. When he entered the interrogation room and shook my hand, he stood so close to me the toes of our shoes touched. He gave me the death grip handshake, rolled his hand on top of mine, and pulled me toward him. I literally had to look straight up to see his face. His introduction was about as dominant as it could have been.

Advantage—me. He very clearly tried to intimidate me before our conversation even started. I now knew that he was likely over-compensating for a lack of confidence and wanted to draw me into a competition for dominance. His attempt at establishing dominance actually put me in the superior position.

I had no hard evidence, and I knew it. If I met him head-to-head on the metaphorical battlefield, I would force him to take a position that he could defend forever. My move was to take the opposite approach. Stay calm, cool, and collected and allow the conversation to come to me. Often, the most unsettling person is the person who can't be unsettled. Once he realized he couldn't draw me into an argument, he had to listen to what I had to say, consider the ideas I shared with him, and determine the source of my calm confidence. Thankfully, he began admitting about thirty minutes in and wrote a multi-page written confession at the conclusion of our conversation.

> Often, the most unsettling person is the person who can't be unsettled.

When people declare their attitudes and intentions, regardless of what they are, they give you the strategic advantage. Like a poker player showing their competitors their cards. Once you know what they are holding, you know how to play them. Stay calm. Stay within yourself and stay focused on your goals.

Legs and Feet

Your counterparts' legs and feet can provide critical intelligence during your conversations. The further any body part is from the brain, the harder it is to control. As stress levels rise and emotions shift, the legs and feet can subconsciously leak a wealth of knowledge. The first thing to look for is the orientation of your counterpart's feet. If their feet are pointed toward you, they are likely engaged with you. If their feet are

> **The further any body part is from the brain, the harder it is to control.**

pointed away from you, they are likely disengaged and preparing themselves to travel in the direction their feet are pointed.

Remember that *when* a behavior changes is more important than *what* behavior changes. I couldn't care less if someone is tapping their feet or not. This can mean many things including impatience, restlessness, nervousness, and more. I care if my counterparts' feet start or stop tapping on time to a specific stimulus. If not, I ignore it.

ADDING VALUE IN CONVERSATIONS AND RELATIONSHIPS

None of the behavior shifts we have discussed in the last two chapters are reliable indications of deception. These behaviors can represent emotional shifts, rising stress levels, and other psychological and physiological shifts. Just because they don't reliably indicate deception doesn't make them less valuable. This makes them more powerful because the potential power of unlocking their true triggers and functions can add layers of value to our conversations and relationships, such as identifying our customers' buying and resistance signals and our employees' hidden fears and motivations.

Detractors will say that we often aren't capable of or successful at evaluating nonverbal behavior. This couldn't be further from the truth. How many parents knew it was time to change their baby's diaper just by the expression on their baby's face? How many dog owners knew it was time to let their dog outside just by watching their dog's behavior? How many times have you looked across a crowded room, locked eyes with your spouse, and you both knew what to do next without ever saying a word? To some degree, we are all experts at evaluating nonverbal communication. Our success decreases when we fail to realize the importance of a conversation, lack situational familiarity, become distracted, fail to complete pre- and post-conversation due diligence, and ignore contextual clues.

We will explore the intricacies of verbal communication in the next chapter. Before we do, I would like to share one more story with you. I'm proud of my former interrogation teammates for many reasons, including their dedication to obtaining the truth, avoiding false confessions, and helping free people who have been wrongly imprisoned based on false confessions. You may not expect this from a team of professional interrogators. When the truth is paramount, their integrity speaks loudly.

One of my former teammates, Dave, was in a meeting with a team of lawyers discussing false confessions. They were largely on the same page, but a few of the lawyers didn't realize it. They made several comments challenging any interrogator's ability to accurately evaluate nonverbal communication and took a firm position against the concept. Dave didn't argue with them and patiently waited for his opportunity to demonstrate the effectiveness of evaluating nonverbal communication. The meeting ran late, as they often do, and one of the lawyers looked at his watch as the clock edged closer to 5:30 p.m. Dave, finally presented with his opportunity, asked the attorney, "Are you hungry?" The attorney replied, "Yes, why?" Dave responded, "Because our meeting is running late, it's almost 5:30, and you just looked at your watch and then out the window. I'm imagining you are pretty hungry and waiting for this meeting to end so you can get dinner." The attorney said, "You're right," and Dave smiled and nodded his head, having clearly, and to his credit, professionally made his point.

There are several ways to practice and improve your ability to accurately identify and evaluate these facets of nonverbal communication. The first one is paying close attention to yourself. Whenever you find your behavior or facial expressions changing, pause and consider what you were feeling or telling yourself at that moment. You can also study videos online of people participating in news interviews, or investigative interviews, and pay close attention to how their behavior changes throughout their conversations. Rewind the videos and compare them to other interviews the subject has participated in. You can also ask for feedback from close friends and family members about what they are thinking and feeling when you see their behavior change. When done properly, it can be a great learning experience for you both.

CHAPTER ELEVEN

WATCHING WORDS

TIM LEVINE'S THOUGHTS ON our missed opportunities to distinguish truth from lies are the opposite of Paul Ekman's. Ekman believes people struggle to detect deceit because they don't spend enough attention evaluating expressive (nonverbal) behaviors.[1] Levine believes the reason most people poorly distinguish truths from lies is that they rely too much on expressive behavior and pay too little attention to the content of what people say.[2]

I find value in both Levine's and Ekman's perspectives. Too many people miss out on opportunities to create value in their conversations because they ignore or undervalue either their counterparts' nonverbal behaviors or verbal content, along with the contextual factors impacting their conversations. To Levine's point, it is perhaps more intuitive for people to focus on the content of their counterparts' words than their counterparts' nonverbal communication.

People communicate "speech attributes" that present a wealth of strategic intelligence on which Disciplined Listeners can capitalize. We often fail to capture this intelligence because we are distracted by other activities in our environment or worse, our internal monologue. Additionally, people miss key verbal clues if they either have no goals or the wrong goals for their conversation.

As a result, they focus on the wrong aspects of their counterparts' messages. Unproductive expectations and inappropriate listening styles, such as valuing time over quality, also regularly reduce the intelligence we acquire.

The final significant barrier to capturing verbal intelligence in our conversations is bias—especially confirmation, diagnosis, and truth bias. If we listen for opportunities to feel comfortable with what we believe, or blindly assume we are getting the whole story, we shut down our ability to capture the nuances of verbal communication that unveil our counterparts' emotions, intentions, fears, and motivations.

Levine and Ekman specifically refer to detecting honesty and deception. Their sentiments apply to our value-seeking approach as well. We are not actively trying to catch people lying in most contexts. We've already outlined the disasters this approach can create in chapter 4. When we evaluate our counterparts' verbal communication, we want to be on alert for emotional shifts, inconsistencies in their messaging, incongruencies in their delivery, indications of withheld information, and clues that they are consciously managing the perception of their messages.

Tim Levine also highlights the importance of assessing the plausibility of the messages we receive.[3] This is where our pre-conversation due diligence pays off. The more familiar you are with a topic and situation, the more likely you will be able to detect implausible or unlikely content in your counterparts' communication.

Your due diligence will help protect you against another common mistake—falling for the friendly extrovert. Levine reinforces the importance of knowing how someone is coming off might not be diagnostic of their internal state.[4] Many people fall for friendly extroverts, who experience a huge advantage in many business and social situations. If you're hiring someone, choosing a business partner, or considering a personal relationship, remember that

there's more to the opportunity than just being a friendly extrovert. This has such a powerful impact on leaders who get sucked
into their counterparts' charisma and forget to dive deeper in the
conversation and complete their due diligence.

Seemingly implausible content doesn't necessarily equal a lie.
If I told you I met and did a favor for Paul Newman when I was
a kid, you would likely think that I'm lying, as that is a highly
implausible statement. Well surprise, it is also 100 percent true.
Identifying implausible information provides you with the opportunity to further investigate the situation and either validate your
counterparts' story or validate your suspicions.

The fact that observing the totality of what people say and
do within the context of a conversation is effort intensive, only
bolsters its importance. As Tim Levine's *Truth-Default Theory*
illustrates, we don't need to be this vigilant in every interaction.[5] It
would be a tiring and miserable way to go through life. However,
you should be aware enough to turn your radar on anytime the
combination of your counterparts, topics, rewards/consequences,
and environment increases the likelihood that someone may be
massaging their messages.

Don Rabon has been a leader in the world of investigative
interviewing for decades, as both a professor and a practitioner.
He contends that every word a speaker uses in a narrative is a
matter of choice.[6] Rabon continues to say that speakers build their
sentences word by word based on the rules of language and their
individual goals. He asserts that every word, pause, and hesitation
has meaning for observers to ascertain. According to Rabon, narrative discourse includes three components: what a person actually
relates, what a person meant to relate, and how an observer inter-
prets what has been communicated. In critical conversations, an
observer's goal should be to align what our counterparts actually
relate with our interpretations as closely as possible.[7]

The dynamic between what people relate and what they mean to relate is an interesting one. There can be a gap between the two as a result of language or cultural barriers. Sometimes people can't find the right words because of their fluctuating emotions. On other occasions, they may literally not know how to communicate exactly what they mean. People also willfully select words, tone, and other attributes to deliver a message they can justify as "accurate" while intending for you to walk away with an entirely different impression.

To this point, Paul Ekman illustrates that when people intentionally manipulate their messages, they tend to be the most careful with their choice of words because they know that they will be held more accountable for their words than for the sound of their voice, facial expressions, or most body movements.[8] Which is why, as David Matsumoto points out, we should focus on the three voice subchannels people communicate through:[9]

1. Our voice subchannel communicates the actual words we speak.
2. Our style subchannel includes our patterns of speech, including our pauses and irregularities.
3. Our tone subchannel includes aspects such as our tone and pitch.

Matsumoto clarifies that most of the time, these three channels should communicate roughly the same message. However, they will occasionally communicate different or even contradictory messages that astute observers will benefit from recognizing.

Unfortunately, listeners often react in a way that makes identifying these contradictory verbal messages difficult. Ed Geiselman found that the biggest mistake interviewers make is interrupting their subjects.[10] Not only does this damage relationships and

rapport, cut off their counterparts' message, and derail their counterparts' train of thought, but it can also cause their counterparts
to alter their post-interruption message. Another grave misstep
is answering questions for people. We often do this when we
think the answer is obvious, we lose patience, or we feel bad for
them. When learning the truth is paramount, it is critical that we
patiently wait for people to answer our questions themselves. A
third mistake is connecting dots that don't actually connect. Our
brains do a wonderful job filling in the gaps in the stories we hear.
And they fill these gaps in with ideas based on our experiences,
perceptions, and expectations, which can actually widen the gap
between your counterparts' words and how you interpret them.

The first four core behaviors of the Disciplined Listening
Method significantly reduce our distractions and mistakes while
simultaneously increasing our opportunity to observe and accurately evaluate everything we see and hear.
Clearly establishing the correct goals for our
conversations and leveraging our perceived
weaknesses to build our communication
strategies allows us to complete a due diligence process that increases our situational
familiarity and provides us with information
to assess the plausibility of what we hear.

**Patiently allow the
conversation to come
to you. The longer
you listen, the
more you learn.**

Patiently allowing the conversation to come to us stops us from
interrupting and answering questions for our counterparts while
significantly increasing the depth and breadth of communication
that we have to evaluate. Remaining focused on the totality of what
we see and hear allows us to capture and evaluate the communication we observe within the context of the situation.

I cannot overstate how important it is to patiently allow the
conversation to come to you. The longer you listen, the more
you learn. Ed Geiselman refers to this as obtaining the untainted

narrative.[11] Essentially, this means quietly capturing your counter-parts' entire story or explanation before responding or interjecting. Or to say it another way, gather as much data as possible before making a decision. Allowing your counterparts to share their full story without interruptions allows you to evaluate the level of detail in their stories, the logical progression and plausibility of their stories, and assess all three verbal communication subchannels. All these observational opportunities are important, and none of them present observers with concrete assessments. Don't forget that honest and dishonest people can appear nervous, confused, composed, or well prepared for any number of reasons. The accuracy of our evaluations typically increases as the data available for evaluation increases. The more red flags we see and hear, the more likely we should be concerned with the message we are receiving.

Tim Levine points out that people often determine what to say while they are talking.[12] These simultaneous activities can cause even the most honest person's stories to include inconsistencies, appear vague at times, fall in and out of logical order, and include changes in word choice and focus. Some of the most organized stories I've ever heard came from suspects I knew for a fact were lying. Just as some of the more inconsistent stories came from victims of traumatic experiences who had to relive those experiences while sharing their stories.

As we begin to evaluate spoken messages, it will be import-ant to heed Levine's advice and pay attention to both the content and the correspondence of our counterparts' messages.[13] When we evaluate the content, we strive to capture and compare the nuances of their verbal and nonverbal communication. Assessing the correspondence refers to comparing what we are told against the facts that our due diligence uncovered. Again, Levine stresses the importance of executing these evaluations within the context of the situation.

STRUCTURE AND SEMANTICS

When we evaluate the content of the messages our counterparts share, we want to adhere to Don Rabon's approach and evaluate both the structure and semantics of the message.[14] The structure of the stories and explanations we receive include three components: the pre-event, the event, and the post-event. All three components should be of roughly equal length and include roughly equal detail.

Recognizing shifts in this structure can be important. If your counterparts labor on with an extended introduction, they may be preparing to omit or minimize critical information in the event portion of their story. If the event portion of their explanation appears to be very short, your counterparts may have omitted critical information or may have fabricated the event and intentionally kept it short so they wouldn't commit themselves to unnecessary details. If the event portion is too long, it may reflect the fact they were fabricating the event as they were speaking. If the post-event is super short, it may indicate that the event portion of the story caused a spike in stress and as a result the story fell off a cliff once they soldiered through the stressful part.

Tense changes are another potential indication worth capturing. When your counterparts share stories that are actually assembled from pieces of several different stories, or if they are fabricating parts of their story, you may catch them transitioning out of both past and present tense. This may also happen if they are having difficulty accessing their memories. An example is when you ask someone if they have done something and they say, "I will."

Another example of tense manipulation comes to us from former Mayor of Toronto, Rob Ford. In 2013, a scandal erupted when it was reported that Mayor Ford had been captured on cell phone video smoking crack cocaine with three men. Speaking at a press conference, Mayor Ford said, "I do not use crack cocaine, nor am I an addict of crack cocaine."[15] The accusations were that he used crack cocaine in the past, and his comment was in the present tense. He was also never publicly accused of being an addict. Shortly after this first press conference, Mr. Ford admitted to using crack cocaine and eventually sought treatment for his drug and alcohol use.

EVALUATING THE LEVEL OF DETAIL

Disciplined Listeners also assess the relative vagueness and level of detail in the explanations they observe. Typically, people with something to hide are more likely to be vague with their explanations. This approach provides several benefits including less detail to commit to, more wiggle room to adapt their story as necessary without appearing to "lie," and easily built-in rationalizations for why they "forgot" to share information. Yes, sometimes dishonest people will share prepared explanations that are very detailed. Statistically, this is far less common. When you are observing stories and explanations, ask yourself if the level of detail your counterparts share is contextually appropriate and if the critical details were included.

This dynamic was most evident to me when I was asked to investigate a theft from a financial institution. A team of local employees had counted and verified that all the money was in the safe on Friday. The following Monday, a corporate auditing team conducted an unannounced audit and found thousands of dollars missing. Their in-house investigations team reviewed CCTV footage from over the weekend and found that two employees had separately entered the office on Saturday. Interestingly, both employees were part of the team that counted the money the previous day.

After the local team was unable to resolve the investigation, I was asked to fly out and interview both employees. I started both conversations with the same question: "Please help bring me up to speed on the investigation." The first woman responded in incredible detail. She walked me through the entire process of how the money was counted and verified on that Friday. She told me she came in briefly on Saturday to get her headphones from her desk so she could listen to music while her daughter was at gymnastics practice. Then she detailed the process of re-counting the money on that Monday after the corporate team found the discrepancy. She even told me how she had previously been interviewed. She swore to me the money was there on Friday and didn't know what happened to it.

When I asked the second woman the same question, she responded, "Well, we counted the money on Friday and I guess they said it was missing the next Monday?" Her initial response had zero detail and zero commitments, which indicated she was likely very concerned with incriminating herself. She also didn't directly acknowledge the money was missing. She said, "I guess *they said* the money was missing." Her lack of detail and commitment meant that I had to patiently ask her to take me back through her experiences to obtain as much detail as she was willing to share.

I started the conversation by asking her to walk me through the process they used to count the money because I assumed she would be comfortable discussing what happened before the theft. Once she talked me through how they counted the money, I asked her to share how she learned the money was missing. Again, she was relatively comfortable telling me what the auditors told her. Her discomfort levels rose when I asked why the auditors talked to her privately. She hesitated before telling me that she came in over the weekend. This opened the door wide enough for me to start leading her deeper into the conversation.

By the end of my conversation with the second woman, I learned that she had been taking money from the safe for months to cover her boyfriend's child support payments. Then when she got paid, she would replenish what she took. In this instance, the corporate auditing team showed up and interrupted her ability to replace the money.

It is very difficult to pick up on these shifts in the structure of your counterparts' stories if you are distracted, talking to yourself, unprepared, or situationally unfamiliar. This is also true for dissecting the semantics or meaning of the words your counterparts share with you. If you find yourself in a situation where you have to engage in a critical conversation with a person who has expertise in a topic that you are unfamiliar with, you have two choices: You can either educate yourself on the topic prior to the conversation, or invite an expert to join you and observe the conversation.

If you recall back to my investigation into the director of consumer marketing, my client didn't want me to get fooled on a technicality because I wasn't familiar with their accounting system. Their solution was to sit me in a conference room with their VP of accounting and teach me their accounting system. Considering that math is not my strong suit, this was not going to be a successful endeavor. Instead, I asked the VP of accounting to sit in on my interrogation as my silent witness. This provided me with a content expert in the room that would most likely stop my suspect from trying to fool me with a technicality. I'll never know the true impact of having him as my witness, but I do know my suspect never tried to dupe me with an accounting technicality.

INSULATE YOURSELF FROM RELATIONAL RISKS

Be smart and protect yourself in your most important conversations. This can take the form of educating yourself both prior to and after your critical conversations. It can mean bringing in a subject matter expert, or at least someone who is more familiar with the situation than you. It can also mean having someone else lead the conversation. In my career, I have handed over interrogation opportunities to teammates

> Be smart and protect yourself in your most important conversations.

on multiple occasions because an objective assessment made it clear that they had a better chance of obtaining the truth from those specific subjects.

This idea translates to business as well. Recently, I was speaking with an executive who was struggling to convince his aging father to relinquish his leadership position in the organization. This executive and I spoke about his motivations, the approaches he had tried, and his father's resistance. Eventually, the executive realized that so much acrimony had built up between him and his father that the situation had likely become personal. He stepped aside, asked his brother to take over the negotiations, and his brother was quickly able to secure their father's commitment to step aside.

Another one of my clients was preparing for a meeting with an important prospect they had a chance to onboard because the prospect's last vendor failed to deliver adequate customer service. During our preparation meeting, the sales reps acknowledged their biggest concern was answering technical questions. I responded with what felt like an obvious question: "Which one of your tech support agents are you bringing with you?" One of the reps looked at me like I was crazy and said, "We're not." When I asked why, he said this was a sales meeting, not a service call. Once they realized this meeting was almost certainly going to focus on service, they saw the wisdom of having a service expert with them. They quickly changed their thinking, prepped their strongest service tech, and brought him with them to the meeting. The move paid off and they onboarded the new client.

THE CORNERSTONES OF VERBAL COMMUNICATION

Evaluating the semantics of your counterparts' communication includes assessing their volume, tone, speed of delivery, pauses, and specific word choices. When you are in a conversation, listen for changes in your counterparts' volume. When someone raises their voice, they may be angry, over emphasizing, or trying to get your attention. When someone lowers their voice, they may be trying to share a secret or avoid embarrassment. They may also have lost confidence in what they are saying.

When you listen to your counterparts, ask yourself, "Does the tone match the message?" Allowing for individual and cultural differences, incongruity between the tone and the message often indicates an emotional conflict with what your counterpart is saying. If they punctuate an affirmative statement with a questioning tone, and it is outside of their behavioral baseline, they aren't telling you, "it's true." They're likely asking you if you believe it's true. One point of additional consideration is the proliferation of upspeak. When people use upspeak, their pitch peaks at the end of their statement, sounding like question mark, even when that is not what they intend to represent. In these cases, this doesn't indicate an emotional shift or deception. It simply indicates how they choose to speak.

Speed of delivery, or how fast or slow someone talks, is another important observational opportunity. It doesn't matter if people are normally fast or slow talkers. It matters if their speed of delivery changes on time to a stressful stimulus. If your counterparts start talking faster, they may be trying to rush past a stressful or inconvenient topic. If your counterparts start talking slower, it may mean they are choosing their words very carefully. Especially if their volume drops and they have a questioning tone. In these scenarios, what they don't say may be more important than what they do say.

Long and short pauses can both be causes for concern. The length of the pause is not what's important. Whether or not the pause fits the question is important. If you ask your counterparts a thought-provoking question and they answer without pause, that likely indicates they prepared their answer, have previously answered the same question, or they made their answer up. If you ask an easy question and they have a lengthy pause before answering, it may indicate they are searching for an answer that pleases you while minimizing any potential consequences.

> **The length of the pause is not what's important. Whether or not the pause fits the question is important.**

Keep in mind that language and cultural barriers will create lengthy pauses. It will certainly take more time if someone has to listen to what you say, translate it to their native language, determine an answer, translate it back to your language, and then deliver their answer. This process may also involve a multitude of facial expressions, nonverbal behaviors, and word changes that reflect translation and confusion, not dishonesty.

Long pauses often make people feel awkward. This awkwardness increases their stress levels, impeding their memories and thought processes whether they are honest or deceptive. People will often reduce the awkwardness of their pauses with words like "ah," "um," and "er." I've found when people cover their pauses by saying "you know," it reflects the fact they currently don't know what to say and they're searching for it. Several years ago, I watched retired FBI agent Jack Schafer speak at a conference.[16] During his presentation he said that he is alerted every time he asks someone a direct question and the first word they answer with is, "Well . . ." His quote was, "Anytime I hear this, I know I'm likely going to get dragged into storyville."

CHOOSING THEIR WORDS

Your counterparts' specific word choice is very important to note. People who are concerned with potential consequences will often avoid harsh words or terms that carry connotations of punishment or judgment. Thieves say, "I took" more than "I stole." Abusers are more likely to say, "I said" instead of "I screamed," or "I grabbed" instead of "I tackled."

The funniest example I ever encountered was during an investigation into the theft of a quarter million dollars of raw materials from a manufacturing facility. I was tasked with interviewing sixty-two employees in two days to determine if it was an inside job. In these investigations, one of the questions we like to ask is, "What do you think should happen to the person who stole $250,000 of raw materials?" Usually, a person not connected to the theft will say something like, "They should get arrested and go to jail," and a person connected to the theft may say something like, "Well they probably shouldn't be allowed to work here anymore," or "I don't know, I just can't say."

One of the gentlemen I interviewed as part of this investigation was a second-generation employee whose father still worked at the facility. I asked him this question at the end of our conversation and he answered, "I think we should all line up and take turns beating his ass!" I bit down on my smile and felt pretty confident this guy and his dad had nothing to do with the theft. Our law enforcement partners eventually found the crew that was responsible, along with other thefts in the area.

Word choice is another great window into someone's emotional state. If a sales team is talking to a prospect and their prospect says, "We've all agreed we need to commit to this," or "I guess we may have to do this," they are reflecting two very different emotional states that the sales team needs to identify and address. All too often, sales professionals fall into a check-the-box listening approach and assume either answer is a positive affirmation, when that is not true.

Hiring managers fall into the same trap when they are interviewing candidates. They may ask a candidate about an experience where they had to work through conflict and they say, "My manager asked Sally to work with me," versus "They gave my project to Sally," or "Sally took the project from me." All three sentences have very different meanings that should be explored in more depth.

Every language has words with multiple meanings as well as tonal and gestural qualities that can impact the perceived meanings of words. Adept storytellers are well aware of this and will often use this to their advantage. They claim "honesty" while intentionally attempting to leave you with another impression. Perhaps the most famous example of this technique comes from Bill Clinton's deposition interviews in 1998.[17] During the interview he was asked, ". . . The statement that there was no sex of any kind, in any manner, shape, or form with President Clinton was an utterly false statement. Is that correct?" He started his answer by saying, "It depends upon what the meaning of the word *is*, is . . ." This response technique is often referred to as strategic ambiguity.

It is also beneficial to capture when your counterparts share unsolicited or irrelevant information. Essentially, they provide information you didn't ask for, information before you asked for it, or information that has no bearing on the situation. Each of these reflects a potential distracting technique. If you are looking at a car in a dealership and the salesperson walks up to you and immediately says, "That's a beautiful vehicle. I can give you $1000 off that sticker price if you buy her today," you should likely get at least $2,500 off the sticker price. Generally, people provide you with unsolicited excuses or information in an attempt to pacify you so you won't follow up and dig deeper. When you catch these, they should register with you as a good place to start the conversation.

Sharing irrelevant information serves a similar purpose. While someone may be confused or struggling to make a point, often when people share irrelevant information, they are trying to improve their perception or change the focus of the conversation from a topic in which they are weak, to a topic in which they are strong.

It is also prudent to listen for misplaced emphasis and overemphasis. Sometimes when people are working to massage the perceived meaning of their messages, they will emphasize the wrong words, or overemphasize certain words. Some of the more entertaining denials I received in my career were when people would say things like, "I didn't say THAT," or "I didn't touch her THERE." Those statements are likely technically true. They also indicate that we are on the right track and they are now debating a technicality, not the overall truth of their actions. Similarly, in business you may hear a customer say, "We aren't interested in THAT," or an employee say, "I didn't do it like THAT." In both cases they are likely emphasizing a technicality while exposing that there are related aspects to discuss.

Pronoun usage is another very valuable source of potential intelligence. Pronouns often connotate ownership, knowledge, and responsibility. When your counterparts are trying to avoid any of these connotations, their pronoun usage may change. Listen for sentences that are lacking necessary pronouns. If they just say, "went downstairs," "said it could get taken care of," or "misjudged the scope of the project," without including a pronoun (I, me, we us, she, they, etc.), then they may be trying to distance themselves from any accountability.

Listen for changing pronouns as well. If someone's explanation starts out with "they and them," and later changes to "we and us," it may be an indication that either the participants changed, or they were more involved than they initially let on. Another verbal tactic for avoiding accountability is using passive language instead of active language. If your counterpart says, "That's when the knife cut her," or "That's when the car crashed," or "That's when the customer got angry," they are leaving out the trigger (the who) that caused these incidents to occur. Someone had to be holding the knife, driving the car, and talking to the customer. If they did not share who, it may be because they are trying to either protect themselves or someone they care about from the potential consequences.

Distancing language works in a similar fashion. If there has been an incident between two people, or a person and an object, that person may want to create distance in an attempt to insulate themselves from potential consequences. Let's say Suzy and Johnny work together and Suzy accuses Johnny of sexual harassment. Their HR manager sits down with Johnny and asks him what happened, and Johnny says, "I never harassed that woman." (Sound familiar to anyone?) Johnny clearly knows Suzy's name. If he says I never harassed Suzy, he is admitting that he knows her, and technically could have been in a position to harass her. When he says, "I never harassed that woman," he is implying that there is so much distance between them that he could not have been in a position to harass her. He may also be avoiding the stress associated with saying her name.

First responders and 911 operators encounter this as well. If 911 answers a missing person call and hears a father say, "That boy is always running off," or "That woman stays out late a lot," they immediately should be concerned for the health and safety of the missing boy or woman. I am not saying this makes the father or husband guilty of a crime. However, this distancing language indicates there is likely trouble in the relationship as he is not using names or relationship titles, or expressing love or concern. We would expect a father reporting his missing son to use phrases such as "my boy" or "my son," just as we would expect a husband reporting his missing wife to use phrases such as "my wife" or "my love."

A more common example occurs when you're eating a meal with your friends. If one of your friends takes a bite of their food and says, "Taste this," they probably liked it. On the other hand, if they take a bite of their food and say, "Taste that," there is a good chance they don't like it. Of course, their facial expressions, tone of voice, and accompanying word choice will also give away their true feelings about their meal.

Proper article use is another valuable indication. For example, if someone says, "That's my car," or "That's Dennis' car," they are being clear on the owner of the vehicle. If they say, "the car," they are indicating they have had some experience with the vehicle previously. If they say, "a car," they could be talking about any vehicle.

If you are asking them to share a story that involves a car, the proper progression would be for them to start with "a car" the first time they saw it, "the car" the next time they saw it, and "Dennis's car" once they learned it was his. If you know that they know it is Dennis's car and they refer to it as "a car" or "the car," that would be a concern. Similarly, if they start their explanation by saying "the car" and then switch to "a car" (assuming they are talking about the same car) you should be concerned as to why they are distancing themselves from the vehicle.

DEVELOPING AWARENESS OF OUR SUBCONSCIOUS CONNECTIONS

As we've mentioned previously, our brains do a wonderful job connecting dots that aren't meant to be connected, and subconsciously filling in gaps based on our perceptions. One of the most common opportunities to fall victim to these traps is to assume someone finished a task when they didn't actually tell us they did.

If someone says, "I started," it doesn't mean they finished. If they say, "I'm heading to," it doesn't mean they arrived at, or went straight to, their destination. Just because they say, "At first I thought," it does not mean they changed their minds later. Yet, all too often we hear these statements and assume the actions were completed without receiving verification.

Another occasion where our brains can connect unrelated events is when people omit information and skip over time in their stories. When you hear people use phrases such as "later on," "after that," or even "then," it is important to consider how much time they just jumped past. They could be linking to the logical next event, or skipping information they honestly do not think is important. They may also be intentionally passing over information they do not want you to know.

It is also worth paying attention to the order of items people include in a list. It is quite common that the first item or person on their list is the one most important to them. The opposite can be true as well when the last item is the most important to them. This happens most often when someone gives you a list of reasons why you should do something, and the first four reasons benefit you, while the fifth reason benefits them. There is a reasonable chance the reason that benefits them is truly what is most important to them.

In my opinion, one of the absolute most valuable verbal sources of intelligence is when people cut themselves off in the middle of a word or sentence, replace the original word with a different word, and continue speaking. One example may be "I'm afr—, I just want to be sure this is the best option." They stopped themselves from saying the word "afraid," adjusted their vocabulary, and continued with their sentence. This is a huge intelligence-gathering opportunity. Clearly, they are afraid of something and they do not want you to know, or they do not want that knowledge to impact your perception of them in this situation. Now you have to determine what they are likely afraid of and how to address it.

> One of the absolute most valuable verbal sources of intelligence is when people cut themselves off in the middle of a word or sentence, replace the original word with a different word, and continue speaking.

When people stop themselves in the middle of a word or sentence, alter their vocabulary, and continue speaking, they communicate several critical pieces of intelligence. They leak what they are really thinking or feeling. They expose that they don't want us to know. And they select new words that clearly demonstrate the impression they are trying to create.

Comparing all of these elements, within the context of the situation, allows Disciplined Listeners the opportunity to paint a much clearer picture of what their counterparts are experiencing and create new approaches to use this intelligence to their advantage.

QUALIFYING STATEMENTS

Another common intelligence-gathering opportunity is when people equivocate or qualify their statements. These qualifiers do not necessarily signal lies. They *do* often signal a lack of confidence and specificity that provides our counterparts wiggle room with their statements. Common qualifying words include: *probably, currently, possibly, usually, about, typically, often*, etc. Anytime you pick up on an equivocating statement, you should consider what specificities they are trying to avoid committing to.

Equivocations have several cousins in the "I don't want to commit to details" family. Idle political statements are an unfortunate reality that we are all too familiar with. Statements like "I cannot confirm or deny," "to the best of my recollection," and "at this point in time," all protect speakers from committing to details now, and afford them the ability and excuse to add or subtract more information later.

Another cousin is relying on an uncheckable source. If someone tells you that you can confirm their story by asking someone who is either impossible to contact, or likely unavailable, that should be a red flag. Similarly, when people exaggerate their answers to the point of absurdity, they may be trying to make you feel foolish for asking the question and let them off the hook. My preferred response to this tactic is to immediately follow up and say, "Thank you. I'd like to ask you again more accurately, what would you say . . . ?"

One of the major targets of George Mitchell's eponymous Mitchell Report outlining the widespread use of steroids in baseball was Roger Clemens.[18] For those unfamiliar, Roger Clemens was one of the all-time great pitchers in baseball history, and prior to the release of the Mitchell Report, a surefire Hall of Famer.

Shortly after the report was made public, Roger Clemens participated in an interview with Mike Wallace on *60 Minutes*.

During the interview, Mike Wallace asked Roger Clemens several direct questions about receiving steroids and other performance-enhancing drugs from his trainer, Brian McNamee. At one point in the interview, Clemens says, "If he's putting that in my body, which is totally false, if he's doing that to me, I should have a third ear growing out of my forehead and I should be pulling tractors with my teeth." Clearly, neither a third ear, or teeth strong enough to pull tractors, are side effects of using performance-enhancing drugs.

There are two specific words that catch my attention when I hear them: *actually* and *just*. When people say "actually" they are typically exposing the fact they considered two alternatives, and only voiced the second.

In another example from years ago, I returned home from teaching in Africa for two weeks, and my wife picked me up at the airport. I felt surprisingly fresh having survived such a long trip home. After giving my wife a hug and a kiss, I asked her if she would like to stop for dinner on the way home. To which she replied, with a look of surprise on her face, "Actually, yeah, I'd love to get dinner." I'll let you determine how she initially expected me to act after a twenty-three-hour trip home. It is worth noting, like with upspeak, that some people may use *actually* more frequently as part of their personal lexicon. If this is the case, we need to treat it as part of their behavioral baseline unless we have contextual clues telling us otherwise.

The word *just* is often used as a minimization tool. If you ask someone where they've been or what they've done and their answer starts with, "I just . . ." there is a reasonable likelihood they may be minimizing their answer and there is more to the story. They may also be highlighting what they didn't do. For many years, I taught an annual three-day seminar for CEOs in Las Vegas. One year, my hosts invited an additional speaker to educate us during dinner.

They informed me that this gentleman had worked in the military and intelligence communities, and I jumped at the chance to potentially learn from him.

I arrived at the seminar room early that morning and started setting up my gear. I looked up when I saw my host walk in with the guest speaker. He introduced us by saying, "Hey, Mike, this is Robert. He's a real-life Jason Bourne." My host fancies himself a funny guy, so I assumed the movie character comparison had some truth to it but was mostly used for effect. Robert immediately followed by saying, "I was just a Ranger." I didn't serve in the military and have respect for those who have, especially those who volunteered for specialist assignments. I've met several Rangers over the years and exactly zero of them have said, "I was just a Ranger." His statement was a clear indication that, yes, he was definitely a Ranger before likely moving on to other roles in his career.

People may even speak using less contractions when they are not being honest or withholding information. For instance, they may say, "I did not" or "I would not," as opposed to saying, "I didn't" or "I wouldn't." Again, it is important to remember that this could be caused by several different stressful situations.

Two responses that are often associated with dishonesty and require further consideration are when your counterparts either repeat the question or answer with a question. These responses do not mean that someone is lying. However, they may likely indicate that your counterparts are stalling for time. They don't have an answer they love at the moment, so they either repeat the question or answer with a question to buy themselves more time to come up with a better response. Before you jump to the conclusion that it is a stall tactic, you have to ask yourself three questions: *Was I clear? Do we speak the same language? Were there any distractions?* If you answer two yeses and a no, then it was probably a stall tactic. If there is doubt about your clarity, language barriers, or distractions, then you need to consider they may have actually needed the clarification.

Another commonly assumed, yet mythical, verbal indication of dishonesty are words such as "honestly," "truthfully," "swear to God," and similar statements. The thought behind this myth is if people have to assert how honest they are, they are likely being dishonest. While this myth can occasionally be true, it very often is not. People will also use these phrases when they are conveying a truthful message they believe their counterparts will have a difficult time believing or adding extra emphasis.

An additional family of verbal behaviors that are often associated with potential deception are signs of nervousness or lacking confidence, speech errors, slips of the tongue, and memory issues. It is true all of these can be caused by someone experiencing an emotional shift, a spike in stress, or trying to consciously manage their communication. All these factors are experienced by honest and dishonest people. People who have suffered brain injuries or experienced traumatic events may display all these behaviors. Disciplined Listeners evaluate everything they see and hear in the context of the situation.

NERVOUS INNOCENCE

The most nervous person I ever interviewed was innocent. And I knew she was innocent when I got there. Remember my interrogation outside Miami that got invaded by the popcorn cruncher? The first person I talked to that day was the manager. She wasn't even employed at that location when the theft occurred. I had to talk to her first to confirm some basic schedule and logistic information and ask for any important insight she may have on each of the suspects.

I arrived at the store at 8 a.m. with the vice president of human resources who had also flown in the night before. I had no idea we were showing up unannounced. The VP of HR knocked on the door and the manager walked over to see who it was. She looked very surprised when she saw us. She opened the door and greeted the VP by name, at which time the VP said, "I'm here with Michael Reddington this morning to investigate the recent theft activity. He is a Certified Forensic Interviewer and he needs to speak with you first."

Imagine coming to work expecting a normal day, getting halfway through your first cup of coffee, and hearing that. This woman literally started shaking and stuttering. I was worried she was going to fall down as we were walking to her office. She was so nervous she couldn't answer basic questions about her staff's schedule. Thankfully, I saw a picture of her at Boston University in her office. I spent over thirty minutes talking about the Green Line, Kenmore Square, and baseball traffic before she could calm down enough to answer my questions. It goes to show that just because someone is nervous doesn't make them guilty. Context is king.

The last three chapters have illustrated a wide range of verbal and nonverbal indications of emotional changes, spikes in stress levels, and withheld information. We are all capable of observing many of these behavior changes, in real time, when we focus on our counterparts and eliminate distractions. I cannot make it clear enough that these behaviors do not represent truth or deception on their own. Disciplined Listeners evaluate the totality of everything they see and hear, within the context of the situation, with the goal of ascertaining what their counterparts are most likely thinking and feeling, and how this intelligence can help them unearth hidden value and achieve their goals.

Observing these behavioral nuances is half the battle. The second half is using them to your advantage and inspiring your counterparts to commit to taking the actions you need them to. Now that we have covered what to look and listen for, we will transition to how we can ethically persuade our counterparts to commit to sharing sensitive information with us.

CHAPTER TWELVE

INCREASE YOUR INFLUENCE

MUCH OF THIS BOOK has focused on how to increase the power of our observations with the Disciplined Listening Method. We are now going to pivot to the persuasive communication elements of the methodology and shift our focus to leveraging our observations and obtaining sensitive information from our counterparts.

In chapter 6, we discussed the first of two critical realizations that led to the development of the Disciplined Listening Method. The cognitive processes leading suspects to say, "I did it," employees to say, "I'll do it," and customers to say, "I'll buy it," are essentially identical.

Now it is time to discuss the second realization: The best leaders and the best interrogators capitalize on the same two core skills—vision and influence. Both communication contexts require leaders to perceive how their actions, and their audiences' actions, impact the big picture, while influencing their audiences to commit to the process necessary to achieve their long-term goals.

SEARCHING FOR LEVERAGE

When people consider changing someone's mind, getting buy-in, or negotiating agreements, they often look for leverage, which is comparable to searching for the high ground. This approach often results in creating division, unnecessary competition, and reinforcing in-group out-group dynamics. The traditional negotiation concept has long been that whoever has the most power in a situation holds the most leverage. This power may be based on title, reputation, money, organizational size, threats, or other factors.

William Ury and his team at Harvard University reframed this argument when they illustrated that leverage resides with the person who has the strongest BATNA (Best Alternative to a Negotiated Agreement).[1] This concept does a much better job leading negotiators to negotiate based on interests, as opposed to staking themselves and their counterparts to positions. Essentially, Ury and his team believe that whoever has the best plan B is the one who is most willing to walk away, and therefore is in possession of the most leverage in the conversation.

There is a third concept of leverage that is often overlooked: the ability to influence others. When we lack traditional power, or a strong plan B, our ability to influence becomes our last source of leverage. Developing the skills necessary to persuade people to commit to your ideas creates powerful advantages in all your conversations.

If you assume you have the leverage because you have the power, you may be correct. You may also be committing to a biased and short-sighted approach, which ultimately sets you up for failure. If you assume that you have the leverage because you have the best plan B (BATNA), you may also be correct. Of course, you may also be underestimating your counterpart's plan B. Even when you believe you have the power and/or the best plan B, possessing the ability to influence others increases your confidence, allows you to put your advantages in your back pocket, and positions you to negotiate to your strengths instead of from your strengths.

As we begin to compose our influential approaches, it will be important to consider that the three foundational elements of influential communications are timing, delivery, and situational awareness. Well-conceived and factually strong arguments are easily wasted when they are delivered at the wrong time and with the wrong approach. There is a reason we spent an entire chapter on situational awareness. Understanding the ripple effects of our actions and decisions in relation to our goals is a critical component of influ-

> **The three foundational elements of influential communications are timing, delivery, and situational awareness.**

ence. If we move too quickly or without proper consideration, we are almost certainly hamstringing our efforts. Our influential efforts are typically far more effective when we communicate reflectively, not reflexively.

A FOUNDATION OF TRUST

It is critical to note that trust serves as the foundation for influence. Your counterparts will be far more open to accepting your influence when they trust you, and far more resistant when they don't. In his book *The Speed of Trust*, Stephen M. R. Covey illustrates the two core components of trust are character and competence.[2] The more your audiences believe that you are of high character and possess a high level of competence in the topic you are discussing, the easier it will be for them to trust you and for you to influence them.

Covey also illustrated that the four core components of credibility are integrity, intent, capability, and results.[3] When people believe you possess a high level of integrity, your intentions are consistent with your actions, you are capable of achieving success in the topics you're discussing, and have produced the results to substantiate your capabilities, they will perceive you as credible.

When we find ourselves in situations where we feel like we need to influence someone immediately and struggle or fail, it is likely because we missed previous opportunities to build trust and set the stage for this moment. Had we taken advantage of previous opportunities to earn trust, demonstrate credibility, and allow our counterparts to consider our ideas, we likely would have avoided these frustrating failures entirely.

Disciplined Listeners don't approach influence as a parlor trick, easy button, or quick solution. We approach influence as a long game. The relationships we have with the people we need to influence give us the opportunity to earn our counterparts' trust by consistently demonstrating our character and competence, then cashing in the trust equity we've built when we need to.

Trust is synonymous with vulnerability. If you want someone to trust you and be persuaded by you, they have to feel comfortable being vulnerable in front of you. Persuaders are problem solvers. Failures to persuade can typically be traced back to trying to solve the wrong problem. Often the real problem we are solving is not how to get someone to say yes or accept our idea. It is how to get someone to justify showing vulnerability in front of us so they will be comfortable accepting our ideas. It is almost always easier for someone to embrace showing vulnerability in front of you after you have shown vulnerability in front of them first.

There is an important difference between trust and faith. All religious connotations aside, we typically trust what we have tangible experience with. We've seen it, touched it, and know it to be true for ourselves. We typically have faith in things that we strongly believe, but with which we lack tangible experiences. All too often, leaders across all contexts expect people to trust them because of their title, expertise, or years of experience, without providing tangible evidence they can be trusted. They feel entitled to that trust, or worse yet, feel that telling someone they can be trusted is enough. In these scenarios, leaders are asking their team to operate on faith, not trust, which is substantially more difficult. Trust is earned over time, especially with members of out-groups.

During my investigation into the stolen handguns, I had to interview several other employees who I was relatively confident were innocent. The first gentlemen I had to speak with was a long-tenured employee and a military veteran. His manager described him to me as their "biker/bouncer." He was substantially older than I and reportedly stubborn.

Sure enough, he entered the interview room, gave me an inquisitive and distrustful look, and sat down facing me with his entire body turned toward the door. I presented him with our consent-to-interview form and he literally leaned away from it as he read it carefully. He eventually signed it and looked at me as if to say, "Now what?"

He clearly did not seem interested in talking about the investigation, so I figured it would not hurt to take a shot at establishing some base level trust and rapport. After all, people like people they believe are like themselves. Of course, they also dislike people who pretend to be someone they are not. I thanked him for signing the form and said, "Your manager tells me that you ride." He replied, "Yeah." I asked him what he rode, and he said, "An old 70 FL" (1970 Harley Davidson Electra Glide). I responded, "I'm a new fish. I'm riding a 2009 Dyna Super Glide." He smiled, nodded his head, and said, "That's alright. Two wheels is two wheels," and as of that moment, we had mutual respect.

I did not pretend to be anything I was not and, in a humorous way, deferred to his experiences. Just those few authentic sentences gave us enough in common that he could begin to drop his guard. During our conversation, I was able to eliminate him from the investigation and he provided additional circumstantial evidence supporting his suspicion that my main suspect was the thief. In the end, he strengthened my hypothesis.

EARNING COMMITMENT VS. FORCING COMPLIANCE

My favorite quote from Sun Tzu's *The Art of War* is, "Subduing the enemy without fighting is the acme of skill."[4] While our counterparts are not our enemies, this quote supports our operational definition of influence, which is *inspiring someone to commit to making the decision you want them to without relying on your title or force.*

It takes almost no skill at all to impose your title on someone and demand they do something because you told them to. Admittedly, this approach may be required on occasion. However, the appropriate occasions for this approach are far rarer than many people think. Leaders may default to this coercive approach because it was how their parents and managers once spoke to them, because they have not been taught any other approaches, or simply because they are being lazy.

> **Kindness and empathy only add to any leader's perceived power, and their ability to influence others.**

Perhaps most disturbingly, people default to a "because I told you" approach because they feel taking any other route would cause them to appear weak and violate their self-image as the person in charge. Kindness and empathy do not equate to weakness, and do not undermine a leader's power. Kindness and empathy only add to any leader's perceived power, and their ability to influence others.

The best results we can hope for when we use the "because I told you" approach is forced compliance. Compliance occurs when people feel forced to obey a command. In these scenarios, people typically apply the minimum required amount of effort for the minimum required amount of time, until the task is completed to the minimum required standards. Forced compliance often results in long-term feelings of resentment, which continue to resurface and negatively impact relationships, performance, and morale. Perhaps the real danger here is that forcing compliance, although realistically a loss, often feels like a win. Leaders walk away thinking, *Great, they are going to do what I asked them to do,* when the long-term damage may be significant.

Earning commitments can feel more time consuming than forcing compliance, but it is far more effective. When people commit to saying or doing something, they feel like they own part of the decision. This idea ownership helps them justify and align new actions with their own self-image and continue in a new direction in the face of challenges, disagreements, and potentially easier alternatives.

This is why torture and other coercive interrogation techniques are nearly always ineffective. Most of us have a limit to the discomfort we are willing to endure in any situation. If we are talking to someone who we feel is being rude or disrespectful under normal circumstances, we might leave the room, hang up the phone, or stop responding to their messages. Suspects in custodial interrogations can be made to feel like they cannot leave the room until they satisfy their interrogators with information, and the pain that they are experiencing is only going to increase the longer they hold out. So, they exercise their only choice and provide their interrogators with false information to end the discomfort.

In the business world, this may result in people ending the conversation by giving us the answer we want to hear, even though it is not true. An employee may say "I've got it under control" when they don't, or "I'll handle it" when they won't. A customer might say "Send me the proposal" when they have no intention of signing it, or "Call me next Tuesday" when they have no intention of answering your call. In each of these examples it was easier for people to get what they want (end the discomfort of the current conversation), by telling you what you want to hear, regardless of their future intentions.

SAVING FACE

The annals of interrogation history are replete with surprising examples of self-image-saving techniques producing results where torture and coercive techniques couldn't. Perhaps the most successful American interrogator in the Pacific theater during World War II was Major Sherwood Moran. He had lived in Tokyo prior to the war, spoke Japanese, and was familiar with Japanese culture. He treated every Japanese Prisoner of War (POW) like a human being, not as an enemy. He began all his interrogations by telling his prisoners that they were safe and inquired about their condition before ever asking tactical questions. At least one prisoner reportedly asked Moran to come back and talk with him every day.

German interrogator Hanns Joachim Scharff is also widely regarded as one of the best interrogators in history. Scharff spoke English and used a rapport-based, friendly approach in his conversations with captured American fighter pilots during World War II. He started his interrogations by saying, "Come in, please," and wove his tactical questions into seemingly innocuous conversations. His approach led him to obtain astounding amounts of information from the American pilots with whom he spoke. One of his techniques was to go on walks with his captured pilots and use much of the seemingly meaningless information he had picked up to convince them he knew much more than he really did. This allowed the pilots to justify giving him more information because they assumed he already knew it. After the war, many of the pilots he interrogated spoke highly of him and even reached out to him. Scharff relocated to the United States, taught his techniques to the US government, and lived the rest of his life as an artist in California.

David Zulawski and Doug Wicklander are extremely influential leaders in the world of interrogation, having created the non-confrontational Wicklander-Zulawski (WZ) Method in the early 1980s. They were among the first groups to systematize a non-confrontational interrogation approach predicated on establishing rapport and encouraging suspects to save face while telling the truth. They learned that often people will tell the truth for one (or a combination) of three reasons:

1. They believe the truth is already known, or will inevitably be known.
2. They have the opportunity to save face and put their spin on the message.
3. They feel guilty enough to come right out and tell the truth.

One of the biggest mistakes that leaders in all contexts make during influential conversations is disrupting the face-saving process. Too often, leaders, parents, sales professionals, and investigators mistakenly feel that their audiences need to admit to being wrong and accept accountability at the beginning of their conversations. Whether they realize it or not, this approach is based on the leader's perception of right and wrong and their need to be acknowledged as the authority figure. It also prioritizes

262 The Disciplined Listening Method

moral superiority over influencing a commitment to changing their audiences' behavior.

Nothing may be more frustrating to leaders facilitating accountability conversations than receiving excuses. This frustration leads them to disrupt the face-saving process by immediately challenging the excuses they receive. Excuses are gold! The excuses leaders receive are typically the result of their counterparts' internal negotiations. Anytime someone gives you an excuse for their actions, they are admitting their actions took place. Half of the battle is now over. More importantly, their face-saving efforts outline their fears and motivations, and provide leaders with the perfect place to start their conversation and work backwards to achieve accountability. The next time someone responds to you with an excuse, please calmly respond, "Thank you, that is a good place to start," and ask them to explain their ideas further. Their excuse will almost certainly come unwound and they will lead themselves to accepting responsibility. It is far more effective to obtain accountability at the end of the conversation than the beginning.

> It is far more effective to obtain accountability at the end of the conversation than the beginning.

It is natural for people to want to withhold or spin information they believe will be harmful to their job, relationships, and reputations. One of the most important lessons I learned as an interrogator was that it was totally acceptable for people to either deny, make excuses for, or lie about their actions. Honestly, this is what they were supposed to do if they had made regrettable decisions and wished to avoid the consequences. There was no serviceable purpose for getting mad at them for simply exercising the last good option they believed they had. Instead, look through these lies and excuses to uncover the intelligence you need to move your conversations forward toward the truth, commitment, or accountability you require.

Sharing sensitive information requires people to change their own mind from "I don't want to tell you," to, "I believe telling you is an acceptable alternative." Even in our daily conversations, this can be difficult. Our brains are wired to prefer our own ideas and resist ideas from others—especially others we perceive to be in our out-groups. When people *commit* to changing their minds, they typically need to experience several factors. As both Moran's and Scharff's approaches illustrated, people need to feel emotionally and physically safe. At the same time people need the opportunity to save face and protect their self-image. They also need to experience respect and recognition while having the opportunity to participate in the conversation in order to feel they own part of the decision-making process.

This process often requires people to overcome the discomfort associated with cognitive dissonance, which occurs when people say or do something that contradicts their previous beliefs. They are deciding it is okay to say or do something they previously committed to not saying or doing. Similar to justifying a large purchase when we feel buyer's remorse, they have to justify their decision to change their mind and align this new decision with their self-image.

Remember, the number one fear that stops most people from accepting new ideas or taking new actions is embarrassment. The number one reason most adults lie is to avoid a consequence that is either real or perceived. It can be much harder to persuade someone to share sensitive information when they have already staked themselves to the position of not sharing the information, especially if they've publicly declared their position. When people take positions, they are forced to defend them—even when their position doesn't appear logical.

Our counterparts' motivations and fears create substantial barriers in persuading them to share sensitive information. It has been well documented that people are typically more motivated by a fear of loss than a motivation to gain. Losing something is tangible. We know what it feels to have something, and we can clearly picture how we will feel if we lose it. It is harder for us to justify exposing our vulnerabilities by picturing how it will feel to gain something we don't currently have. This is why people may choose to stay in unhealthy relationships, jobs that make them unhappy, or avoid difficult conversations. They believe resigning themselves to the misery they are familiar with is easier than risking the vulnerability necessary to achieve something better.

Similarly, it is hard for people to open up in stressful and ambiguous circumstances. Ambiguity breeds stress, and stress kills our ability to trust other people, reframe problems, and create new alternatives. In his book *The Trust Factor,* Paul Zak illustrates how our brains secrete oxytocin (a.k.a. the love drug) when we experience trust.[5] He writes how our brains produce cortisol when we experience stress, and that cortisol is an oxytocin inhibitor. Our brains are therefore rendered incapable of trusting when our stress levels rise. When we feel stress, our brains focus on protecting ourselves and alleviating the stress as quickly as possible. This often causes us to make short-term, tactical decisions while failing to consider more productive, long-term strategic options. There are times we need to influence people under stressful circumstances. Other times, we may create unnecessarily stressful circumstances by either imposing time constraints, adding pressure, or offering too many options.

Therefore, Disciplined Listeners prepare for their conversations by asking themselves, "Why shouldn't my counterparts commit to what I need them to?" "Why haven't my counterparts already committed to what I want them to?" and, "What do my counterparts need to experience before committing to what I need them to?" Answering these questions should get you much closer to your counterparts' fears and motivations, which will serve as the building blocks for your persuasive strategy.

KEEP IT CLOSE TO THE VEST

In chapter 6, we outlined the seven stages of potentially contentious conversations. The pre-conversation stage offers our counterparts the first opportunity to create their defensive strategy. Dave Zulawski illustrates that the two most common strategies our counterparts employ when they have information, they prefer not to share are either "deny until they die," or force our hand to reveal any evidence we've uncovered.[6] In doing so, they give themselves an educated opportunity to choose what information to share and withhold.

Leaders often feed into both strategies by accident. People who are withholding information love to hear direct accusations as soon as possible. Any time we make a direct accusation, we expose what we know (or believe) and allow our counterparts to publicly take a position of denial. As a result, they gain confidence based on what they've learned and simplify their defense by repeating the same denial for the remainder of the conversation.

We also hand the advantage to our counterparts when we expose what we know too early in the conversation. Leaders often assume that showing someone evidence of a transgression will immediately motivate them to tell the truth. Unfortunately, this is often not the case because sharing the truth might be embarrassing and create consequences. The natural reaction in this situation is for people to try and explain away the evidence in a manner that either justifies their actions or shifts accountability away from themselves. The research behind the Strategic Use of Evidence interrogation technique has proven that there are indeed risks associated with showing evidence too early, and benefits of withholding the evidence for as long as possible.[7]

Exposing what we know too early in a conversation also eliminates our ability to use our knowledge as a validation tool. Remember, knowledge doesn't create power. Successfully applying our knowledge in the context of the situation creates power. Often, the power of what we know is maximized by withholding our knowledge. Withholding our knowledge allows us to compare everything we hear to what we already know without impacting the direction of the conversation. We have a huge advantage when people don't know what we know. They have to choose what to tell us, and we will likely learn much more than we would have otherwise.

> **Often, the power of what we know is maximized by withholding our knowledge.**

A funny example occurred more than once when clients called to ask for help with their investigation. The conversations went something like this:

Client: "We caught an employee stealing."

Me: "Okay. What did you do next?"

Client: "Well, we sat him down and showed him the video."

Me: "How did that go?"

Client: "Surprisingly, not well. He said it wasn't him even though it clearly was."

In reality, this reaction is not a surprise whatsoever. The thief was confronted with clear evidence of his theft and resorted to the

only face-saving and consequence-avoiding option he had left—
"That isn't me." This result is as predictable as the tides.

The same situation often plays out when sales professionals
call out their customers for making a mistake, failing to keep their
end of the bargain, or talking with competitors. In these scenarios,
the customers are often forced to deny the allegations to save face
and avoid conflict. Leaders can generate the same response when
they confront employees with evidence of mistakes or failed commitments. Employees often react immediately by claiming they
don't recall, blaming someone else, or denying ever receiving the
initial instructions. In each of these examples, the sales professionals and leaders have compromised their ability to achieve their
goals by exposing what they know, forcing their counterparts to
take defensive positions, and creating unnecessary conflict.

COSTLY MISTAKES

There are several other common mistakes people make when they
attempt to persuade people to share sensitive information.

One mistake, in addition to forcing their counterparts to
defend positions, adding unnecessary pressure, and exposing what
we know, is trying too hard to build rapport. When we try too
hard to build rapport with someone, we impinge our trustworthiness because it appears that we are setting them up to get more
information from them. This occurs when we point out too many
similarities too quickly, offer unsolicited similarities, and provide
people with unnecessary and/or untrue compliments.

Committing to ineffective approaches is another common mistake. I've seen too many C-Suite executives drive themselves crazy
trying to find rational solutions to emotional problems. It is easy for
persuaders to engage their counterparts with a strategy that makes

perfect sense from their own perspective but is entirely misaligned with that of their counterparts. Through this approach, we see a decision as logical and fail to recognize emotional attachments. This rational approach has several built-in opportunities to fail. Anytime we present opinions or facts, we create the opportunity for our counterparts to spin them in defense of their ideas or positions. In fact, the stronger someone's belief is, and the more their belief is wrapped around their self-image, the less effective this rational approach will be. The information we share to persuade them away from their position typically has the reverse effect and only serves to reinforce their position.

Poor word choices are costly as well. These may be words that invoke consequences, violate someone's self-image, generate unproductive emotional responses, or create relationship imbalances. One oft-quoted study clearly illustrates the impact of our word choice.[8] Elizabeth Loftus and John Palmer used filmed car accidents to illustrate their point. After viewing the videos, their participants were asked to give an account of what they saw and answer a few specific questions. As part of this questionnaire, participants were asked how fast the cars were going using one of the following words: *contacted, hit, bumped, collided,* or *smashed.* Everyone watched the same video, yet the average perceived speed changed with each verb used. The participants who received the "contacted" question guessed 31.8 miles per hour. The participants who received the "hit" question guessed 34 miles per hour. The participants who received the "bumped" question guessed 38.1 miles per hour. The participants who received the "collided" question guessed 39.3 miles per hour. The participants who received the "smashed" question guessed 40.5 miles per hour. Just changing one word in the question generated a perceived difference of nine miles an hour. Don't underestimate the unintentional impact our word choice can have on our audiences.

I applied this principle to my advantage when I was asked to help free a multimillion-dollar negotiation from a protracted impasse. One of the parties had intentionally stalled the negotiations for over five years in an effort to wear down the other two parties while profiting along the way. We were able to restart the negotiations through his lawyer and 100 percent of our communications were shared via email. As expected, his first offer was laughable, insulting to my clients, and quite advantageous to him. It was also as good a place as any to start because it revealed a few of his motivations.

The first key adjustment we made with our responses was removing any potentially combative language. Any phrases such as "you said," "our previous agreement mandates," "it is your responsibility," and most importantly, "our counteroffer." While all these statements were true, they also could've easily created a defensive response—and he'd already stalled the negotiations for half a decade.

Removing the term "counteroffer" was of particular importance. This term connotes that the previous offer (and offeror) wasn't good enough, and the new offer (and offeror) is superior. Thus, producing a competition to see who can win by forcing the other negotiator to lose more. Losing less shouldn't equal winning. We replaced "counteroffer" with "updated proposal" to avoid triggering these mental traps. We also used the underlying motivations he revealed in his offers to justify our offers.

The negotiation process wasn't entirely without issue. However, we were able to successfully resolve the negotiation over the course of several months, and six total emails, using this strategy. Thankfully, we were able to collaborate on payment terms that resulted in my clients receiving over one million dollars above the original offer they received. Our strategy continues to pay off as the value of the assets we negotiated for has increased fivefold since the agreement was finalized.

Last but certainly not least, another common misjudgment that impedes persuasive efforts is engaging with people at the wrong time. Remember, if we need someone else to give us information, they are in control of the conversation whether we like it or not. Yet all too often, we approach people at times that are convenient for us, such as the moment the idea strikes us, or when they are emotionally unprepared for the conversation. While there is almost never the perfect time to persuade someone to share information or take action, you must pause and consider an appropriate time to broach your persuasive conversations with your counterparts based on your goals and their likely needs.

THE ART OF PERSUASION

Robert Cialdini's research is revered in the world of persuasion. Through his research, he has identified the seven automatic mechanisms of persuasion.[9] Anytime these mechanisms are triggered, they create what Cialdini calls a "*click, whrrr*" response and cause us to accept outside influence. We are going to focus on ethical applications for these mechanisms, to increase our influence during our conversations. His seven automatic mechanisms are:

1. Liking
2. Reciprocity
3. Authority
4. Social Proof
5. Consistency
6. Scarcity
7. Unity

Liking. It should come as no surprise that we are easily influenced by people we like. We typically like people with whom we share important similarities. It is the perceived authenticity of these commonalities that creates potential problems. The issue that leaders in all contexts often run into is trying too *hard* to be liked. People usually like us less when they perceive us as trying too hard because they believe we are going to try and get something from them. Often, the best way to be liked is to add unsolicited and unexpected value to someone's life.

Reciprocity. This may be intuitive as well. We all feel the need to do something nice for people who have done something nice for us. Again, the perceived authenticity and sincerity of our actions will impact the sense of reciprocity that our counterparts feel. A common error people make is doing something nice for someone and then immediately asking for a favor in return. This creates the impression they did something nice only to set up the opportunity to ask for a favor. For our purposes, one of the most effective ways to ethically leverage reciprocity is to share information and demonstrate vulnerability prior to asking your counterparts to do the same. Once they see us set the example it will be much easier for them to follow suit.

Authority. When we think of leaders as experts and not as power figures, the concept of authority creates opportunities across all contexts. We can increase our persuasive power when people perceive us as experts. Two great ways to fail at this are to tell people you are an expert or to ask a series of questions without providing any insight along the way. Leaders and sales professionals often fall prey to both. It is hard to be perceived as an expert if all you do is ask questions. Experts are expected to share insightful information and ask fewer, more powerful questions.

Social Proof. This is another concept we are all likely familiar with. Amazon and other online retailers have weaponized social proof by adding their star ratings. If one item has 500 5-star ratings and another item has 1,200 5-star ratings, we think the second item must obviously be better, even if we have no idea who wrote those reviews and if we have anything in common with them. We all love to feel included with groups of people with whom we perceive to share important traits (our in-groups). This creates an enormous opportunity for leaders to encourage their counterparts to save face by associating their counterparts with groups they see themselves a part of.

Consistency. This is the strongest driver of the seven mechanisms. People possess a strong desire to believe they are thinking, speaking, and acting in a manner that is consistent with their self-image. I would argue that encouraging someone to align your ideas with their self-image represents at least 80 percent of the persuasive battle. The more aligned you are with your counterpart, the more persuasive you will be in a given situation. The wider the gap between your perception, the actions you are asking them to take, and their perception of themselves, the more challenging the persuasive battle may be.

Scarcity. Essentially, the rarer something is, the more valuable it is. This does not just apply to products and experiences. It applies to people as well. Leaders across contexts leverage the perception of scarcity based on how they treat and communicate with the people around them. Your persuasive abilities increase exponentially when people perceive you to be a scarce, authoritative figure. This does not mean that your expertise is scarce, although that is helpful. It means that they believe you are a scarce resource because you treat people in a way that is not often experienced.

Unity. The tighter our perceived in-groups, the stronger our feelings of unity are toward the people in them. In many cases, we feel more unity with our family members than our coworkers. Perhaps the strongest way to create the feeling of unity is through shared sacrifices. Leaders across contexts can significantly reduce the ever-present outgroup mentality between employees and leaders by sharing sacrifices with their teams. These sacrifices can include working with employees side-by-side, helping them with the hardest parts of their jobs, and dedicating extra time to help them learn new skills or tasks.

THE APPROACH

There are two general approaches we can take when we try to persuade someone. The first and most common approach is asserting our point and then substantiating it with additional facts or opinions. This typically works best when we are "preaching to the choir" and persuading someone who we believe will be in almost total agreement with us, based on what we have in common.

The second approach is the opposite. We start by providing the substantiation for our main point prior to asserting it. This approach possesses more persuasive power, although it is typically used less often. This approach works much better anytime we are attempting to persuade someone who may be motivated to resist our requests.

Disciplined Listeners default to this second approach because *people react the strongest to what they hear first*. You can unknowingly encourage people to take defensive positions if you ask them to do something they do not want to do, or if you ask them a question they do not want to answer honestly. Once they take this position, they will listen to any additional reasoning you provide, not as a reason to agree with you and change their mind, but to validate and fortify their defensive position.

One of the most important influential tactics that Disciplined Listeners utilize is to, "Illustrate before you investigate."

You create a real persuasive advantage and limit resistance when you provide your counterparts with reasons or excuses to agree with your statement or request prior to presenting it. You allow your counterparts to align their self-image with your illustrations when you show understanding of the situation, give reasons to agree that satisfy their interests and excuses, and allow them to save face prior to making your statement or asking your question. Once they have aligned their self-images with your illustrations, it becomes substantially easier for them to agree with your statement and honestly answer your request because they no longer feel the need to take a defensive position.

> **You create a real persuasive advantage and limit resistance when you provide your counterparts with reasons or excuses to agree with your statement or request prior to presenting it.**

As an example, you may need to ask someone on your team to take on extra responsibility to satisfy a difficult customer. If you just ask them directly, you will make it easy for them to say no and then resist your ensuing persuasive efforts. However, if you give them the reason first, you will likely short-circuit their defensive response. That request may sound like "We can all vaguely remember how excited we were when we won this contract because it introduced us to a new market and represented 20 percent of our new customer revenue this year. They've clearly been more demanding than we anticipated but this is still a critical opportunity for us. I need someone who's demonstrated the ability to handle tough clients and deliver us the win we are all expecting. I know we are all stressed at the moment. How much additional support might you need to step up and be the point person on this project moving forward?" This approach frames their decision around the greater goals, aligns their self-image with the request, and avoids yes or no answers.

There is an offshoot of this concept that is exceptionally effective. Several of my early goals in any sales conversation, negotiation, or difficult conversation are to establish my credibility, resonate with my audience, violate any potentially negative expectations, and induce a feeling of reciprocity that will encourage my audience to share more information without me having to ask. I typically look to achieve these goals by illustrating my understanding of the situation before I ever ask any questions.

How my audience perceives my illustration usually determines the success of this approach. With this in mind, I preface my opening illustrations by saying, "Please correct me *where* I'm wrong . . ." This statement is substantially different than, "Please correct me *if* I'm wrong . . ."

Saying, "If I'm wrong," implies that I expect to be correct. This can come off as arrogant and assumptive. If it doesn't turn my audience off completely, they likely will not be fully focused on what I say next.

Saying, "Please correct me *where* I'm wrong," creates an entirely different effect. First, starting the statement with "please" is helpful because it is polite and respectful—that never hurts. Second, saying, "where I'm wrong," now encourages my audience to listen for opportunities to correct me, which forces them to listen more intently. Now that I've captured their full attention, my message will be more powerful.

Once I've completed my illustration, I pause and wait for a response that generally falls into one of two categories. The first is when they say, "You're not wrong." This is fantastic for me because they just verified my credibility before the conversation truly starts. The second option is they say, "Close . . ." and fill in all the information I missed. This option is even better for me because now they feel it is necessary to supply me with much of the information I am looking for, without me having to ask for it.

This approach has become one of the closest techniques I have to a silver bullet. It consistently helps me establish credibility and solicit much more information without me having to ask for it. Often, people are happy to tell me what I want to know without having to ask. I want to make it clear that I do not intentionally make mistakes with this approach to try and trick people into sharing information with me. If they sniff out any trickery this early in the conversation, I'll ruin any chance I have at establishing a relationship. I provide honest illustrations and let the chips fall where they may.

I use this technique in the early stages of nearly all my sales meetings. Several years ago, I received a call from a potential client who was considering me as a candidate to keynote their annual sales kick-off meeting. Their director opened the call by introducing herself and asking me about my background. Before I could answer, an unidentified man (later confirmed to be the VP of Sales) spoke over her and asked, "Mike, before we go any further, how much experience do you have in our industry?"

The honest answer was zero. If I had responded with "None, but we are focusing on universal aspects of communication," or "you would be my first client in your industry," I would've been dead in the water.

Instead, I responded, "Great question. Please correct me where I'm wrong. From what I understand, your team leverages an indirect sales model. They sell to retailers who sell to the end users. In my previous experience with teams who leverage that model, they often have to compete with other wholesalers their retailers represent, fight to keep their retailers motivated, and struggle to ensure their retailers are reflecting their culture."

My answer stripped away the unnecessary focus on their industry and illustrated my understanding of the challenges their team faces. The director responded by saying, "You're not wrong."

I didn't hear from the VP for the rest of the call, and I had a signed contract by the end of the week.

BE CAREFUL SAYING *YOU*

Previously, we discussed the risks associated with inadvertently offending someone's self-image. One of the most common ways leaders accidentally offend their counterparts is by overusing the word *you*. *You* is one of the most potentially offensive words in the English language. Every time we say the word you, we stab our counterparts directly in their self-images. This can come across as threatening, assumptive, judgmental, and embarrassing. Once people start feeling these emotions, they are far more likely to shut down and become defensive.

Imagine how it would feel if a leader was trying to encourage you to open up with them and they said, "Normally you're on the ball. I'm sure you just made a mistake because you've got a lot on your plate and you're under some pretty tight deadlines. I can understand if you're stressed out right now. I really just need you to tell me what happened so I can help you make this right." In fairness, this leader is likely trying to show empathy and understanding. In reality, you may perceive that he is treating you like a child, accusing you of making a mistake because you are stressed out, incapable of handling stress, meeting deadlines, or juggling everything on your plate . . . and you need him to rescue you. All of which should immediately create a defensive reaction.

Now imagine how it would feel if the same leader said, "We've all been under more stress recently as our deadlines creep up on us. These situations make it easy for even our strongest team members to make oversights as they juggle everything on their plates. I'd appreciate it if you could please walk me through where we are in this process so we can work through some alternatives for getting back on track." In this example, the parental communication style and accidental accusations disappear. The leader includes themselves in the stressfulness, includes you in the strongest team member category, helps you save face by swapping "mistake" for "oversight" and includes you in the process of improving the situation. There is no real opportunity for your self-image to feel attacked or your resistance levels to rise in this example.

These two statements essentially deliver the same message, but generate drastically different emotional reactions and levels of commitment. We create several significant advantages when we limit our use of "you" and shift to setting up our questions in the third person. First, we increase the perception of our credibility because we create the impression that this isn't our first rodeo and we've successfully navigated these scenarios previously. Second, we allow our counterparts to protect their self-images because they don't feel attacked, and they can experience a feeling of safety in numbers because they are all in the same boat.

Additionally, we invoke all seven of Cialdini's persuasive mechanisms. By avoiding the word "you" and the associated accusatory tone, we are more likable and create the perception that we are a scarce resource because no one else has likely ever spoken to our counterparts this way. Illustrating our understanding of the situation increases the perception of our authority. We invoke social proof and consistency to encourage our counterparts to include themselves in positive in-groups. Bringing them into the decision-making process after illustrating our understanding invokes unity. Providing this illustration before asking for their input, invokes reciprocity. Not bad for three sentences.

THREE OPTIONS

There are three general options we have when we engage in persuasive conversations:

1. We present people with what we know or believe and hope it changes their mind. There are occasions where this may indeed work. However, we have previously outlined the dangers of this approach.
2. We ask our counterparts questions that motivate them to open up to us. We will cover this option in detail in chapter 13.
3. We leverage a narrative, or story-based, approach.

Walter Fisher published his narrative paradigm in 1984. His conceptual framework essentially states that human beings are storytelling animals and we experience life through a series of stories.[10] He continues to say that people do not deliberate whether or not they should buy into a story. We buy into stories when we can identify with them based on our life experiences and when they provide good reasons to change our actions.

Stories are so powerful because they allow listeners to be drawn in and make emotional connections with the content and characters. Every human being shares hundreds, if not thousands, of common experiences. People from the same geographic area, with similar interests, shared experiences, and similar aspirations have even more in common.

We run the risk of raising doubt and suspicion when we tell someone we understand their situation or have something in common. We encourage them to avoid feeling threatened, protect their self-images, and decide for themselves when we demonstrate that we understand their situation and share our insights through stories.

Great stories have protagonists and antagonists. They proceed logically. These stories feature challenges or problems that have been overcome. They illustrate the approach used to solve the problem and tie it back to the current situation while illuminating new options for our audiences. These stories shouldn't be overrun with details. They should include the specifics necessary for your audience to perceive your credibility and become emotionally invested in the story.

For many of us, the most persuasively challenging conversations we participate in are with our family. My personal, most difficult application of this storytelling technique came when my neighbor and close friend was struggling through his final days. Chuck was eighty-two, and forty-seven years older than me, when I moved in next door to him. We became very close over the years that we were neighbors. Chuck was a Renaissance man. Photography and classic cars were two of his hobbies that we bonded the most over.

Unfortunately, our trips to car shows decreased and our trips to the emergency room became more frequent as Chuck's body started breaking down. His health quickly deteriorated to where he was admitted into an assisted living facility. The original plan was for this to be a temporary stop to help him recover and return to his house. After a few weeks, it became apparent he probably wouldn't be able to return home.

Chuck's mind remained razor sharp to the end and he was a master of persuasion in his own way. To his credit, he tricked the doctors at the assisted living facility to allow him to return home. We were taken by surprise and circled the wagons to support him the best we could. Within hours of Chuck returning home, it became crystal clear he couldn't stay in the house by himself. The assisted living facility told us that excluding a medical emergency, they could only take him back if it was his decision.

The following day, his daughter and son-in-law tried to talk him into going back. It played out like so many tough family conversations, with the children (i.e., subordinates) telling the parent (i.e., superior) what the parent needed to do. This reversal in perceived roles creates layers of defensiveness that often only results in arguments that no one wins.

Sure enough, this was exactly how the conversation with Chuck played out. His daughter and son-in-law walked into his house, told him he wasn't healthy enough to stay, that they weren't able to take care of him, and he needed to go back to the assisted living facility. Both their approach and their desired result were in direct conflict with what Chuck wanted and the role he perceived he had in the decision-making process. As a result, they both dug themselves deeper into their respective positions.

Thankfully, after several unproductive hours, they called me and asked me to talk to Chuck. I waited for them to leave his house before I entered. I walked in, found him sitting at his kitchen table, and pulled up a chair to sit with him. I asked him, "How are you?" This was almost certainly the first time anyone had asked him how he felt and what he was thinking that day. Chuck took a deep breath and unloaded everything he was feeling and why. How he felt physically, mentally, and emotionally. How he felt his children were treating him and why he wanted to stay in his home. He admitted that he knew it wouldn't be easy to stay home but he couldn't stop thinking about how to "engineer" solutions to his problem. His answer was cathartic for him and provided volumes of intelligence for me. He clearly knew he would struggle to stay in his home and was trying hard to create mechanical solutions to make it possible.

When he finished, I let the silence linger for several minutes. Then I asked, "Do you remember that black F-150 I almost bought?" He laughed and said, "Yeah, it was really nice." I said,

"Do you remember how I screwed that up?" He looked at me inquisitively and said, "I don't."

I continued, "I walked into the dealership convinced I couldn't get the price I wanted, so I abandoned my normal negotiation strategy. By the time I realized I probably could get the price I wanted, it was too late. The salesman had locked himself into a price structure I couldn't get him out of. The payment was at the very top end of my budget and the years were way too long. I dropped the ball bigtime." Chuck nodded his head and laughed. I continued, "I really wanted the truck, so I came home to think it through. Over the next two days, I asked Brooke for her opinion several times, and you twice. I also called my brother, my father, and my father-in-law. On the second night, Brooke and I were getting ready for bed and I asked her about the truck again. She looked at me and asked, 'Mike, when was the last time you asked five people their opinion on anything?' and right then I knew I couldn't buy the truck." Chuck cut me off and said, "It was the right call." I agreed and responded, "You're right, and I learned two important lessons. Never assume failure and abandon a good strategy, and the harder ~~I~~ you have to work to justify a decision, the more the right decision becomes obvious."

We sat together silently for another minute or so until he said, "Will you please help me pack my bags?" Listening to Chuck first, then sharing that story, eliminated the perceived roles of the conversation, removed the defensive reactions, established common interests, and used an example we both clearly understood to illustrate the right decision without ever asking Chuck to make it. We lost Chuck a few months after that conversation. I think back to it frequently and wonder if I did the right thing.

This storytelling technique is an extremely valuable component of the most successful interrogation technique I ever used. Dave Zulawski and Doug Wicklander realized the power stories have to illustrate credibility, help interrogation suspects save face, and encourage these suspects to choose to tell the truth. As a result, it became a core component of their eponymous WZ Method of interrogation.[11]

I could clearly see the impact that this technique had on the suspect responsible for stealing the two handguns. During that interrogation, I told the suspect a story that illustrated how my friend's business was forced to close when his partner betrayed him. I continued to share how this affected him and his family, along with the sacrifices and struggles he experienced as he struggled to take care of his wife and four kids. The suspect and my friend both had small construction businesses fail and they both struggled to support their family. It was a perfect match. My suspect started nodding along and let out a large exhale about halfway through the story. I wrapped up by saying that the experience left me with a firsthand understanding of how hard it is, and how far people will go to support their families. He confessed to stealing the guns within minutes of me finishing the story without ever denying responsibility.

Credibility is key. We should not tell stories that expose our lack of experience, understanding, or expose ulterior intentions. As an example, one of my CEO clients, Joe, applied for a business loan from a bank. In these situations, banks will often investigate their applicants' financial credibility and personal integrity. During the interview process, a security executive from the bank told Joe a story about how this executive's father had stolen money when he was growing up. Joe, who is as honest as they come, quickly recognized this as a ploy the security executive likely used on every applicant to try and make them feel comfortable discussing previous acts of dishonesty. This obviously insincere tactic motivated Joe to partner with another bank.

Stories also work wonderfully to reduce resistance and defuse arguments because they are impersonal and don't force people to take positions. Additionally, they also allow our audiences to save face, change their mind, and back down from arguments.

The best time to solve a problem is before the problem actually materializes. One of the best ways to handle resistance is to avoid causing it. More often than not, we should be able to anticipate how, when, and why our counterparts may either become upset or counter our thoughts. In these cases, we can use the anticipation to our advantage, acknowledge their perspective before they do, and take their argument away from them. We refer to this technique as "taking bullets out of guns."

> One of the best ways to handle resistance is to avoid causing it.

If you are confident that your employee is going to say, "You have no idea what it's like in the field," you can eliminate their excuse by saying, "I know it can be hard for me to truly understand what it's like working in the field every day." If you believe your customer might say, "You don't have a lot of experience working with companies in our industry," you can take the chance away from them by saying, "Over time we've learned that, regardless of industry, there are three core opportunities all of our clients share." Anticipation is one of the most important facets of persuasion. Typically, the sooner we can identify and address an issue, the easier it is to influence our counterparts to accept our ideas.

Letting people finish their rant is another simple and effective alternative. Most of the time, we resist this option because we are focused on time and run out of patience. Or because our egos do not allow us to let them finish, and we feel forced to interject on behalf of our own self-images. Letting people finish their rant gives them the stage and perceived control when they want it most. It also gives us the opportunity to listen and gather intelligence while they exhaust their energy. Many emotional rants often conclude with a large exhale and a pause to see how we will respond. When you recognize this, patiently wait a few seconds and calmly start your response with, "Thank you."

Accept-Reframe-Justify

When Disciplined Listeners respond to challenging questions or statements, we follow a three-step process: Accept-Reframe-Justify. The best way to end the argument your counterpart is trying to start is by initially accepting their point of view. This does not mean that you agree with it. It simply signifies that you are validating their perspective. Your counterparts will find it really hard to argue with someone who won't argue with them.

Now that we have cut off the argument before it could start, we want to reframe the conversation. Whenever possible, we want to reframe the conversation around an idea or perspective that is universally agreed upon. Once we have done so, we want to close this technique by offering our counterparts a justification for accepting our idea or perspective.

As an example, let's say that your counterpart tells you, "I don't have to listen to you." They are likely trying to trick you into saying, "Yes, you do," so they steal control of the conversation and argue that point until you give up and go away. A more productive response would be, "Of course you don't. I'm thankful when people do listen so we can find a way to work through this together. It's been my experience that people generally like putting these situations behind them as fast as possible and that's what I'd like to try and do today."

Another example could be when your counterpart says, "Why should I bother? What I have to say doesn't matter." I like to respond with, "You don't have to bother, that's okay. The project has to proceed one way or another. Our goal is to get everyone's input before making a decision and we appreciate anyone who wants to take the time to help."

This approach applies to a common challenge sales professionals receive. The next time a prospect challenges you by saying "Why should I choose your company?" calmly respond with, "You shouldn't if you don't believe we can give you the best opportunity to surpass your goals. All our clients have taken the opportunity to research their alternatives and select the best partner. Our job is to honor our selection by dedicating ourselves to exceeding our commitments."

As our frustration mounts, it can be harder to use these techniques and easier to default to ultimatums, threatening consequences, exposing what you know, or bluffing. All these techniques are dangerous. Ultimatums should only be used as a last resort, when all other attempts have failed and when you are willing to execute your threats. However, using ultimatums in most situations creates more problems than they solve, and can irreparably harm your credibility.

Threatening consequences often has a similar effect. We assume that people will cooperate if we remind them what the consequences of not cooperating are. Unfortunately, this approach often has the unanticipated effect of motivating people to create a new alternative that allows them to escape the consequences, while avoiding what we want them to do.

Bluffing integrates the risks of both ultimatums and exposure of what we know. We put our credibility on the line every time we bluff, and we lose ground every time someone calls our bluff. The biggest issue here is we may not know they called it. We can bluff someone and they can know we're bluffing and not tell us. Now our credibility is shattered and we don't even know it. Similar to ultimatums, we should only bluff when we've exhausted all other options and we can't make the situation any worse than it already is.

The Disciplined Listening mantra is: *Focus on the issue, not the person. Focus on the resolution, not the consequences.* Focusing on the issue allows us to avoid confronting our counterparts' self-images, allows our counterparts to save face, and creates an opportunity to work together on resolving the issue. Focusing on the resolution gives us a positive end state to work toward whereas focusing on the consequences reminds people they need to be on the defensive.

> **Focus on the issue, not the person. Focus on the resolution, not the consequences.**

Influence should be approached as a long game. Study your counterparts as you build your relationships. Take note of how they like to make decisions, who they look up to, how they process information, what types of rewards or feedback are important to them, and what fears or concerns usually slow them down. I have worked with people who need to be presented with an idea that is 100 percent buttoned up and ready to go. I have worked with others who need to have the opportunity to point out where I'm wrong so they can feel superior and receive credit. I have worked with some people who like making quick, gut-feeling decisions. I have also worked with people who need to see that someone else they respect is doing it before they will. I have even worked with a few executives that only cared about the financial bottom line. We can ethically leverage all of these approaches once we are aware of them and present our ideas the way our audiences need to receive them.

Ethical, goal-oriented influence should never be about receiving credit, avoiding blame, tricking people, or taking advantage of others. Influence should always focus on ethically motivating the people around us to protect their self-images and commit to helping us achieve the goals we honestly believe in.

An integral part of influence is asking questions. Asking the right question at the right time can unlock a series of new alternatives. Asking the wrong question at the wrong time can kill conversations and relationships. In the next chapter, we will explore how to enhance our questioning skills and integrate the most important influential concepts.

CHAPTER THIRTEEN

GET WHAT YOU ASK FOR

QUESTIONS ARE AN INTEGRAL part of listening. Great questions confirm what you have heard, demonstrate that you are interested in both the conversation and your counterpart, and move the conversation forward. Great questions also generate intelligence-laden responses that move us closer to our goals and bolster our relationships. On the other hand, poor questions can expose our disinterest, our lack of attention and preparation, and destroy our credibility, thereby damaging relationships.

Whether we realize it or not, most of the time we get exactly what we ask for, and that is not always a good thing. The timing, quality, and delivery of our questions can either unearth stunning revelations or play right into our counterparts' defensive, or at least deflective, strategies. Former Toronto Mayor Rob Ford provides us with another stellar example. After he admitted to trying crack cocaine, a reporter asked him why he previously lied about it. Mayor Ford responded by telling the assembled crowd of journalists, "If you ask the question properly, I'll answer it . . . I wasn't lying. You didn't ask the right questions."[1]

Dan Ariely's research made it clear that we are all capable of dishonesty to the degree that we can justify it, within our self-images.[2] There is a direct link between the questions we ask and the results we achieve. Asking better questions yields stronger information, leads to better decisions, and creates better results. Asking impulsive and poorly conceived questions stops us from obtaining critical information and negatively impacts our decisions and results. A great way to help people justify lying, massaging, or withholding information is to ask an improperly timed, poorly worded, or harshly delivered question. They use our bad questions as their justification for feeling good about not sharing the information we are asking for.

This is true for decisions up and down the scale of importance. Readers who have traveled extensively know that sometimes little conveniences make a big difference on the road. For many years, it felt like my home was the Hilton and my residence was a storage facility. Then, my travel requirements changed for a year and I lost my Diamond status with Hilton. Losing the status mattered less than not being able to partake in the free breakfasts.

After losing my status, I knew that asking a desk associate, "Please book me on the executive floor," when I checked in, would almost certainly result in them explaining to me why they couldn't. I needed to create another avenue to make it easy for them to give me what I wanted, which was just the breakfast (and maybe the occasional beer in the evening). The approach I went with was to arrive at the desk and wait until they were in the process of confirming my reservation on their computer. Once I was confident they were in my account, I'd ask, "Excuse me, which floor is the executive lounge on?" The desk agent would tell me the floor every single time because I wasn't asking them to book me on it. Once they told me the floor number, I was halfway home. I'd follow up by saying, "Thank you. I slept in my own bed a few extra times last year and lost my Diamond status. I know the rooms up there are limited and I don't want to take one. I have early morning meetings all week and I'd be grateful if you could set my key card up so I could just sneak into the lounge for a quick breakfast." My success rate with this approach was nearly 100 percent. It may not seem like a big deal to others, but it made a big difference to me out on the road. After all, breakfast is the most important meal of the day.

AXIOMS FOR INQUIRY

Disciplined Listeners follow seven axioms for inquiry across their business and personal lives. These axioms combine to set a series of guidelines for questioning that increases the quality of the information we obtain while lowering the resistance we encounter. We will explore each of them individually.

First axiom: Know what is more important: asking the question or obtaining the answer

At first glance, this statement may appear trite; however, it is equally overlooked and under-considered. Some people covet a reputation for asking tough questions. My response to that moniker is "Congratulations, but how often do you obtain truthful information?" Asking tough questions may satisfy someone's ego, create a desired reputation, and feel satisfying or powerful. But unnecessary tough questions can do more harm than good when they cause your counterparts to feel defensive and answer in a way that protects them from potential consequences.

There are a few situations where asking the question is more important than obtaining the answer. These situations typically involve circumstances that make it extremely unlikely your counterpart will answer honestly, or the rules of engagement may not allow you to phrase a question the way you would like—investigative journalists and lawyers often fall into these two categories. In these scenarios, it may very well benefit you to ask a tough question that illustrates your knowledge, gives your counterparts important information to consider, or serves to influence public opinion in your favor when obtaining the truth is a long shot. However, these situations are generally few and far between.

One of the biggest mistakes leaders make is asking questions based on what they want to say, as opposed to what their counterparts need to feel in order to own the decision to respond honestly. Leaders often deliver their questions based on their emotions in the moment, the information they want to obtain, and their perception of their own superiority. People typically answer questions in a manner that they believe will help them save face, avoid consequences, and satisfy their questioner. This results in a sizable gap between the information we want to obtain and the information we often receive.

The next time you find yourself in an emotional conversation and a question pops into your mind, stop yourself from immediately asking it. Pause, and think through how the question may make your counterpart feel. If you believe that there is any chance it may cause your counterpart to feel defensive or embarrassed, refrain from asking it just yet. Rephrase the question to avoid these negative impacts, encourage your counterpart to save face, and then deliver it.

Second axiom: Questions create problems that need to be solved

This is true for both the person asking the question and the person answering the question. The person receiving the question has to listen to the question, determine the questioner's motives, consider their own goals, think through the consequences they'd like to avoid, and then create the best available answer. The person asking the question has to address the ripple effects caused by their counterparts' responses. Their counterparts may become more defensive, aggressive, or submissive. The answer they provide may open new doors, slam the conversation shut, or add additional discomfort. This axiom is yet another illustration of why it is critical to develop our situational awareness and ask questions that are more likely to reduce rather than increase the problems we need to solve.

Third axiom: Questions can be perceived as invitations or attacks

When your counterparts perceive a question as an invitation, they are more likely to respond honestly and accept your ideas. When your counterparts perceive questions as attacks, they are more likely to respond defensively and resist your ideas. Your tone, word choice, speed of delivery, and body language all contribute to this perception. Avoid using jargon that your counterpart does not understand. This can cause them to feel embarrassed and stop them from providing you with the information you need. It is typically more productive to speak in commonly understood language and to ask questions with a curious tone rather than a threatening or patronizing tone. It is also helpful to remove any harsh accusations or words, and display welcoming body language.

These recommendations are especially helpful for technical experts such as IT professionals, SaaS (software as a service) sales professionals, and other experts. People in these positions may not always realize their word choice, acronym usage, perceived impatience, and pointed questions often put their audiences on the defensive. Technical experts are more likely to view a situation as simple when their audiences are more likely to find the situation confusing. If they aren't careful, they can exacerbate this disconnect with their delivery. These experts can save time and avoid much of the resistance they receive by slowing down, using common language, and recognizing their counterparts' confusion.

I lived by these considerations in the interrogation room. Often, when I asked a question that I believed might make my subject feel vulnerable, I would lean back and away from them as I turned my hands over and faced my palms to the sky. These movements created additional space, a welcoming appearance, and helped to ease any tension in the room.

I have seen opposite behaviors create negative reactions. On one particular occasion, I brought an investigator I was training with me to a theft investigation at a jewelry store. My goals were to provide her with more experience and assess her skill set.

My new teammate asked to conduct the first interview. We brought the employee in and they both sat approximately four feet in front of each other while I sat about six feet behind, and off to the side, of the subject. During the interview, my teammate asked about twenty questions while never breaking eye contact, shifting her posture, or varying her verbal delivery.

At the conclusion of the interview, she asked how she had done, and I responded with, "Easy on the bullet eyes." From my vantage point, I could see my teammate's questioning style made the subject extremely uncomfortable. Thankfully, it didn't have an appreciable effect on our ability to eliminate the employee from the investigation. We will never know what other information this employee may have shared with us if the conversation had felt different. In the end, we were still able to resolve the investigation.

Fourth axiom: How questions are set up is more important than the questions themselves

Aligning our counterparts' self-images with reasons or excuses to answer our questions, prior to asking them, significantly reduces the resistance we encounter. The more uncomfortable you believe a question may make your counterpart feel, the more important it is to set it up with an appropriate illustration. This is why we preach "illustrate before you investigate." I look back at my career in interrogation and laugh at the bad questions I managed to salvage by setting them up well. I also still shake my head at the great questions I wasted because I didn't set them up. Dave Zulawski used to preach to avoid asking someone a question before they were ready to answer it as often as possible. Our persuasive illustrations change our counterparts' mindsets and prime them to honestly answer our questions before we ask them.

I use this technique a lot, especially when I'm selling to CEOs. I know they see themselves as kings and queens of their castle and I never want to offend their self-images. I also know they are so busy that they don't have the time or bandwidth to know exactly what all of their people are saying and doing. As such, I don't want to ask them questions that force them to embarrass themselves by answering "I don't know." Setting up my questions with quality illustrations increases the perception of my credibility, makes it easier for them to share sensitive information, and helps me move agreements forward. As an example, I may say, "The CEOs we work with are often so focused on growing their business that they trust their managers to bring any significant issues to their attention without having to micromanage them. Unfortunately, their managers often try to resolve these issues themselves and only alert the CEO when they are all out of options, which limits the impact the CEO can have on the situation. With that in mind, I'm curious: How many times in the last quarter have your managers brought issues to your attention long after they've accidentally made the situation worse?"

Fifth axiom: Lead to your most important question, not with your most important question

We can expect our counterparts' resistance to be the highest at the beginning of our conversations. This is when they are trying to determine what the conversation is about, what impact the conversation could have on them, and what they should or shouldn't say.

Unfortunately, this is also the time our stress levels may be the highest. When we are under stress, we go to what we know. The stress we feel, our focus on saving time, and our egos can all drive us to ask our most important questions right away. This forces our counterparts to receive our requests with maximum defensiveness. Not only does this typically result in our questions failing to produce the information we want, but it also exposes what we are looking for, further increases our counterparts' defensive posture, and eliminates our ability to effectively use the same question again later in the conversation.

Leading to your best question allows you to shift your counterparts' perceptions over time. This technique also helps you prime them to answer your question by encouraging them to share less threatening information first. Once your counterparts have been primed, and have reduced their defenses, you can ask your most important question and significantly increase the odds that you will obtain the information you're looking for.

For example, I have a client who used to sell advertising to car dealerships. During his discovery process, it was critical for him to uncover how much his target dealerships were spending on advertising each month. However, he was aware his prospects would never come right out and tell him. On the flip side, he knew the industry average dealers spent on advertising per car sold. Dealers love bragging about the number of cars they sell. As a result, he would start by asking his prospects how many cars they sell per month. Once they answered he congratulated them, quickly did the math in his head, and assumptively asked them about their advertising budget. The conversation flowed as follows:

> **Sales executive:** "Your lot's impressive and you've got a ton of guys working today. How many cars do you sell per month?"
>
> **Dealer general manager:** "We consistently put a hundred cars a month on the road."
>
> **Sales executive:** "That's awesome. I'm sure it drives your competitors crazy. Considering how competitive this market is, I assume a dealer this size must be spending about $60,000 a month in advertising to stay ahead."
>
> **Dealer general manager (option 1):** "We spend more than that! We want everyone to know we are the best store in town and our consistent messaging keeps it that way."
>
> **Dealer general manager (option 2):** "Not quite. We only have to spend about $40,000. Our reputation does a lot of marketing for us."

By leading with a question, the dealer is usually happy to answer; the sales executive gathers helpful intelligence, encourages the dealer to start providing information, and creates the opportunity to lead the dealer into sharing the information the sales executive really needs.

Sixth axiom: The direct path is the path of most resistance

One of the many downsides to the time-focused and task-oriented listening styles is directly shooting for the information you are seeking. You may feel like this approach will save you time. In fairness, it may be true—but only in the most convenient of circumstances. Often, this approach will most likely increase your counterpart's resistance.

As mentioned previously, there is a reason that rivers don't flow in a straight line. It would require too much force to cut through the sediment. Instead, rivers ebb and flow in a circuitous fashion as they find the path of least resistance from their source to their destination. It may feel like a waste of time to influence our counterparts' perspectives, establish credibility, create a productive conversational tone, and set up your critical questions. This time is actually an investment that pays off at the critical moments in your conversations.

Usually, it is most productive to use a funnel approach when you are trying to obtain sensitive information from reluctant people. Start at the top of the funnel with open questions on a broad overarching topic, and patiently work your way down the funnel. Each level of the funnel should capitalize on a piece of information your counterpart has previously provided, further tightening the funnel. Only once you've allowed them to lead you to the bottom of the metaphorical funnel do you ask for the real important information you're looking for.

For example, let's say you have a manager who you believe is not taking the time to coach and develop his people. You could take the direct path and confront him with your thoughts by saying, "Why aren't you developing your people?" "It doesn't appear that you are developing your people," or even, "Do you believe you are taking the necessary time to develop your people?" Each one of those questions will likely cause the manager to protect himself by answering defensively. A better approach is to wind down a question funnel that leads your manager to accept that he isn't spending enough time developing his team. The funnel may unfold as follows:

CEO: How does your team feel about hitting their sales goals this month?

Manager: It sounds like they feel pretty confident.

CEO: That's good to hear. What has the client feedback sounded like this quarter?

Manager: It's been pretty strong. Our team is definitely making their calls and staying in front of their prospects.

CEO: How does that line up with what your team is telling you?

Manager: It actually lines up pretty well.

CEO: What are some of the reasons your team is giving you for missing their sales goals?

Manager: It's been tough out there. Budget issues and market uncertainty are keeping prospects from moving forward.

CEO: How does that line up with what you've observed?

Manager: It lines up. I know they are working hard.

CEO: How many hours have you spent coaching them in the last quarter?

Manager: Well, ahh, honestly, probably not as many as I should. I've been busy putting out fires and keeping an eye on their numbers.

In this progression, the CEO patiently walks the manager down a funnel and gives the manager every opportunity to surprise him with great answers. In the end, the manager acknowledges his lack of coaching without being accused of failing and takes ownership for improving how he coaches his team.

Seventh axiom: Great questions are concise questions

Shorter questions are most often better questions because they are easier for our counterparts to hear, internalize, and respond to. It is easy to ask compound and run-on questions when we are nervous, upset, unprepared, or trying to obtain multiple answers at the same time. Convoluted and confusing questions complicate our counterparts' cognitive processes and reduce the value of the answers we receive.

> **Convoluted and confusing questions complicate our counterparts' cognitive processes and reduce the value of the answers we receive.**

One of the most common mistakes hiring managers make during their candidate interviews is asking compound questions. One example could be asking a candidate, "Please tell me about a time when you experienced conflict at work, what the conflict was about, who was involved, how it got started, how you responded, and what you learned from the experience." This is a classic example of asking a question based on what the interviewer wants to know and not what the candidate needs to feel.

This hiring manager just asked six questions at one time. There is almost no chance the candidate will remember to answer each aspect of the question, or that the interviewer will remember to listen for answers to all six components. The candidate's brain is going to get scrambled trying to create their answers, which creates misleading nonverbal and verbal communication. The interviewer may even run out of patience with the candidate's answer and cut them off.

This mistake can easily be fixed by asking the candidate, "Please walk me through the last time you had to navigate conflict with a manager at work." The question is concise, and it directs the candidate to a specific memory. This adds significant value to the hiring manager's evaluation of the candidate's communication and allows the candidate to recount the story in a manner that is most valuable to him or her. This creates the opportunity for the hiring manager to obtain far more intelligence from the candidate's answer and ask any necessary follow-up questions, one at a time, after the candidate completes his or her initial answer.

Following these axioms reduces the resistance that questioners face, increases the value of the information they acquire, and safeguards them from many of the common mistakes leaders make.

Additional Mistakes to Avoid

There are a few additional mistakes worth noting. The first is issuing accidental accusations. Anytime you ask someone, "Did you," "Why didn't you," "Do you," or "Why don't you," or any of their cousin questions, we create an accusatory environment. We may feel like we are simply checking to see if someone did what they were supposed to, while they can feel like you are accusing them of not doing it. This is a frequently unrecognized conversation killer. Instead of asking someone, "Did you send the client the proposal?" ask, "Has the client confirmed receiving the proposal?" Instead of asking, "Did you ask Steve if he completed his project?" ask, "When did Steve give you his last progress report?" This even works at home. Instead of asking, "Did you feed the dog?" ask, "Does the dog still need to be fed?" Great questions

> Great questions focus on addressing the issue, not saddling your counterparts with unnecessary accountability.

focus on addressing the issue, not saddling your counterparts with unnecessary accountability.

A related mistake is asking questions with implied expected answers. Again, we often get what we ask for. All too often, we ask questions that allude to obviously correct, and obviously incorrect, answers. As a result, our counterparts give us the obviously correct answer whether it is true or not. This is not an intentional, premeditated lie. Their answer represents a reflexive response to a bad question. When leaders find out they have been misled in response to these faulty questions, they typically get angry and fail to realize it was their fault they did not get the truth because they asked a question with an obvious correct answer.

As an example, you may ask an employee, "Have you finished the proposal?" This is a fair question, with an obviously correct answer. You imply the expected answer is yes. If they answer "yes," they satisfy you. If they answer "no," they create potential consequences. Instead, ask the question, "How many more hours will the proposal take to finish?" This second question is infinitely better. The question is now about the proposal, not the person. This should eliminate or reduce any resistance to answering. The implied expectation is that the proposal isn't finished yet, which makes it much easier for the employee to be honest. It sets them up to give you an excuse, helping them save face and opening up the conversation so you can get the full story. This is another example of asking questions based on what your employee needs to feel, not what you want to say.

Perhaps the most common question that betrays a leader's best intentions with an implied expected answer is, "Do you have any questions?" When a leader (read: expert) follows up their instructions by asking, "Do you have any questions?" the implied expected answer is "No," regardless of how eager the leader is to answer any questions. To make matters worse, their counterpart may be afraid to ask a question and risk being judged as inattentive, incompetent, or lacking confidence. As a result, the employee reflexively says, "no," walks away, and struggles to solve problems their leader could have helped them with.

There is an easy way to avoid these negative dynamics: The next time you attempt to confirm your counterparts' understanding after you give them directions, you can say, "I may not have explained that as clearly as I thought I did. What questions did I create?" or "Usually the first two questions I receive at this point are . . . how many questions did I create this time?" Now the implied expectation is there should be follow-up questions, and you take responsibility for creating the follow-up questions. This will help your audience save face, and help you save time, by clearing up any ambiguity immediately.

Several other common mistakes include forcing people to take positions they will have to later defend, challenging your counterparts' self-images, appearing to lack confidence in your question, and asking irrelevant questions that reveal you are either unprepared or not paying attention. Asking too many questions is another common mistake. Question fatigue is real. The value of the information you receive will drop as your counterparts tire of the number of questions you're asking them. Most of the time, questioners make these mistakes inadvertently and don't realize the problems they've created. The real danger with all these mistakes is not just the unobtained information and aroused emotions. It is blaming your counterpart for not sharing information that they may have likely shared if you approached them differently. It is often our fault when people get defensive and withhold what we are looking for, and we rarely realize it.

HOW TO GENERATE GOOD QUESTIONS

Disciplined Listeners follow a five-step question generation process to increase their opportunity to obtain sensitive information and minimize mistakes. The **first step** is to contemplate the goals you are looking to achieve with your conversation. With these goals in mind, the **second step** is to clarify the information you need to receive. There is a significant difference between building your questions based on the information you need to obtain versus building your questions based on what you want to say. What you may initially want to say is often impacted by your emotions and biases.

Once you have identified your goals and the information you need to obtain to achieve them, the **third step** is to consider any fears that may stop your counterparts from sharing this information with you. This is why we ask ourselves, "Why shouldn't they answer this question?" We know the number one reason why people withhold or massage information is to avoid consequences that range from embarrassment to losing valuable privileges. Scripting questions based on what your counterparts need to experience before answering honestly requires you to first consider the fears and motivations that may stop them from answering.

After considering why your counterparts may not want to answer your question, the **fourth step** is choosing how to reduce those fears and align your counterparts' self-image with sharing the information you need prior to asking the question. We know that how we set up our questions is more important than the questions we ask. This step forces us to pause and consider what statements, stories, or illustrations will give us the best chance to shift our counterparts' perspectives and prime them to answer our questions.

The **fifth step** is to craft the actual question based on what you believe your counterparts need to experience to answer truthfully.

These questions should be phrased in a manner that reduces resistance and motivates your counterparts to answer. Be careful to avoid harsh terminology, unnecessary implications of accountability, and implied expected answers. Your questions should make your counterparts feel comfortable sharing the information you are looking for.

As an example, I applied this approach to an unexpected witness during my investigation in Oklahoma. I was interviewing a woman who I was relatively certain was not involved in the theft. However, she appeared to be very nervous discussing the missing products. It dawned on me that she likely knew something she was too nervous to share.

I quickly ran through the five-step checklist in my head. My goals were to resolve the investigation and protect her while she shared any potential knowledge with me. I figured she didn't want to get in trouble for not telling anyone sooner and she likely didn't want the thief to know she told me. I felt confident I could illustrate that I commonly encounter these fears and protect witnesses before I asked her what evidence she had.

With that thought process in mind I told her, "I commonly talk to people who have evidence that someone else made a regrettable decision, and aren't comfortable sharing it. Usually, they don't want to share because they don't want anyone to think they were involved or don't want anyone to think they were holding back, and they don't want the offender to know they shared the information. That's why I come in from the outside. I know firsthand how nerve-wracking it can be to have evidence and how worrisome it can be to share it. One of my most important jobs is to protect witnesses by creating the impression I discovered the evidence on my own. With that in mind, I would like to ask you this: What is the strongest piece of evidence you've seen linking someone to this theft activity?"

She rubbed her hands together, breathed deeply, and looked down at her feet before looking back up at me and saying, "No one can know it came from me." She went on to tell me she came in on a Saturday and found copies of bank records on the office printer. She had kept them in her desk for months, waiting for a time when it would be okay to reveal what she knew. She said she felt bad for the thief because she knew how tough his personal situation was, and the longer she held onto the records, the more she worried about getting in trouble for not going to leadership sooner.

After talking through the situation with her, we created a plan that allowed her to go back to her desk, get the documents out of her drawer, conceal them in her calendar, and bring them to me at a time when we were confident the suspect wouldn't be in the office. Thankfully, the plan worked perfectly. She felt a tremendous sense of relief and I had the evidence I needed to come back and re-interrogate the suspect the following morning.

> **Every question we ask should serve a specific, goal-oriented purpose. If we cannot articulate how a question is going to improve our situation, we should not ask it.**

Every question we ask should serve a specific, goal-oriented purpose. If we cannot articulate how a question is going to improve our situation, we should not ask it. Asking the wrong questions, irrelevant questions, uninformed questions, or too many questions can seriously damage our credibility and our relationships.

OBTAINING THE TRUTH

Certified Forensic Interviewers (CFIs) acquire questioning approaches like tools for their toolbox. The more types of questions they are comfortable using, and the more interview and interrogation techniques they're comfortable executing, the more successful they will be. Each interrogator has their own strengths and weaknesses. Every investigation, and every interview subject, provides their own unique opportunities and concerns. The same holds true for business leaders, sales professionals, and parents. Every conversation they participate in offers unique variables and opportunities that need to be addressed including the people, relationships, information, potential consequences, goals, environment, and beyond. Cultivating the ability to use the right tool for the right job can make all the difference between obtaining the truth and creating resistance that can't be overcome.

CFIs typically rely on six types of questions to obtain the truth during their investigations: Closed, Open, Expansion, Assumptive, Choice, and Enticement questions. All of these offer different benefits and drawbacks. The chart on the next page outlines benefits, drawbacks, and examples of each of the six types of questions CFIs utilize.

Type of Question	Benefits	Drawbacks	Examples
Closed	verifying information someone has already shared establishing non-threatening facts breaking the ice when your counterparts are reluctant to speak with you	answered with a yes or no may force your counterparts to take a position that they will later have to defend provide very little evaluation opportunities significantly limit follow-up question alternatives	Starting a question with: "Can you . . ." "Would you . . ." "Have you . . ." "Do you . . ." Ending a question with: "right?" "correct?" "isn't it?" "is that true?"
Open	creates the opportunity for our counterparts to share information they believe is valuable, in more depth	If your counterparts detect even a hint of sarcasm or judgment, these questions will backfire	"Please walk me through . . ." "Please take me back to . . ." "Please help me understand."
Expansion	encourages your counterparts to add valuable information to their initial answer	If these questions are asked in a tone or at a speed that makes people feel defensive, they will likely backfire	"What happened next?" "What were you feeling when that happened?" "What else happened?" "What else did she say?" "Please continue . . ." "Take all the time you need . . ." "That's a great start . . ." "And then . . ." or A pregnant pause.

Type of Question	Benefits	Drawbacks	Examples
Assumptive	add to your perceived credibility typically kick off your counterparts' cognitive processes add to the nonverbal communication you can evaluate in conjunction with their verbal responses leave the window open for your counterparts to save face if necessary in business: should be utilized to great effect during the sales conversation to establish elements of the deliverables, not at the end to force a deal	Avoid using assumptive questions for closing sales. While there may be occasions where this is appropriate, this can damage your credibility and hurt relationships at the last and worst possible moment	"How many hours will it take you to finish your homework?" "What is the largest obstacle your team is facing?" "How do your customers prefer to be contacted?" "What is the most amount of money you've ever taken?" "When was the last time you took on a project of this magnitude?" "How many people would you need to hire to meet our production needs?" "When was the last time your team had to hit such an ambitious deadline?"
Choice	often have the same credibility-boosting effects as assumptive questions with built-in face-saving mechanisms provide your counterparts with built-in excuses to answer your questions; the juxtaposition encourages them to accept the face-saving option or deny the face losing option	If the options you provide are irrelevant, don't resonate with your counterparts, or don't help your counterparts save face, the question can backfire	"Did this happen because you felt rushed for time or because you were frustrated with the situation?" "Looking back, was this your idea or were you talked into it?" "Had you seen that approach work before or was this the first time you tried it?"
Enticement	work well when you have information serve as a substitute for bluffing when you don't have information—as long as the information you imply having is credible If your counterparts pause to seriously consider that it does exist, it could be an indication that there is more to their story	Presenting this question too early can completely close the person off Basing this question on unrealistic evidence can destroy your credibility	"Is there any reason you can think of that . . ." "Could there be any reason why . . ."

Disciplined Listeners take responsibility for their counter-parts' communication experiences. The framing, phrasing, and delivery of questions play a substantial role in these experiences. Disciplined Listeners exhibit levels of situational awareness that empower them to avoid falling prey to the temptation to ask the easy direct, or surface level, questions and thoughtfully compose open or assumptive questions that invite their counterparts to share sensitive information. For Disciplined Listeners, the result is the motivation.

Occasionally, this approach pays off with a single, well-crafted question. More often, the payoff is revealed at the end of a stra-tegic sequence of questions. These sequences often start with an open question such as, "Please walk me through this situation in as much detail as you can remember."

After patiently listening to the entire answer, the sequence continues with assumptive questions such as, "When did you first realize?" "How many alternatives did you consider?" "What was the priority at that point in the process?" or "Where do you believe that response came from?"

Should your counterparts' answers feel incomplete, you can encourage them to share more details with an expansion question. This could be a simple pause and head nod or repeating the last word they said such as "Last week?" "The whole team?" or "In the second phase?"

If your counterparts start to shut down, you may be able to recharge the discussion with a choice question like, "I understand our managers may want to hold off on telling me about these sit-uations—either because they think it will just go away or because they believe they can handle it themselves. Was this a situation where you believed you had it under control and there was no need to bother me?"

As a last resort, you can use an enticement question to reframe their perspective and motivate them to continue adding value to the conversation. As an example, you may ask, "Is there any reason you can think of that the customer may have felt compelled to call me directly?"

Enticement questions have been a great tool for getting me out of jams I got myself into. I typically don't want to use these questions too early or too many times (i.e., more than once) in a conversation. That doesn't mean they cannot accidentally work if they are used too early.

On one occasion, I was advising an HR client who had to interview a manager who was alleged to have shown naked pictures of his girlfriend (an hourly employee in his office) to his coworkers. After we reviewed my client's interview strategy, she asked me what she should do if he wouldn't admit. I recommended asking an enticement question. I told her that if all else failed she could ask him, "Is there any reason you can think of that one of your coworkers may have forwarded me nude pictures of a female coworker that they received from you?"

The day of the interview, I called to ask her how the conversation went. She said, "Great, thank you so much for your help. I started the interview by asking him 'Is there any reason you can think of that one of your coworkers may have forwarded me nude pictures of a female coworker that they received from you?' and he confessed right away." She was super excited, and I didn't have the heart to tell her she used the question too early. We just put it in the win column and moved on.

My most memorable enticement question became necessary after I committed a series of mistakes. During a routine safety and security evaluation, I learned a security guard was rumored to be smoking marijuana on the job. This was a problem considering security guards at this location drove patrol vehicles, responded to emergencies, and carried handguns.

To be fully transparent, my ego got the best of me. The tip I received appeared to be fully credible and I was audio/video recording all my interviews at the time. Instead of focusing on getting the truth about the drug use, I opted to try and make a great video. I decided to try and obtain a theft confession before the drug use confession because it wasn't a huge leap to think a person using drugs at work could also be stealing from their employer. This decision was wrong on many levels, and it backfired.

During the interrogation, it quickly became clear this gentleman wasn't a thief, and he was angry I had asked him about potential theft activity. Now that I had pissed him off, I still needed to learn the truth about the drug rumors. I hadn't done myself any favors.

I needed him to calm down, and I needed time to come up with a plan B. I accomplished both by thanking him for patiently answering my questions and asking him to walk me through his typical day. During his illustration, he mentioned how he worked long shifts in the hot summer sun. When he completed his story, I told him that I could easily understand if he needed to take a few extra breaks to rest and cool off. He immediately admitted to doing just that.

Thankfully, this was about the time I remembered that the owners of this property had told me they hang camouflage game cameras every year to track the deer on their property. Now that my suspect had locked himself into taking a few extra breaks in the summer (which is totally understandable), I had him in position to use an enticement question because if he was smoking marijuana at work, it was likely on one of these extra breaks.

I set the question up by asking him if he was familiar with the game cameras and he answered that he was. After locking him into acknowledging the cameras were used on the property, I asked him, "Is there any reason you can think of that I could've seen game camera footage of you smoking marijuana on the property?" He looked at me like he saw a ghost and completely froze. I realized he wasn't quite ready to tell the truth and helped him save face by illustrating I understood some people occasionally use drugs to relieve stress.

By the end of the conversation, he admitted to smoking marijuana on the job an average of three times a day, every day, for over three years. Thankfully, my enticement question worked beautifully. More importantly, I learned from my mistake and never prioritized making a video over obtaining the truth again.

My honest opinion is that everyone is capable of sharing sensitive information ~~that exposes their vulnerability~~. It requires the right person, with the right approach, to ask the right question, at the right time. Anything is possible when all these pieces are skillfully assembled.

SUMMARY

Committing ourselves to goal-focused approaches, putting our egos in our back pockets, increasing the intelligence we observe, maximizing our situational awareness, and encouraging our counterparts to save face, places us in positions to obtain information we never thought possible from people we never imagined would share it. Anytime you attempt to obtain sensitive information under stressful circumstances, it is critical you choose an approach that is based on what your counterpart needs to experience, not what you want to say. These conversations are most productive when we prioritize achieving our goals over assuaging our emotions.

CONCLUSION

SUCCESS IN ANY CONVERSATION can be attributed to three components: *strategy, process,* and *communication.* Disciplined Listeners address all three components to create conversational experiences that lead their counterparts to choose to share sensitive information, embrace outside ideas, and commit to new actions.

The truth is often hiding in plain sight. We just need to be alert enough to identify it, aware enough to recognize its value, and adept enough to take advantage of it to achieve our goals. Adjusting our mindsets and our conversational approaches unlocks a whole new world of intelligence, opportunities, and success across our personal and professional lives.

As communicators, we often focus on solving the wrong problem. It is easy to ask yourself, "What do I need to say or do in order to influence person X to commit to action Y?" This focuses our mind's eye on *us,* not *them.* Answers to this question will be largely driven by our biases, perceptions, and expectations. Yes, the solution you arrive at may work. However, it also creates a substantial risk of increasing the resistance you encounter along the way.

Solving the right problem highlights the importance of focusing on how every important conversation you participate in can get you at least one step closer to your goals. Developing an acute sense of situational awareness is a foundational component of the Disciplined Listening Method. This situational awareness includes recognizing the potential significance of any interaction based on who you are speaking with, the topic, the timing, and the potential rewards or consequences. It also involves embracing the totality of your counterparts' experiences including their fears, motivations, and perspectives.

Prioritizing your counterparts' experiences leads you to build your communication strategies from your perceived weaknesses, not your perceived strengths. The most important question Disciplined Listeners consider is, "Why shouldn't they commit to what I want them to commit to?" This also means accepting the fact that anytime we need other people to share information, we are not in control of the conversation. Controlling our own emotions and egos is another difficult and essential step to the Disciplined Listening Method. Disciplined Listeners question their own motivations and explore their default listening styles. They identify when these styles are inhibiting their ability to achieve their goals and make the necessary adjustments.

Patience prevails in our critical conversations. Disciplined Listeners allow the conversation to come to them because they know the more they observe, the more they learn. It isn't natural to maintain a learning mentality while we listen; our brains are wired to listen for opportunities to defend or confirm what we already believe. We often have to force ourselves to keep an open mind, push through the discomfort we feel, and observe for unexpected value.

The most important part of listening is talking. Truly listening to learn requires us to limit our internal monologue. This allows us to listen for intelligence as opposed to information. These seemingly inconsequential nuances of conversation are what typically enlighten us to new alternatives. Showing our counterparts respect, acknowledging their value, and patiently observing the totality of their communications maximizes our intelligence-gathering efforts and leads us to better decisions and stronger relationships.

Context is king. Disciplined Listeners evaluate everything they see and hear within the context of the situation. We don't focus on catching people lying. Again, that is an us-focused endeavor. Often, we want to catch people lying so we can satisfy our self-images, assert moral superiority, and dish out consequences. These actions are rarely helpful as we try to connect with our counterparts and obtain sensitive information during our critical conversations.

Instead of listening for lies, observe for indications of comfort and discomfort. This forces you to prioritize your counterparts' experiences and empathize with their perspectives. It also helps unlock what they are thinking and feeling in real time. Understanding why someone may be uncomfortable, or withholding information, is infinitely more valuable than simply determining they lied to you. Integrating your observations with your situational awareness allows you to make the adjustments necessary to activate the truth.

The truth you've observed can be rendered meaningless if you can't encourage your counterparts to protect their self-images. Saving face is the lynch pin that holds the Disciplined Listening Method together. Any persuasive communication process needs to be predicated on helping your counterparts avoid feeling embarrassed and align what we want them to commit to with their self-image. Again, the Disciplined Listening Method isn't about what we need to hear, see, or say. It is all about understanding and communicating what our counterparts need to experience, in order to commit to the actions we require.

True influence cannot be exercised without trust. Despite all the attention-signaling behaviors the traditional active listening model recommends, the only way to prove to someone that you listened to them is to provide tangible evidence—after the conversation. Following up is the final place Disciplined Listeners differentiate themselves. Leaders across all contexts earn their trust equity over time and often cash it in during unexpected, stressful conversations. Leaders will be rewarded for building their trust equity long before they need to cash it in.

Once again, the Disciplined Listening Method is not an interrogation or lie-detecting technique. It is a goal-oriented communication approach which focuses on creating value and accepting responsibility for our counterparts' communication experiences. Disciplined Listeners apply a curious, investigative, and solution-oriented mindset to the communication problems they encounter every day. It prioritizes learning over defending, empathizing over correcting, and creating value over winning.

Yes, committing to the Disciplined Listening Method requires increased effort and awareness. The rewards are more than worth the effort. However, listening, influencing, and questioning are all perishable skills. The more you intentionally practice them, the better you will become. The more you interrogate your own reactions and actions, the more tuned in you will be to yourself and others.

It will take consistent effort to integrate these behaviors and perspectives into your important communications; such preparation, awareness, and focus does not manifest overnight. As we conclude this book, it is wise to revisit the questions we posed in the introduction:

1. What are the most valuable lessons you took from this book?

2. What relationships will you impact with these lessons?

3. What new opportunities will you create with these lessons?

4. How can your previous successes and missed opportunities reinforce these lessons?

I wish you nothing but success as you communicate your way toward achieving your business and personal goals. May all your ethical efforts be rewarded.

Take care of each other.

ACKNOWLEDGMENTS

FIRST AND FOREMOST, THANK YOU to my beautiful wife, Brooke, and my wonderful son, Gabriel. Their love, encouragement, perspectives, and sacrifices mean the world to me. They have made me a better person and have made this book possible. Thank you as well to my father, Dale; mother, Donna; and brother, John. Their love, support, guidance, and belief in me have enriched my life. The same needs to be said for Dennis Donovan, Jason McConville, Aaron Williams, Tom Maida, Mark Patterson, Justin MacIntyre, and Mike Walker. Thank you all for always being there.

Thank you to Clint Greenleaf, Lauren Hall, and the whole team at Content Capital for putting up with all my idiosyncrasies and bringing this book to life. Clint, your mentorship, motivation, and support have been instrumental. Thank you as well to Ali Forrest, Bella Griffin, and Dale Reddington for your research assistance.

I'd also like to extend a significant debt of gratitude to Dave Zulawski, Doug Wicklander, Shane Sturman, Wayne Hoover, Brett Ward, Dave Thompson, Chris Norris, John Guzman, Tom McGreal, Tony Paixao, Sue Thompson, Pattie Mathison, Mercedes Balcer, and the whole team at Wicklander-Zulawski & Associates. Your love, guidance, education, and friendship have been life-changing. The integrity your organization brings to the world of interrogation, as well as your commitment to adhering to moral and ethical standards, has truly made WZ the torchbearer of the industry.

I wouldn't be where I am today without a small army of mentors who have chosen to share their time, insight, and expertise with me. They have helped mold me into the critical thinker and Disciplined Listener I've become. Thank you, Joe Wein, Padraig O'Ceidigh, Rudy Karsan, Anastasios Economou, Neville Crawley, Jeff Dudan, Becky Rodgers, John Delaney, Gregg Smith, Adam Ostrowsky, Bob Losik, John Morris, and Chuck DeMund for your guidance.

And thank you Bobby Masano, Carole Chaski, David Matsumoto, Edward Geiselman, Don Rabon, and Tim Levine for contributing to my education and investigative approach.

Thank you, Michael Slater, Raymond Watt, Paul Venter, Walt Van Der Westhuizen, Carole Calma, Jennifer Johnsgard, Wilhelm Helmbold, Jennifer Dunn, and Hendre Coetzee, who contributed so much time and energy into my development.

Thank you to all of my clients for the wonderful opportunities to learn, teach, and grow together.

Thank you to everyone I've interviewed and interrogated. The perspectives and understanding of the human experience you've provided me with are priceless.

I could easily write another complete book detailing the contributions of everyone listed above, and the dozens of names I've inevitably and pre-apologetically missed. I am absolutely the result of the energy and ideas so many people have poured into me. To the readers, please stop often to reflect on the people who have poured themselves into you, and share your own insights, ideas, and expertise with as many people as you can.

ABOUT THE AUTHOR

MICHAEL REDDINGTON, CFI is an expert at moving people from resistance to commitment. He is an executive resource, President of InQuasive, Inc., and the developer of the Disciplined Listening Method.

Growing up in New England, Michael wanted to be a special education teacher and baseball coach—although he had no idea interview and interrogation techniques would later become the foundation of his educational programs. He did both for a short time before being enticed by the financial industry, where he lasted two years, one month, and two days before returning to college to earn his business degree.

A twist of fate led Michael to his first investigations job while he was completing his degree, and what began as an opportunity to pay the bills has since morphed into a completely unexpected career. Michael was quickly promoted into a management role, and after successfully resolving several investigations early in his tenure, Michael was enrolled in his first Wicklander-Zulawski & Associates (WZ) non-confrontational interview and interrogation techniques training course. During the course the clouds parted, the sun burst through, a rainbow appeared, and Michael knew exactly what he wanted his focus to be.

He continued to take on additional investigative responsibilities and attained several promotions. Michael's success in the interrogation room fostered his fascination with why people choose to share sensitive information in the face of consequences. He attended additional training programs and earned his Certified Forensic Interviewer (CFI) designation—the highest available professional designation in his field. Recruited shortly after by Wicklander-Zulawski & Associates to join their staff of investigators and trainers, he spent a decade working for WZ running their investigations division, developing new content, and traveling the world teaching investigators how to apply rapport-based interrogation techniques.

In his investigations role, Michael conducted and managed a wide variety of interrogations across the public and private sector. He created and taught seminars for law enforcement personnel, federal investigators, private sector investigators, and human resource professionals around the world. For this work, Michael received the Homeland Security Outstanding Contributions Award in 2011.

During this time, Michael had the opportunity to start teaching CEOs how to apply interrogation techniques in their business conversations. These training programs quickly opened Michael's eyes to the similarities his executive clients' negotiations, leadership conversations, and sales conversations shared with his interviews and interrogations. As a result, Michael dove into research from across the world of business communications and arrived at two important realizations. First, the best leaders and the best interrogators capitalize on the same two core skills: Vision and Influence. Second, the cognitive process that leads customers to commit to saying, "I'll buy it," employees to commit to saying, "I'll do it," and interrogation suspects to truthfully commit to saying, "I did it," are essentially identical.

Michael realized he could teach executives how to reduce missed opportunities and increase commitments to action. He founded InQuasive, Inc. and created the Disciplined Listening Method by integrating research and best practices from the worlds of business communications and investigative interviewing. The resulting educational content represents a new and in-depth approach to applying strategic, ethical observation and persuasion techniques across the full spectrum of business conversations.

Michael has been invited by companies, government agencies, and executive groups to facilitate his seminars and presentations across North America, Europe, Africa, and the Middle East. He has led thousands of programs and educated tens of thousands of participants from over fifty countries on how to activate the truth in the areas of leadership communication, sales, negotiation, conflict resolution, customer service, candidate interviews, family conversations, and influential instruction. Michael is also a frequent guest contributor for various media outlets and podcasts.

Michael goes well beyond facilitating and advising. He applies customized content specifically designed to meet the needs of each participant with a humorous and intelligent delivery style. His diligent preparation, attention to each participant's concerns, and added context coalesce to drive home the learning objectives. It's never just a presentation, seminar, or advisory session—it's always an experience.

Michael is excited to raise his son, Gabriel, with his wife, Brooke, and continue to inspire people to evolve their communication approaches and embrace the rewards.

NOTES

INTRODUCTION

1. Stephen R. Covey, *The 7 Habits of Highly Effective People: Powerful Lessons in Personal Change* (New York: Simon & Schuster, 1989), 239.
2. Ruth G. Newman, Marie A. Danziger, and Mark Cohen, *Communicating in Business Today* (Lexington: D.C. Health and Co., 1987).
3. Carl R. Rogers, *A Way of Being* (Boston: Houghton Mifflin, 1980).
4. Simon Sinek, Twitter Post, October 2, 2012, https://twitter.com /simonsinek/status/253238772366471168?lang=en.

CHAPTER ONE

1. Ruth G. Newman, Marie A. Danziger, and Mark Cohen, *Communicating in Business Today* (Lexington: D.C. Health and Co., 1987).
2. Buster Benson, "Cognitive Bias Cheat Sheet," *Better Humans*, September 1, 2016, https://betterhumans.pub/cognitive-bias-cheat-sheet -55a472476b18.

CHAPTER TWO

1. Kelby K. Halone, Terry M. Cunconan, Carolyn Gwynn Coakley, and Andrew D. Wolvin, "Toward the Establishment of General Dimensions Underlying the Listening Process," *International Journal of Listening* 12, no. 1 (1998): 12–28, https://www.tandfonline.com/doi/abs/10.1080/109 04018.1998.10499016.
2. Judi Brownell, "Exploring the Strategic Ground for Listening and Organizational Effectiveness," Cornell University School of Hotel Administration Site (2008), https://ecommons.cornell.edu /handle/1813/72469.
3. Kittie W. Watson, Larry L. Barker, and James B. Weaver III, "The Listening Styles Profile (LSP-16): Development and Validation of an Instrument to Assess Four Listening Styles," *International Journal of Listening* 9, no. 1 (1995), https://www.tandfonline.com/doi/abs/10.1080 /10904018.1995.10499138.

4. Graham D. Bodie, Debra L. Worthington, and Christopher C. Gearhart, "The Listening Styles Profile Revised (LSP-R): A Scale Revision and Evidence for Validity," *Communication Quarterly* 61, no. 1 (2013): 75–93, https://www.tandfonline.com/doi/abs/10.1080/01463373.2012 .720343.

5. Jack Zenger and Joseph Folkman, "What Great Listeners Actually Do," *Harvard Business Review*, July 14, 2016, https://hbr.org/2016/07/what -great-listeners-actually-do.

6. Margarete Imhof, "The Social Construction of the Listener: Listening Behavior Across Situations, Perceived Listener Status, and Cultures," *Communication Research Reports* 20, no. 4 (Fall 2003): 357–66.

7. The character Raylan Givens, episode "Justified" in *Hole in the Wall* (2013).

CHAPTER THREE

1. Charles F. Bond Jr. and The Global Deception Research Team, "A World of Lies," *Journal of Cross-Cultural Psychology* 37, no. 1 (January 2006): 60–74, https://journals.sagepub.com/doi/10.1177/0022022105282295.

2. Richard Wiseman, Caroline Watt, Leanne ten Brinke, Stephen Porter, Sara-Louise Couper, and Calum Rankin, "The Eyes Don't Have It: Lie Detection and Neuro-Linguistic Programming," *PLOS ONE* 7 (July 2012), https://journals.plos.org/plosone/article/authors?id=10.1371 /journal.pone.0040259.

3. Timothy R. Levine, *Duped: Truth-Default Theory and the Social Science of Lying and Deception* (Tuscaloosa: The University of Alabama Press, 2020), 25.

4. Paul Ekman, *Telling Lies: Clues to Deceit in the Marketplace, Politics, and Marriage* (New York: W.W. Norton & Company, Inc., 1985, 1992, 2001, 2009), 91, 94.

5. Richard Hunsaker, *Understanding and Developing the Skills of Oral Communication*, 2nd Edition (Englewood, CO: Morton Publishing Company, 1990).

6. Rodney J. Korba, "The Rate of Inner Speech," *Perceptual and Motor Skills* 7, no. 3 (December 1, 1990).

7. Kerry Patterson, Joseph Grenny, Ron McMillan, and Al Switzler, *Crucial Conversations Tools for Talking When Stakes Are High* (New York: McGraw Hill, 2012), 109.

8. Phil McAleer, Alexander Todorov, and Pascal Belin, "How Do You Say 'Hello'? Personality Impressions from Brief Novel Voices" *PLOS ONE* 9(3): e90779 (2014), https://journals.plos.org/plosone/article?id=10.1371 /journal.pone.0090779.

9. Janine Willis and Alexander Todorov, "First Impressions: Making Up Your Mind After a 100-Ms Exposure to a Face," *Psychological* 17, no. 7 (July 2006): 592–98, https://journals.sagepub.com/doi/10.1111/j.1467 -9280.2006.01750.x.

10. Tiffany A. Ito and Geoffrey R. Urland, "The Influence of Processing Objectives on the Perception of Faces: An ERP Study of Race and Gender Perception," *Cognitive Affective & Behavioral Neuroscience* 5, no. 1 (2005): 21–36.

11. Mahzarin R. Banaji, and Anthony G. Greenwald, *Blind Spot Hidden Biases of Good People* (New York: Delacorte Press, 2013), 73.

12. Dan Ariely, *The Honest Truth about Dishonesty: How We Lie to Everyone—Especially Ourselves* (New York: Harper Perennial, 2012), 206.

13. Robert Cialdini, *Pre-suasion: A Revolutionary Way to Influence and Persuade* (New York: Simon & Schuster, 2016), 54.

14. Steven Levitt and Stephen Dubner, *Think Like a Freak* (New York: William Morrow, 2014), 8.

15. Timothy R. Levine, *Duped: Truth-Default Theory and the Social Science of Lying and Deception* (Tuscaloosa: The University of Alabama Press, 2020), 94.

16. Norman Anderson, "Likableness Ratings of 555 Personality Trait Words," *JPSP* 9 (1968): 272–79.

17. Levitt and Dubner, *Think Like a Freak*.

18. Levitt and Dubner, *Think Like a Freak*, 87.

CHAPTER FOUR

1. Vasudevi Reddy, "Getting Back to the Rough Ground: Deception and 'Social Living,'" *Philosophical Transactions of the Royal Society* (February 2007), 621–37.

2. Paul Newton, Vasudevi Reddy, and Ray Bull, "Children's Everyday Deception and Performance on False Belief Tasks," *British Journal of Developmental Psychology* 18 (2000): 297–317.

3. Yudhijit Bhattacharjee, "Why We Lie," *National Geographic,* June 2017.

4. David Zulawski, "The History of Interrogation According to Wicklander-Zulawski," *Loss Prevention Magazine*, December 6, 2017.

5. Zulawski, "The History of Interrogation According to Wicklander-Zulawski."

6. "The Truth about Lie Detection in Ancient and Modern Times," last modified September 27, 2014, https://www.ancient-origins.net/myths-legends/truth-about-lie-detection-ancient-and-modern-times-002125.

7. Martina Vicianova, "Historical Techniques of Lie Detection," *Europe's Journal of Psychology* 11, no. 3 (2015): https://ejop.psychopen.eu/index.php/ejop/article/view/919.

8. Employee Polygraph Protection Act, https://www.dol.gov/agencies/whd/polygraph.

9. Bella M. DePaulo, Deborah A. Kashy, Susan E. Kirkendol, and Melissa M. Wyer, "Lying in Everyday Life," *Journal of Personality and Social Psychology* 70, no. 5 (1996): 979–95.

10. Robert S. Feldman, "Self-Presentation and Verbal Deception: Do Self-Presenters Lie More?" *Journal of Basic and Applied Social Psychology* 24, no. 2(2002): 163–70.

11. Pamela Meyer, "10 Research Findings about Deception That Will Blow Your Mind," liespotting.com, https://liespotting.com/2010/06/10-research-findings-about-deception-that-will-blow-your-mind/.

12. Timothy R. Levine, *Duped: Truth-Default Theory and the Social Science of Lying and Deception* (Tuscaloosa: The University of Alabama Press, 2020), 94.

13. Emma E. Levine and Maurice E. Schweitzer, "Prosocial Lies: When Deception Breeds Trust," *Organizational and Human Decision Processes* 126 (2015): 88–106, https://www.sciencedirect.com/science/article/abs/pii/S0749597814000983?via%3Dihub.

14. Pamela Meyer, *Liespotting: Proven Techniques to Detect Deception* (New York: St. Martin's Griffin, 2010), 35–39.

15. Levine, *Duped*, 166.

16. Levine, *Duped*, 166–67.

17. Levine, *Duped*, 152.

18. Dan Ariely, *The Honest Truth about Dishonesty: How We Lie to Everyone— Especially Ourselves* (New York: Harper Perennial, 2012), 23.

19. David E. Zulawski and Douglas E. Wicklander, *Practical Aspects of Interview and Interrogation*, 2nd Edition (Boca Raton: CRC Press, 2002), 206–14.

20. Francesca Gino and Dan Ariely, "The Dark Side of Creativity: Original Thinkers Can be More Dishonest," *Journal of Personality and Social Psychology* 102, no.3 (2012): 445–59, DOI: 10.1037/a0026406.

21. Albert Virj, *Detecting Lies and Deceit*, 2nd Edition (Hoboken: Wiley, 2008).

22. Levine, *Duped*, 96.

23. Levine, *Duped*, 206.

24. Levine, *Duped*, 257.

25. Levine, *Duped*, 283.

26. Levine, *Duped*, 287.

27. David Matsumoto, Hyisung C. Hwang, Lisa G. Skinner and Mark Frank, "Positive Effects in Detecting Lies from Training to Recognize Behavioral Anomalies," *Journal of Police and Criminal Psychology* (2012), http://davidmatsumoto.com/content/2014%20Matsumoto%20et%20al%20JPCP-%20Positive%20Effects%20in%20Detectin%20gLies%20from%20Training....pdf.

28. R. Edward Geiselman, Ph.D., Emiline Musarra, Natalya Berezovskaya, Cory Lustig, and Sandra Elmgren, *Training Novices to Detect Deception in Oral Narratives and Exchanges—Part II* 31, no. 1 (2013), https://www.forensicpsychology.org/31113.pdf.

CHAPTER FIVE

1. Mica Endsley and Daniel J. Garland, *Situational Awareness Analysis and Measurement* (Boca Raton: CRC Press, 2000), 5.

2. Endsley and Garland, *Situational Awareness Analysis and Measurement.*

3. Debra G. Jones and Mica R. Endsley, "Sources of Situation Awareness Errors in Aviation," *Aviation, Space and Environmental Medicine* 67, no. 6 (1996): 507–12.

4. Endsley and Garland, *Situational Awareness Analysis and Measurement*, 19.

5. Graham D. Bodie, Debra L. Worthington, and Christopher C. Gearhart, "The Listening Styles Profile Revised (LSP-R): A Scale Revision and Evidence for Validity," *Communication Quarterly* 61 (2013): 75–93, https://www.tandfonline.com/doi/abs/10.1080/01463373.2012.720343.

6. Dan Feldman, "Warriors Coach Steve Kerr: 'I Lied,'" NBC Sports, June 12, 2015, https://nba.nbcsports.com/2015/06/12/warriors-coach-steve -kerr-i-lied/.

7. Margarete Imhof, "The Social Construction of the Listener: Listening Behavior Across Situations, Perceived Listener Status, and Cultures," *Communication Research Reports* 20, no. 4 (Fall 2003): 357–66.

8. Andy Stumpf and Jason Tuschen, *Cleared Hot* Podcast, Episode 165 (January 25, 2021).

CHAPTER SIX

1. Judee K. Burgoon, "Cross-Cultural and Intercultural Applications of Expectancy Violations Theory" (Intercultural Communication Theory 1995).

2. Edward T. Hall, *The Hidden Dimension* (New York: Doubleday Anchor, 1990).

3. David E. Zulawski and Douglas E. Wicklander, *Practical Aspects of Interview and Interrogation*, 2nd Edition (Boca Raton: CRC Press, 2002), 241–42.

CHAPTER SEVEN

1. Stephen R. Covey, *The 7 Habits of Highly Effective People: Powerful Lessons in Personal Change* (New York: Simon & Schuster, 1989), 97.

2. Skye Schooley, "SWOT Analysis: What It Is and When to Use It," *Businessnewsdaily.com,* December 1, 2021, https://www.businessnewsdaily .com/4245-swot-analysis.html.

3. Matthew Dixon and Brent Adamson, *The Challenger Sale: Taking Control of the Customer Conversation* (New York: Penguin, 2011), 58.

4. Robert Cialdini, *Influence: The Psychology of Persuasion* (New York: Harper Collins, 1984, 1994, 2007), 57.

5. Crystal Raypole, "What It Really Means to Have a Type A Personality," healthline.com, November 9, 2021, https://www.healthline.com/health /what-is-a-type-a-personality.

6. NASA Glenn Research Center, "Newton's Laws of Motion," https://www 1.grc.nasa.gov/beginners-guide-to-aeronautics/newtons-laws-of-motion/.

CHAPTER EIGHT

1. Robert Cialdini, *Pre-suasion: A Revolutionary Way to Influence and Persuade* (New York: Simon & Schuster, 2016), 54.
2. David E. Zulawski and Douglas E. Wicklander, *Practical Aspects of Interview and Interrogation* 2nd Edition (Boca Raton: CRC Press, 2002), 169.
3. Zulawski and Wicklander, *Practical Aspects of Interview and Interrogation*, 111–15.
4. Paul Ekman, *Telling Lies: Clues to Deceit in the Marketplace, Politics, and Marriage* (New York: W.W. Norton & Company, Inc., 1985, 1992, 2001, 2009), 21.
5. Timothy R. Levine, *Duped: Truth-Default Theory and the Social Science of Lying and Deception* (Tuscaloosa: The University of Alabama Press, 2020), 97.
6. Nina Porzucki, "Suzanne Massie Taught President Ronald Reagan This Important Russian Phrase: 'Trust, but Verify,'" The World, March 7, 2014, https://theworld.org/stories/2014-03-07/suzanne-massie-taught -president-ronald-reagan-important-russian-phrase-trust.

CHAPTER NINE

1. Paul Ekman, *Telling Lies: Clues to Deceit in the Marketplace, Politics, and Marriage* (New York: W.W. Norton & Company, Inc., 1985, 1992, 2001, 2009), 91, 94.
2. David Matsumoto, Mark G. Frank, Hyi Sung Hwang, *Nonverbal Communication Science and Applications* (Los Angeles: Sage Publications, 2013), 4.
3. Ekman, *Telling Lies*.
4. Matsumoto, Frank, Sung Hwang, *Nonverbal Communication Science and Applications*, 15.
5. CBC The Nature of Things, "The Seven Universal Emotions We Wear on Our Face," https://www.cbc.ca/natureofthings/features/the-seven -universal-emotions-we-wear-on-our-face.
6. Matsumoto, Frank, Sung Hwang, *Nonverbal Communication Science and Applications*, 25.
7. *Nonverbal Communication Science and Applications*, 26, 30.
8. *Nonverbal Communication Science and Applications*, 29, 34–36.
9. *Nonverbal Communication Science and Applications*, 104.
10. Rachel E. Jack, Oliver G. B. Garrod, and Philippe G. Schyns, "Dynamic Facial Expressions of Emotion Transmit an Evolving Hierarchy of Signals Over Time," *Current Biology* (2014), https://www.sciencedirect.com /science/article/pii/S0960982213015194.

11. Ekman, *Telling Lies*, 116.

12. Aleix M. Martinez, Yong Tao, and Shichuan Du, "Compound Facial Expressions of Emotion," PNAS (2014), www.pnas.org/lookup/suppl /doi:10.1073/pnas.1322355111/-/DCSupplemental.

13. Paul Ekman, *Emotions Revealed: Recognizing Faces to Improve Communications and Emotional Life* (New York: St. Martins, 2007), 215.

14. Matsumoto, Frank, Sung Hwang, *Nonverbal Communication Science and Applications,* 37.

15. *Nonverbal Communication Science and Applications,* 38.

16. Ronald P. Fisher, Ph.D. and R. Edward Geiselman, Ph.D, *Memory-Enhancing Techniques for Investigative Interviewing: The Cognitive Interview* (Springfield, IL: Charles C Thomas, 1992), 13.

17. *Memory-Enhancing Techniques for Investigative Interviewing,* 13.

18. *Memory-Enhancing Techniques for Investigative Interviewing,* 13.

19. Timothy R. Levine, *Duped: Truth-Default Theory and the Social Science of Lying and Deception* (Tuscaloosa: The University of Alabama Press, 2020), 130.

20. Thomas R. Masano, CFI, "What Their Eyes May Be Saying," *CFInsider, Journal for the Certified Forensic Interviewer,* no. 1 (2009).

21. Carolien G. F. de Kovel, Amaia Carrion-Castillo, and Clyde Franks, "A Large-Scale Population Study of Early Life Factors Influencing Left-Handedness," *Scientific Reports* 9 (January 2019): 584, https://www .nature.com/articles/s41598-018-37423-8.

22. David Zulawski, "The History of Interrogation According to Wicklander-Zulawski," *Loss Prevention Magazine,* December 6, 2017.

23. Ekman, *Telling Lies,* 133.

24. Ekman, *Telling Lies,* 83.

CHAPTER TEN

1. Paul Ekman, *Telling Lies: Clues to Deceit in the Marketplace, Politics, and Marriage* (New York: W.W. Norton & Company, Inc., 1985, 1992, 2001, 2009), 81.

2. David Matsumoto, Mark G. Frank, Hyi Sung Hwang, *Nonverbal Communication Science and Applications* (Los Angeles: Sage Publications, 2013), 12.

3. Albert Mehrabian, *Silent Messages: Implicit Communication of Emotions and Attitudes* (Belmont, CA: Wadsworth, 1980).

4. As quoted in Matsumoto, Frank, Sung Hwang, *Nonverbal Communication Science and Applications.*

5. *Nonverbal Communication Science and Applications,* 101, 104, 109.

CHAPTER ELEVEN

1. Paul Ekman, *Telling Lies: Clues to Deceit in the Marketplace, Politics, and Marriage* (New York: W.W. Norton & Company, Inc., 1985, 1992, 2001, 2009), 81.

2. Timothy R. Levine, *Duped: Truth-Default Theory and the Social Science of Lying and Deception* (Tuscaloosa: The University of Alabama Press, 2020), 63.

3. Levine, *Duped*, 194.

4. Levine, *Duped*, 244.

5. Levine, *Duped*, 95.

6. Don Rabon, *Investigative Discourse Analysis: Statements, Letters, and Transcripts* (Durham: Carolina Academic Press, 2003), 16.

7. Rabon, *Investigative Discourse Analysis*, 47.

8. Ekman, *Telling Lies*, 81.

9. David Matsumoto, Mark G. Frank, Hyi Sung Hwang, *Nonverbal Communication Science and Applications* (Los Angeles: Sage Publications, 2013), 53.

10. Ronald P. Fisher, Ph.D. and R. Edward Geiselman, Ph.D, *Memory-Enhancing Techniques for Investigative Interviewing: The Cognitive Interview* (Springfield, IL: Charles C Thomas, 1992), 20.

11. Fisher and Geiselman, *Memory-Enhancing Techniques for Investigative Interviewing*, 148.

12. Levine, *Duped*, 105.

13. Levine, *Duped*, 97.

14. Rabon, *Investigative Discourse Analysis*, 34.

15. "Toronto Mayor Rob Ford Denies Use of Crack Cocaine," Global News, May 24, 2013, YouTube https://www.youtube.com/watch?v=DCChaBjeK-k.

16. Jack Shafer "Catch a Liar," International Association of Interviewers Elite Training Day, Chicago, April 4, 2017.

17. "USA: President Clinton Lewinsky Testimony Video Highlights," YouTube, July 21, 2015, https://www.youtube.com/watch?v=z4vHBE8hwNk.

18. George J. Mitchell, "Report to the Commissioner of Baseball of an Independent Investigation into the Illegal use of Steroids and Other Performance-Enhancing Substances by Players in Major League Baseball" (MLB, 2007), http://files.mlb.com/mitchrpt.pdf.

CHAPTER TWELVE

1. Roger Fisher, William Ury, and Bruce Patton, *Getting to Yes: Negotiating Agreement Without Giving In* (New York: Penguin Books, 1991), 99.

2. Stephen M. R. Covey with Rebecca Merrill, *The Speed of Trust: The One Thing That Changes Everything* (New York: Simon & Schuster, 2008), 30.

3. Covey and Merrill, *The Speed of Trust*, 54–55.

4. Sun Tzu, translated by Samuel B. Griffith, *The Art of War* (Oxford: Oxford University Press, 1963, 1971), 77.

5. Paul J. Zak, *The Trust Factor: The Science of Creating High Performance Companies* (New York: Amacom Books, 2017).

6. David E. Zulawski and Douglas E. Wicklander, *Practical Aspects of Interview and Interrogation*, 2nd Edition (Boca Raton: CRC Press, 2002).

7. Maria Hartwig, Pär Anders Granhag, Leif A. Stromwell, and Ola Kronkvist, "Strategic Use of Evidence During Police Interviews: When Training to Detect Deception Works," *Law and Human Behavior* 30 (November 2006): 603–19, https://www.researchgate.net/publication/6816747_Strategic_Use_of_Evidence_during_police_interviews_When_training_to_detect_deception_works.

8. E. F. Loftus and J. C. Palmer, "Reconstruction of Automobile Destruction: An Example of the Interaction Between Language and Memory," *Journal of Verbal Learning and Verbal Behavior* 13, no. 5 (1974): 585–89.

9. Robert Cialdini, *Pre-suasion: A Revolutionary Way to Influence and Persuade* (New York: Simon & Schuster, 2016), 171–73.

10. Walter Fisher, "Narration as a Human Communication Paradigm: The Case of Public Moral Argument," *Communication Monographs* (1984), https://doi.org/10.1080/03637758409390180.

11. Zulawski and Wicklander, *Practical Aspects of Interview and Interrogation*, 21.

CHAPTER THIRTEEN

1. "Toronto Mayor Rob Ford Admits He Has Smoked Crack Cocaine," CBC News: The National. November 5, 2013, https://www.youtube.com/watch?v=qQTwGO047E8.

2. Dan Ariely, *The Honest Truth about Dishonesty: How We Lie to Everyone—Especially Ourselves* (New York: Harper Perennial, 2012), 23.

9 781954 020191